A TUDOR JOURNAL

A Tudor Journal

The Diary of a Priest in The Tower 1580-1585

by

BRIAN A. HARRISON
Supernumerary Yeoman Warder and Member
of the Queen's Bodyguard
of The Yeomen of the Guard Extraordinary

ST PAULS

ST PAULS Publishing
187 Battersea Bridge Road, London SW11 3AS

ISBN 085439 578 4

Copyright © ST PAULS (UK) 2000

Text copyright: Brian A. Harrison
The rights of Brian A. Harrison to be identified as author of this work have been asserted by him in accordance with the Copyright, Designs and Patents Act, 1988.

All rights reserved. No part of this publication may be reproduced, stored in a retrieval system, or transmitted, in any form or by any means, electronic, mechanical, photocopying, recording or otherwise, without prior permission of the copyright owner.

A CIP catalogue record for this book is available from the British Library.

Set by TuKan, Fareham, Hampshire
Produced in the EC
Printed by Società San Paolo, Roma, Italy

ST PAULS is an activity of the priests and brothers of the Society of St Paul who proclaim the Gospel through the media of social communication

ACKNOWLEDGEMENTS

In the process of assembling these records over the past twenty years, it has been my honour and privilege to meet and correspond with many people from all walks of life who, in their own ways, have been helpful in assisting me to piece together the details of individual case histories.

In particular, I would like to thank the staff of the British Library, the Guildhall Library, the Catholic Reference Library (when it was based in Mount Street), the Public Record Office when it was conveniently sited at Chancery Lane, the PRO at Kew – more especially my former army colleague Peter Slade, head of security, for letting me see behind the scenes – and the Royal Armouries at the Tower.

From the many other individuals who assisted, I would like to single out the special yet valuable assistance provided by:

Supernumerary Yeoman Warder G. Abbott, Sword Bearer to the Mayor of Kendal, who, as my 'mentor' on arriving at the Tower, encouraged my enduring interest in history, and his late wife Shelagh, for their constant advice and for the many gifts of books and other 'goodies' for my perusal;

Father Patrick Barry of the Office of Vice Postulation for the Cause of English and Welsh Martyrs, for information regarding beatification and canonisation of certain Tower Prisoners;

Sarah Barter-Bailey, librarian of the Royal Armouries, for so much historical and research advice, not least of these being the accurate translation of John Hart's Diary;

Miss Frances Devereux, FSA (Scot) former Archivist of the Royal Regiment of Fusiliers, for opening my eyes to the contents of the British Library and supplying me with countless references to sources;

Francis Edwards SJ, the acknowledged author, for his time and trouble in reading the work and for adding so much constructive criticism before publication;

Mary Hamilton-Dann, the American authoress, for her expertise on the various plots surrounding Mary, Queen of Scots and for her friendship and encouragement;

Fathers Hilary and Paul of Mount Saint Bernard Abbey, for their friendship and assistance in translating Latin inscriptions;

Tom Mc Coog SJ, the American Jesuit, for his friendship and kindness in presenting me copies of his English and Welsh Jesuits 1555-1650.

Doctor Geoffrey Parnell, curator of Tower History, for his assistance whenever called upon;

Supernumerary Yeoman Warder 'Pip' Piper who, during his term as Clerk of the Chapels Royal of the Tower, evoked my admiration in the diligent and dignified manner in which he performed those duties and yet was only too pleased to give up much of his leisure time in assisting me as we transcribed the ancient handwritten entries in the Burials Register for the Chapel of St Peter ad Vincula;

Yeoman Warder Terry Radley for his constant and accurate advice to a novice on the intricacies of operating a word processor; and for continuing the work begun by 'Pip' Piper on the Chapel Records;

Miss Lisa Severn from Stonor for taking the trouble to advise me of the later fortunes of the family ancestor, John Stonor, who had the misfortune to suffer imprisonment at the Tower.

CONTENTS

FOREWORD	9
INTRODUCTION	11
ORIGINS OF THE DIARY	13
WHO WROTE THE DIARY	17
SCENARIO	21
Religious changes in England	21
Jesuits	22
Recusants and schismatics	22
The Queen's excommunication	23
Overseas ordinations	23
Missionary priests	24
The Secret Service	25
Anti-Catholic sentiments	25
The new martyrs	26
1580	27
THE DIARY TRANSLATED – NOTES	33
THE DIARY TRANSLATED	35
CONFLICT OF EVIDENCE	67
ANALYSIS	68
SUMMARY	71
APPENDICES	
1. The Latin Version of the Diary as printed by Bayley	75
2. The Tower Bills 1580-1585	87
3. Elliot's report of the capture of Edmund Campion	101
4. Prisons of London	111
5. Torture and punishment	123
6. The order for exile	131
7. The journey into exile	137
8. Canonisation of the Forty Martyrs	141
9. The Oath of Supremacy	145
10. The Tirwhit martyr	147

Annx. 1. The Declaration of Richard Smith	157
Annx. 2. The undated petition of William Tirwhit	162
11. John Hart's letter of submission to Sir Francis Walsingham	163
12. Yeoman Warders of 1580	167
13. Brief biographies of the persons named in the Diary	169
BRIEF BIBLIOGRAPHY	229
INDEX	233

ILLUSTRATIONS

View of the Tower of London in 1597
Plan of the Tower of London
Map of London showing the eleven prisons
The Beauchamp Tower
The Lieutenant's Lodgings (Queen's House)
Thomas Miagh's Inscription in the Beauchamp Tower
John Colleton's Inscription in the Beauchamp Tower
Inscription on the tomb of Sir Robert Tyrwhitt
Tomb of Sir Robert Tyrwhitt
Tomb of Sir Robert Tyrwhitt – front view
Lyford Grange, Berkshire
The Scavenger's Daughter
The Rack in use at the Tower

FOREWORD

On assuming the office of Resident Governor of the Tower of London, I was given two pieces of very sound advice on history by my predecessor. 'Firstly,' he said, 'in order to understand the history of the Tower, start with the Tudors and work outwards.' Nine years later, I am just emerging from the early Tudors into the fascinating era of the Elizabethans.

'Secondly,' he added, 'you will get a steady stream of historical questions from members of the public. When you do so, send for Yeoman Warder Harrison.' In following this advice, it soon became apparent to me that Mr Harrison had been taking more interest than the other 150 or so residents in the Tower Prisoners and their case histories. By his careful studies of original records, he became not only my 'historical expert' but also a most helpful colleague.

Many were the letters I received and passed to Mr Harrison and they were always promptly returned from his flat in the top of the Middle Tower with a reply bearing the hallmarks of his labours. I always enjoyed and learned from these brief but comprehensive writings.

I was therefore delighted to hear from Mr Harrison again and to learn that, although he had retired after more than twenty-one years as a member of the Yeoman Body, he is still using his literary talents.

This 'Diary' captures the atmosphere of its times and holds special memories for me. My family and I were proud to live in Queen's House for five years, the same period as the Diary; Sir Owen Hopton lived there too, although for twenty years, including these five. The Diary recalls Catholic prisoners being forcibly dragged into the Chapel of St Peter ad Vincula and subjected to hours of sermonising against their will. I personally happened to be the first Roman Catholic Governor since the Reformation and had the freedom to enjoy taking my official pew for Matins in the Chapel and to invite Jesuits and priests to say private Masses in the Bell Tower, where SS Thomas More and Bishop John Fisher had been held.

It was with great pleasure that I accepted Mr Harrison's request to write this foreword and it was no surprise to find his usual depth of scholarship and fine detail in this fascinating work.

Major General C. Tyler CB
Resident Governor, H.M. Tower of London, 1989-94

INTRODUCTION

Irrespective of the author's beliefs, opinions, political persuasions or morals, any and all ancient documents that recount intimate and explicit insights into contemporaneous events must deservedly be consulted as primary source material by historians. The valuable and charming works of such writers as John Stow, Henry Machyn, John Evelyn, Samuel Pepys and many others have illuminated the pages of our island's history by virtue of their meticulous attention for fine detail without which researchers would be left groping in the dark.

The fascinating and mysterious document we are about to examine is never likely to gain as much fame as the works of those named above; and yet, without full recognition, it has been consulted and repeatedly quoted by many authoritative historical writers since the sixteenth century purely because it is one of those rarities which helps to throw a faint glimmer of light into what would otherwise be a dark corner of the Elizabethan era.

Whereas this particular document from the archives has occasionally passed under the popular title *Diarium Turris* (Tower Diary) or more commonly as *Rishton's Diary*, it has taken some considerable time to decide on a more fitting title for this work, not for reasons of sensationalism but because the previous titles have often led to a somewhat bogus impression.

To have selected the former name might mislead the reader into thinking this was some form of official publication maintained by the Tower authorities; on the other hand, to use the latter heading would certainly have left the reader wondering at the choice when Edward Rishton really does not merit a mention in the title as shall be proved as we progress.

ORIGINS OF THE DIARY

In order to pick up the tangled thread of this journal, we need firstly to travel back to the year 1576 when a Jesuit priest named Nicholas Sander or Sanders put pen to paper to compose a most scathing attack against the religious revolution known as the Reformation. Sander's Latin manuscript – which was never published but was secretly copied out in longhand for subversive circulation – passed under the title *De Origine ac Progressu Schismatis Anglicani* (The Rise and Growth of the Anglican Schism or split with the Church of Rome). It is often referred to as *De Schismate* (About the Schism).

Being one of the more fanatical Catholics of his day – he would die in Ireland fighting for his cause in 1581 – Sander pulled no punches in his literary assault on those who had brought about the breach from Rome. His manuscript provided startling and specific details as proof that Queen Anne Boleyn was actually the illegitimate daughter of King Henry VIII. It was therefore patently obvious to the readership that the king's marriage to her was not only polygamous but also incestuous. The author also submitted that the king's chancellor, Sir Thomas More, was opposed to the royal betrothal as he was personally aware of Henry's liaison with Anne's mother and yet, out of love and fellowship for his monarch, had maintained the secret by his silence even to the scaffold and grave.

In those dark days of superstition, Sander reaped a rich harvest of propaganda from the death of Henry's only son, Edward VI, which fell on the precise anniversary of the execution of 'The King's Good Servant'. More had been beheaded upon Tower Hill on 6th July 1535 and Edward passed away on July 6th 1553. Is it any wonder that those who opposed these many aspersions chose to nickname the author 'Doctor Slander'?

His manuscript of 1576, which as we have seen was never published but existed in a number of hand-written copies, was slowly forgotten and allowed to gather dust for the next nine years. Then, in 1585, one of the longhand copies was handed over to Father Edward Rishton with instructions from his superiors that he was to update the Latin chronicle of the Anglican Schism by means of a continuator in preparation for printing and distribution in more substantial numbers. His allotted task was, quite simply, to recount details of the continued persecution of the English Catholic community since Elizabeth's accession. It is known that Sander had made a start on this aspect; but Father Rishton chose to discard this section in favour of rewriting the account from 1558 to date.

Later the same year, his fully revised edition was published from Cologne, which was given the classical name *Aggripinae* on the title page. That this first edition was an overnight success would be an understatement. Those few copies that found their way onto the English market (and the many others dispersed throughout Europe) created havoc and a popular demand for more copies. To put it mildly, Rishton had written a best seller and so, to meet popular demand, a second edition was published from Rome the following year.

This new edition was even more popular because, whilst the text composed by Sander and Rishton remained unaltered, the new volume was even further expanded by the inclusion of an extra appendix at the rear. This is when the confusion started. Carrying the eye-catching title *Diarium Rerum Gestarum in Turri Londinensi* which was often abbreviated to *Diarium Turris* but without the name of an author, it was believed that this must be the personal Diary of Edward Rishton who had just recently returned to Europe from five years in prison in London. How mistaken they were...

It is known that Rishton's work was later translated into English, French, Italian and Spanish but, despite a most exhaustive search for an English translation, it was only possible to locate the anonymous *The Rise and Progress of the English Reformation, with Additions and Improvements by the Rev. Edward Rishton* (J. Christie, Dublin, 1827) and the more recent and popular translation *The Rise and Growth of the Anglican Schism with a Continuation by Edward Rishton* translated and edited by David Lewis (London, 1877). On inspection, however, it was found that each of these was a translation of the later third edition, also published from Rome, but in 1587.

This discovery came as something of a shock because closer examination revealed yet another alteration to the format from the first and second editions. With no apologies or explanations, the editor had deleted the entire *Diarium Turris* in favour of a much larger appendix entitled *Annals of the Schism*. This comprised a very useful almanac of momentous dates from the start of the Reformation – deemed to have opened in 1471 with the birth of Wolsey at Ipswich – up to the time of printing in 1587.

In checking through this new almanac, it was noticed that, of the original ninety-one *Diarium* entries, only eighteen had been retained but in slightly altered wording; the remaining seventy-three had been totally discarded, irrespective of their merits. If we accept that the two aforementioned translations are the only ones ever produced, it naturally follows that the entire *Diarium Turris* has never been the subject of a full English translation – until now!

Admittedly, some extracts from the Latin Diary have occasionally found their way into historical writings of the Elizabethan period; to have ignored them would have been a grave oversight. But those historians who did so were usually well versed in reading original Latin material and did not see a need for a complete translation. For example, John Lingard's *History of England* (London, 1819) contained a paragraph as a footnote which was easily recognised as coming directly from the preface of the Latin *Diarium* and was Lingard's own rapid translation.

Whilst modern authors tend to lean very heavily on David Lewis's 1877 translation of *De Schismate* – and very useful it can be – it simply means that the only occasions when mention might be given to the *Diarium* are those eighteen entries that survived in the almanac *Annals of the Schism*. Only occasional mention is given to the other seventy three 'deleted' entries, many of which still remain unquoted in the English language.

There is every probability that the original *Diarium* would have continued to retain its secrets if it were not for a reproduction of its Latin format in *The History and Antiquities of the Tower of London* by John Whitcomb Bayley *(2 Volume edition, T. Cadell)* [see Appx 1]. Unfortunately, this author omitted to add a footnote to indicate the source from which he had gleaned those pages of Latin for which reason it is now impossible to ascertain whether Bayley had found an original manuscript in the archives – he was, after all, the assistant keeper of the Tower Records – or if he might have extracted the appendix from a copy of the 1586 edition of *De Schismate*. For simplicity's sake, we shall assume he copied the latter.

In the cheerful confusion of a nineteenth century printing shop, certain errors found their way into Bayley's pages *(Appx to Part II, pp. lxxii – lxxxii)* which did not fully agree with the original Latin *Diarium*. Two entries had been omitted in entirety and many of the datings had either been misplaced or misquoted. These latter errors, which shall be commented upon and corrected by footnotes, had been occasioned by the compositor's change of format. Whereas the 1586 version had been tabulated into two columns per page with dates alongside, Bayley's reproduction placed all dates at the start of the diary entries with the text running across the full width of the page. Admittedly, the overall impression was much neater but it did not cater for the many instances in which dates were offset further down a column or, in the cases of double- and treble-dating, in varying positions down the columns.

Even more confusion arose in Bayley's Index. In listing the Latin names given in his appendix, Bayley inserted his own translations which were nothing more than immature anglicisations. Some of these were so unusual that they only tended to confuse what had already proved to be a rather muddied trail. As a prime example, we find the Latin name 'Rodolphus Cervinus' had been literally taken to mean 'Rudolph Cervin', instead of the famous martyr St Ralph Sherwin who was intended.

Nonetheless, at the time of putting together his most valuable reference books on Tower history, the diligent study of archives was still very much in its infancy so we can forgive Bayley his minor faults especially in light of the fact that he did, at least, have the forethought to incorporate the Latin appendix which inspired this present translation and investigation. In so doing, his printing and translational errors may finally be corrected.

Now that the complete circuit of the Latin Diary has been tracked from its early inception up to the present time, it can more readily be appreciated that, with such a devious and chequered record, the original manuscript that was used by the printers in Rome – whatever it might have looked like – has either been lost to the ravages of time or still lies dormant, neglected and forgotten in the archives of some little known European library or seminary. Whatever might be the case, it is unlikely that the scraps of paper or parchment on which the imprisoned priest had composed his secret and illegal dossier will ever again see the light of day. On the credit side, we can be grateful to John Whitcomb Bayley for having the forethought to include the Latin pages in his wonderful works of reference. These were the pages that aroused sufficient curiosity in one of his readers to inspire this particular investigation and eventually the first full and complete translation of *The Diary of a Priest in the Tower*.

WHO WROTE THE DIARY?

From remarks given in the preface to the *Diarium*, we shall discover that the author of this secret journal was certainly a Roman Catholic priest who spent slightly more than four years as a prisoner of conscience in the Tower of London; he underwent various sufferings at the hands of his gaolers; was kept isolated from all contact with the other inmates; faced the travesty of a trial; was then sentenced to death but was eventually reprieved and banished the realm.

Because the diarist failed to put his name to his important notes and as the pen picture given above could apply to many imprisoned priests of that era, there has always been a great deal of divided opinion over just who might have taken the time and trouble to compose this, albeit incomplete, dossier of the sufferings of Elizabethan Catholic prisoners. By examining the evidence in a little more detail, it is hoped that this chapter will finally dispel all controversy.

Comment has already been passed on how the *Diarium* often passes under the popular epithet *Rishton's Diary* but this has proved to be founded on purely circumstantial evidence. Admittedly, Father Edward Rishton fills just about every one of the qualifications set out in the preface but for one overriding factor that appears to have been overlooked by most recusant writers. We shall examine Rishton a little later but, in the one solitary mention of his name in the *Diarium*, we notice but a brief allusion to his appearing in court with other priests charged with conspiracy. We shall also examine other contemporary documents that provide irrefutable proof of his being brought to trial from another prison and that he went elsewhere after sentence of death had been passed. Quite simply, he was never held as a prisoner in the Tower of London although, we must accept, he was a known figure to most of the other accused priests who appeared in court that day with him.

It suffices to glance briefly through the *Tower Bills* of the period (Appx 2) to see that not a single claim for fees is entered in the name of Rishton. As a priest, he would not have had the wherewithal to finance his own 'diett and fees' as were exacted from those with private means of support. We must not forget, however, that he was certainly numbered amongst the first batch of twenty-one Catholic exiles who were loaded onto a galleon at Tower Wharf in January 1584-5 for the journey to the coast of Normandy.

Moreover, upon reaching the safe refuge of his seminary-college, we know that his superiors set him the task of writing the continuation to Nicholas Sander's manuscript attacking the English Reformation. The book published in the first instance in 1585 was solely his work. It was only as a result of the second edition in 1586, into which the *Diarium* had been appended, that the readership and later historians came to believe that these added pages had also been composed by Rishton during his known term of imprisonment.

Then came the controversial third edition of 1587 which made a particular point of erasing most of the *Diarium* entries in preference for an almanac entitled *Annals of the Schism*. This was the edition that was eventually translated into English; but it now appears that, after Rishton's death, the duties of editor passed into the very capable hands of Father Robert Parsons SJ (1546-1610). This is really momentous news because, in the introductory notes to his translation, David Lewis submitted that the printers at Rome were responsible for feeding up-to-the-minute details into their third edition that concluded with the execution of Mary, Queen of Scots on 8th February 1586-7. Nonetheless, the printers would not have had authority to remove the *Diarium* or the ability to compose the very detailed *Annals* almanac; this was solely Parsons' prerogative. Well might we wonder what may have inspired this drastic alteration to the format of a book that had already proved its worth. Even the eighteen extracts from the *Diarium* had been subjected to heavy amendment action, as we shall soon discover. But why should this be?

There is no doubting that Parsons was an astute and well educated individual who was receiving news and intelligence reports from a wide network of informers in England and elsewhere. From them he would have learned – and as the analysis will show – that the *Diarium* contained far too many errors that could be slated and refuted by Elizabeth's experts, more especially Sir Francis Walsingham, the queen's secretary of state. By discarding the *Diarium* and composing his more accurate *Annals of the Schism*, Parsons produced a more reliable and accurate breakdown of more notable events that could not so easily be criticised by Walsingham's propaganda machine.

Parsons knew exactly what he was up against as he had once served on the English Mission during which time he had found and won many useful friends and contacts. When his close companion Edmund Campion was captured and conducted to the Tower with other captives in July 1581, Parsons appreciated that their interrogation (often by means of torture) and the follow up process of the next few weeks would be concentrated on seeking him out. He therefore fled the country with the next available boatload of Catholic refugees some time between 14th and 21st August 1581. As he was never apprehended and was in Europe for the remainder of the time covered in the *Diarium*, it cannot represent a record of his own experiences.

In view of this assurance that neither Rishton nor Parsons compiled the *Diarium* – although each had been indirectly touched by it – it is still necessary to cast around among the ranks of the other Catholic priests who are known to have held the same qualifications as those set out in the preface with a view to determining, once and for all, which one really was the secret diarist.

We first begin to notice a subtle change of opinion over the author in Volume 3 of the Catholic Record Society's *Miscellanea* series. In the process of editing his valuable article *The Tower Bills 1575-1589*, John Hungerford Pollen (1820-1902) raised a convincing case suggesting that John Hart must have been the man responsible because, as he wrote, 'his term of imprisonment coincides with the Diary whereas Rishton never seems to have been in the Tower at all'. Father John Hart will come in for much closer scrutiny as we progress but, at this early stage, it suffices to say he fills each and every qualification of the preface. Moreover, he makes more appearances in the entries than anyone else; but probably most significant of all yet unmentioned in Pollen's article, it is needful to draw attention to further relevant evidence that can only strengthen this theorising even more.

Comment has already been passed on the prolific writings of Robert Parsons after he fled the country but, of all his compositions in support of the Catholic cause, the most pertinent statement was discovered in a brief aside to his projected *Life of Edmund Campion*. Tucked away within the body of his preparatory notes we actually find Parsons making just one allusion to 'Hart's Diary' and, as no other similar diary of a priest who was held in the Tower from 1580 to 1584-5 has ever come to light, we must finally concur that the one we are about to study is indeed that of Father John Hart.

SCENARIO

Whilst not wishing to write a potted history of the Reformation, it would be remiss in a work of this kind to omit all mention of the events that directly contributed in some way to the diarist and his fellow sufferers being cast into the Tower to be treated the way they were. By the same token, it would not be a bad thing to clarify some of the terminology of the period to assist the novice. Those who feel they are *au fait* with these aspects might prefer to scan through this section or even move directly to the translation at page 35.

RELIGIOUS CHANGES IN ENGLAND

Sufficient has already been written elsewhere about the breach from Rome during Henry VIII's divorce crisis and the subsequent Dissolution of the Monasteries. It is not intended to cover that ground again. It suffices to say that, in the eleven years since Henry's death (1547-1558), the religion of England had swung back and fro like a pendulum at the virtual whim of Henry's three children, Edward VI, Mary I and Elizabeth I.

When Elizabeth I came to the throne in 1558, a new Act of Supremacy declared it an act of treason for anyone to maintain the Pope's authority over England. The Oath of Supremacy (*see* Appx 9) called for acknowledgement of the queen as Supreme Governor in Earth of the Church in England. The title *Supreme Head*, as assumed by Elizabeth's father, was considered but rejected on sexist grounds.

It was one thing to write religious changes into the statute books but quite another to ensure each and every citizen conformed to those new laws. Changing religion is not as simple as changing a television channel. Even if it were, there can be no certain guarantee that all viewers have changed at the same time or moved over to the same channel. It might be argued that another change of monarch could result in yet another change of religion; it could not go on unabated. It was therefore tacitly agreed that wealthy Catholics – many living in the remote wilds in the north of England – who made no secret of their opposing opinions could be excused the Oath and even gain appointment to high office so long as they were not hostile to the government of the day. Their presence in parliament often made for healthier debates on important matters when the extreme Protestant element might have bulldozed through more bigotted and harsher legislation.

JESUITS

In 1535, the Spanish ex-soldier Ignatius de Loyola founded the Society of Jesus having gained papal sanction for the venture. His organisation was dedicated to theological studies, preaching, the education of young men and the furtherance of foreign missions throughout the world. Its members were trained to be soldiers of Christ with a code of discipline as severe as that of any elite forces unit, they also being bound by a vow of poverty and celibacy. By the time of General de Loyola's death in 1556 his so called Jesuits were established in all Catholic countries of Europe and also in Africa, India and South America. For his devotion to the faith, Loyola was canonised in 1622.

Throughout the Elizabethan era, these Jesuits would find themselves in the forefront, acting as shock troops, in the Counter-Reformation, that is the Roman Catholic backlash to the Protestant Reformation sweeping through northern Europe. It will be noticed that the first year of the *Diarium* coincided with the arrival of the first Jesuits on English soil. The government of the second half of Elizabeth's reign looked upon them as extreme activists or Hispano-Catholics determined to overthrow the order of the day until the world was subject to papal domination.

RECUSANTS AND SCHISMATICS

In Elizabeth's first year, the Act of Uniformity restored the use of Edward VI's *Book of Common Prayer*, banned the Mass and enforced compulsory attendance at Protestant worship. Later acts would declare it an act of treason to even refer to the queen as a heretic, to bring papal bulls into the realm, to be reconciled to the Roman Church or to induce others to do so. This latter offence was termed 'persuading to popery'.

Those whose consciences would not permit them to conform to the new laws and rituals were classified *Recusants* – another name for nonconformist – and, by means of their continued recusancy, could be fined, compelled to undergo religious re-education, or even imprisoned in an effort to gain their conformity or information on other recusants. In some outlying districts, local sheriffs or officials who held responsibility for raising these fines were often themselves in sympathy with such offenders and tended to turn a blind eye.

On the other hand, those who supported the breach or schism from Rome were reviled by Romanist propaganda as *Schismatics* or, more often, heretics. It would be a simple matter if these had been the only two divisions; but there were countless citizens who felt their loyalties torn between the law of the land and the faith of their forefathers. Such persons were content to join their neighbours in public worship in their parish church and would then delight at the opportunity to slip away secretly to attend Mass if the opportunity arose. These could expect little sympathy from either side once their duplicity was uncovered.

THE QUEEN'S EXCOMMUNICATION

Things made a dramatic change for the worse on 25th May 1570 when John Felton was accused of affixing the papal bull *Regnans in Excelsis* to the door of the Bishop of London's palace. So called from the preamble beginning 'He that Reigns on High...', the contents of this declaration caught everyone, including the English government and Philip of Spain, totally unawares. The bull proclaimed in the strongest possible terms that the queen, as a 'servant of wickedness', was excommunicated and all of her subjects absolved from their allegiance to her. The culprit who had dared to publicise this scandalous and treasonable document, was tried as a traitor, condemned and executed by hanging, drawing and quartering near the scene of his offence on 8th August 1570. Felton has since been beatified.

Because Pope Pius V had composed *Regnans in Excelsis* from unreliable and out of date intelligence, the uprising of the English he had hoped to provoke never materialised. On the contrary, his publication inspired an early example of that peculiar trait of the English character that has since been called *The Dunkirk Spirit*. Whilst Elizabeth was deemed to be an outcast from the rest of European Christendom, she must have been delighted in finding herself ever more idolised by her subjects after excommunication. To demonstrate her contempt for Rome still further, she released Thomas Howard, 17th Duke of Norfolk from the Tower on 3rd August 1570 on the clear understanding that he would relinquish all thoughts of marriage to Mary, Queen of Scots. Pius Quintus died two years later and was succeeded by Gregory XIII; but the latter's refusal to revoke the tenor of *Regnans in Excelsis* would eventually lead to the phrasing of the infamous *Bloody Question* over loyalties, 'If a papal army landed in England, which side would you take?' On the advice of the Catholic priests and leading Catholic dignitaries, the recusants were advised that such a hypothetical question deserved a hypothetical answer, 'When and if such a day shall come, I shall act according to my conscience'.

OVERSEAS ORDINATIONS

Subsequent to the legislation of the first year of Elizabeth I, young men who felt themselves drawn towards a career in the clergy could only seek ordination into the Protestant Church. The government was confident that the few Catholic ministers still at large would, albeit gradually, fade from the scene by natural wastage to be succeeded by the increasing number of Anglican clergymen. This might well have been the case had it not been for the work of William Allen (1532-94).

In 1568, with assistance from Philip of Spain, Allen founded a seminary college at Douai, close to the Franco-Belgian border. Being aware of the pro-Catholic atmosphere at Oxford University (having been a student there before leaving the country), Allen arranged for word to be passed on this newly founded seat of learning where adventurous young men, probably excited at the prospect of being anti-establishment, could be formally trained for the Catholic priesthood. To differentiate the college from the town, it became common practice to refer to the former as Doway or Douay.

Later, in the face of anti-Catholic persecution, the college at Douay withdrew to smaller premises at Rheims on 22nd March 1577-8. Due to limited space, an overflow college was established in Rome in 1579. Here, at the very heart of Catholicism, English students were expected to undergo a more rigorous course of instruction under the aegis of the Society of Jesus. Later seminaries were founded at Valladolid (1589), Seville and St Omer (1592) and Lisbon (1629). Students ordained from these establishments were thenceforward known as *seminary priests* as opposed to seculars who had been ordained at home.

MISSIONARY PRIESTS

In the initial stages, William Allen's successful seminary students were drafted to minister to various Catholic churches in Europe. At a later stage he was informed by his superiors that he was to prepare his scholars for service in England. It was a slow and gradual process. The first four priests made the dangerous Channel crossing in 1574; seven more followed in 1575; a further eighteen in 1576; fifteen more in 1577. By 1580, as the Diary opens, there were about a hundred of his old boys ministering secretly throughout the length and breadth of England. Filling the hiatus created by the demise of the regular clergy, these men came to be known as *missionary priests.*

Despite the sparsity of numbers, these subversive elements were looked upon by the government as enemies of state. To continue with their work, the missionaries adopted cunning disguises, aliases, secret signs and code words and many other ploys to evade detection, betrayal, capture and death. Being constantly on the move from one safe house to another and steering clear of political activity, they struggled with their task of ministering to those whose only desire was to worship God in their own way.

THE SECRET SERVICE

To counter the threat of enemy incursion – the missionary priests and Jesuits were only one part of a major invasion threat – Sir Francis Walsingham, the queen's secretary of state, established the foundations of a secret intelligence agency, firstly at his own expense and later with generous grants from the privy purse. Operating out of taverns, embassies, ports and suspect households, the total number of agents in his employ has never been truly ascertained. To these agents must be added law enforcement officials such as local mayors and sheriffs and other petty officials who were always ready to feed Walsingham with local snippets of information. Then there were those malcontents who might have undergone a part of their seminary training at one of Allen's colleges and had returned disillusioned at the ascetic life style but with a good memory for the faces they had seen whilst abroad. Last, and certainly by no means least, were those villains clinging to the edges of society who were solely attracted by the rewards and benefits that accrued from priest-hunting. With such a secret army at his disposal, it may then be appreciated how heavily Walsingham's hand rested on the pulse of the nation.

By 1580, he is also known to have four agents in Spain, twelve in France, nine in Germany, four in Italy, three in the Low Countries and operatives working out of Algiers, Tripoli and Constantinople. It has been estimated that all of his counter-insurgency measures must have been costing as much as £3,000 to £4,000 per year and opinions of his secret service fall into two camps. There are many who say that, for its time, it was a brilliantly managed operation using the money wisely and laying a firm foundation for the British Secret Service. Others are wont to condemn his work as incompetent and a disgraceful waste of money.

Be that as it may, Walsingham, one of the leading proponents of the Protestant cause in his day, never allowed religion to cloud his actions. A talented and most intelligent statesman, he viewed his role as nothing more than that of a faithful servant implementing his employer's every whim and fancy. Papers bearing his signature throughout his career contain regular notes on the queen's decision to be sought touching certain matters. He was just one of the many talented courtiers who rallied around the throne to provide stability and enforce royal policies.

ANTI-CATHOLIC SENTIMENTS

Before Henry VIII's reformation of the English Church, as much as a third of all cultivated land was held by the Church. After the dissolution of the monasteries, the king presented much of this valuable property to supporters of his new ideals. Some of the monastery buildings were converted internally into stately mansions; others were ripped apart to provide the necessary materials for building even more impressive residences. Passing rapidly through the reign of Mary Tudor, when some attempt was made to recover church property, there were many *nouveaux riches* landowners still comfortably ensconced on former church property. By 1580, some of these men were holding down positions of great national importance and could not accept that the Romanists only sought freedom of worship. In their opinion, a return of Catholicism could only mean demands for the return of Catholic Church property.

By this time, all European monarchies were adopting the policy *cuius regio eius religio* – the religion of a country is that of its ruler – and to adopt any other creed could only be an act of treason to that ruler. In England, this was a powerful weapon in the hands of the landowners who cherished their property deeds and felt themselves endangered by the Catholic threat.

This threat, if it can be classed as such, was best reflected in the reading matter of the day. After the Bible and Book of Common Prayer, the most widely read publication was Foxe's *Actes and Monuments*, a fearsome dossier covering the history of the martyrs of the Marian persecution of Protestants. More commonly known as *The Book of Martyrs*, John Foxe's catalogue reminded his readers, if they needed a reminder, of all the terrible sufferings of the many Protestants who had opposed Mary's return to the Catholic fold. One only needs to read a page or two at random to notice how Foxe dwelt on the long drawn out pains of the victims as they suffered the traditional death of a heretic by burning.

Having read such blood curdling accounts, children were wont to suffer awful nightmares. Is it any wonder that the monarch who had ruled over such an age was known as Bloody Mary? Many children weaned on bedtime stories from Foxe had now matured to adulthood yet could never erase from the backs of their minds those childhood nightmares. It might almost be classed as a form of brain washing but, when those childhood fears of Protestant sufferings are added to the threatened loss of personal estates, it can more easily be appreciated how much the Catholics were so reviled.

THE NEW MARTYRS

Confident in the certain knowledge that a martyr tradition could prove a double-edged weapon, Elizabeth was loathe to emulate the actions of her half-sister in dealing with her religious opponents. This could only result in Catholic martyrs around whom legends, on a par with Foxe, could be woven. It was not until nineteen years after her accession that one of the missionary priests named Cuthbert Mayne was singled out to be the proto-martyr of her reign. He was hanged, drawn and quartered at Launceston, Cornwall on 30th November 1577. Mayne was canonised in 1970.

Almost three months later, on 3rd February 1577-8, another missionary was similarly dealt with at Tyburn in London, a venue destined to witness many more horrific scenes in the years that followed. In this instance, the victim was John Nelson, a Yorkshireman who, like John Mayne, had been in England for little more than a year, both being former students at Douay. Nelson has since been beatified.

The third victim of this new hard-line policy was not a priest but simply a linen draper who was apprehended in Chancery Lane, close to where the modern Record Office now stands, whilst settling a few final business arrangements. His name was Thomas Sherwood and it seems quite likely that his visit to Chancery Lane was connected in some way to his plan for leaving the country to seek training for the priesthood at Douay. He enters our annals as the very first recusant to come to the Tower of London where he spent a time confined to the 'dungeon among the Ratts'. He was later subjected to torture on the rack in an endeavour to discover something more about the organisation which spirited young men out of the country for training at Douay. Sherwood was tried at Westminster on the same day as John Nelson was executed. Being condemned to the same fate, he suffered at Tyburn four days later and has since been beatified.

These three executions over as many months marked the start of a new *Reign of Terror* and also a new martyr tradition. They were destined to be the forerunners of almost three hundred to take place in the remaining years of Elizabeth's reign, virtually tallying by grim coincidence with the numbers who had died for their own opposing tenets in the previous reign. Whereas Mary had sent her opponents to the fires of Smithfield to suffer the death of a heretic under the revised statute *De Comburendo Heretico* of 1401, the Catholic enemies of Elizabeth were cast as traitors and were fated to suffer death by the process of hanging, drawing and quartering.

———•———

1580

We now reach the momentous year 1580. At forty-seven years of age, Elizabeth I is at the pinnacle of her power at the halfway stage of her eventual forty-five years as monarch. She is still single but proposals for her marriage and the possible conception of an heir to her throne are still being considered and rejected. The present candidate for her hand is François, Duke of Alençon and Anjou, a French Catholic twenty years the queen's junior. An unusual match but a wise political choice, even though, in secret, Elizabeth refers to him as 'my frog'. Diplomats are constantly encouraged to believe that the wedding will soon take place; but their expectations are doomed to failure by the duke's death in four years time.

Spies have been planted everywhere including the royal laundry whence Spain is kept regularly informed of the condition of the queen's undergarments but, by remaining chaste, Elizabeth is providing the English Church with a surrogate Mother of Christ. Whilst Catholics traditionally offer up prayers to the Blessed Virgin Mary, English Protestant churches exalt their Virgin Elizabeth in all their services.

The covert arrival of the missionary priests in England is just one of the minor causes for concern. Financed by Pope Gregory XIII, led by Gerald Fitzgerald, Earl of Desmond and his cousin James FitzMaurice, and supported by Spanish and Portuguese mercenaries, an uprising in Ireland has been the cause of a great deal of concern, being viewed as an endeavour to establish a springboard for invading the mainland. From July through to December 1579, the queen's forces have been ruthless in crushing these rebels. In his capacity as papal nuncio to Ireland, Nicholas Sander is now on the run and the rebellion has almost come to an end. The earl's massive estates in south-west Ireland, covering some half a million acres, are later confiscated and presented to English settlers.

Due to the flight of their queen and her incarceration in the north of England, Scotland is very unsettled yet is confident that James, the son of Mary, Queen of Scots, must surely one day succeed to both thrones on Elizabeth's demise. In view of James' Catholic upbringing, it is considered that he will introduce more lenient legislation to Catholics on both sides of the border. A further twenty-three years will need to elapse before James VI of Scotland succeeds to the throne as James I of England.

Spain is in occupation of the Low Countries and is slowly being bled dry by the expense of maintaining her garrison troops by seaborne convoys having to run the gauntlet along the English Channel. It is an age of piracy on the high seas, more especially in the western Atlantic.

Having lost Calais to France towards the end of Mary's reign, England no longer has a foothold on the mainland of Europe and is now totally isolated, living in constant fear of a surprise French or Spanish invasion or, worse still, a Franco-Spanish Catholic alliance against Elizabeth. To counter this likely contingency, the queen has entered into an alliance with the French against their own inherent dread of a two pronged Spanish assault from the north and south. Apart from Rome, the remainder of Europe is in financial chaos and disorder.

There are a few prisoners in the Tower of London but, as usual, there is sufficient space to accept more. Some building lie silent and deserted, the wind whistling through the arrow loops to blow away all traces of former occupants. The concentric fortress bears many remarkable similarities to those now examined by twentieth-century tourists who are permitted to meander aimlessly through the complex seeking out traces of their ancient ancestors who might well have been held here.

In the centre of the grounds stands the Conqueror's great Norman Keep glistening in the sunlight after a fresh coating of whitewash has been daubed over the stonework. The Inner and Outer Ballium Walls encircling the White Tower echo to the noise of many employees moving hither and thither about their business. The countless shops and as many as six taverns in the Outer Bailey cater for their customers' demands. The drumming sound of horses' hooves beat a hollow tattoo across the surface of the stagnant water of the moat as riders arrive and canter gracefully over heavy wooden drawbridges, automatically ducking their heads as they pass beneath the portcullises set into the various archways. Heavy carts, laden with all manner of goods and drawn by tired horses, seek permission to enter. But this is no place for idle sightseers – admission by appointment only – yet the cacophony of noises is as confusing as any summer's day at the height of a modern tourist season.

Meanwhile, far off in Rome, the overflow of English students from William Allen's seminary at Rheims are diligently applying themselves to their religious studies. Their Jesuit instructors are most impressed with the enthusiasm, devotion and high standards achieved by their students, some of whom have proved themselves so akin to the aims of the Society of Jesus that they have been persuaded to enlist as members. At William Allen's own request, it has been accepted that some of these new English Jesuits could serve a very useful purpose by working on the English Mission with some of the seminary priests from Rome. It has also been agreed that, to maintain discipline between the two factions when they reach England, Thomas Goldwell, the former Bishop of St Asaph in exile since 1560, will travel with them to England.

A select group of fifteen assembles together to receive final blessing from the Pope. As they move off through the Flaminian Gate on 18th April 1580, every Englishman residing in Rome has turned out to see them off. For the younger element, it seems very much like the old days when others had set out to serve in the Holy Land in the Crusades. The older ones take turns in riding the two horses they share between them. Fully indoctrinated with a religious zeal that borders almost on insanity, they reflect on the fate of those many early Christians who had been jeered as they travelled along this same Via Dolorosa; but now the crowds are cheering, applauding and kneeling down in anticipation of a blessing from this daring band about to invade the bastions of the new 'Infidels' of Protestantism.

Clutching their newly presented *Agnus Dei* medallions to their breasts, the group of fifteen trudges steadily onwards and northwards into the solitude of the countryside. The procession takes on the air of a school outing as the roars of the crowds recede behind them. The first stage is to follow the muddy tracks that lead to Rheims where they are to be given a final briefing from William Allen. The constant downpour of rain cannot dampen their morale, even though some of the more elderly priests begin to show signs of fatigue as their days on the road lengthen into weeks.

Observers and spies are sending back regular reports of their progress to Sir Francis Walsingham even though their departure from Rome has been about as secretly managed as the triumphal return of a successful football team from Europe. All along the east and south coasts of England, ports and landing places are at full alert. Descriptions of some of the men have been distributed; anyone anxious to reap a handsome reward for apprehending a priest or Jesuit is heading for the coast in expectant enthusiasm. The security screen thus erected will take a great deal of cunning to penetrate.

Meantime, on Tuesday 31st May, amid scenes of great jubilation, the weary band of fifteen footsore travellers arrives at Rheims after more then six weeks of heavy going. Old friends are reunited, reminiscences of the intervening years are exchanged and prayers of thanksgiving are offered for their safe arrival. Unfortunately, it is patently obvious that Bishop Goldwell is too ill to travel any farther or serve any useful purpose in England. Even whilst they are seeking out papal dispensation for him to abandon his alloted mission, a fresh outbreak of plague forces his companions to speed up their preparations for the next most dangerous stage of their journey. From the fact that they do not appear to have reached England, we must assume that five of the other elderly priests remain behind.

Caught up in the excitement of the arrangements, three new volunteers come forward and offer to fill the vacancies. They are Doctor Humphrey Ely, Thomas Cottam and, the man in whom we are most interested, John Hart. It should not pass unnoticed, however, that Cottam has only recently arrived in Rheims having made a dash from Lyons when he had heard about some old friends leaving Rome. For a part of his journey, Cottam has travelled quite innocently in the company of one Charles Sledd or Slade, little suspecting that his road companion is, in fact, one of Walsingham's most successful agents. Yet another description is already winging its way back to England to be handed over to the secretary of state.

William Allen, whilst giving full approval and blessing for the three volunteers to join the others, begins to have misgivings. Appreciating that the large contingent from Rome can not have passed through the heart of Europe without someone reporting their moves, and in his concern of the probability of an anti-Jesuit backlash that could harm the priests, he advocates that the group of twelve would be best advised to break themselves down into smaller groups of twos and threes each travelling by way of different routes to different seaports, Dieppe, Rouen, Dunkirk and Boulogne. Ely, Cottam and Hart are appointed to travel on the Dunkirk to Dover ferry.

On Trinity Sunday, 5th June, after slightly more than eleven years away from home, John Hart moves out with his two new found companions waving a cheerful adieu to his many friends, some of whom he will never see again and others he will only learn about whilst a prisoner. Nothing eventful seems to have happened on the one hundred and fifty mile march to Dunkirk and it must have been mid-June by the time they all reach Dover.

Confident they can bluff their way past the customs officers waiting at the quayside, they split up and stride nonchalantly down the gangplank hoping to melt into the mass of humanity around the dockside. But Hart and Cottam are singled out and called forward for questioning. From the written descriptions they have, the searchers find no difficulty in identifying them but, even then, the captives try to argue their innocence. All is to no avail and they are placed under arrest pending further confirmation and interrogation in London.

Thomas Andrews, one of Lord Cobham's deputies and a personality well known to the customs men, is asked to escort them to the capital and gladly agrees if he can have an assistant. A bystander detaches himself from the inquisitive crowd and explains he will be glad to assist as, by coincidence, he is also headed for London. The willing helper is recognised by the searchers from his previous business trips through the Channel port and so his kind offer is gladly accepted. As the escort leads the captives away, the customs men notice a peculiar look on the faces of the prisoners but do not stop them to ask what has amused them. Even if they had, Hart and Cottam would not admit the truth that the kindly helper is none other than their bosom friend, Doctor Humphrey Ely.

Little if anything is known of the circumstances but it must be patently obvious to the reader that, at some later stage of the journey to London, the group of four splits into two thereby permitting Ely to 'lose' his captive. More surprisingly, the daring doctor then has the effrontery to report to Walsingham to tender an apology for allowing Cottam to escape. Still fully unaware of Ely's credentials, the secretary of state explodes in a fit of temper and issues order for Ely to be sent to the Tower, not for any religious offence, but for permitting an escape.

Thomas Andrews completes his part of the errand and is suitably rewarded with a gift of one hundred shillings (£5) for delivering John Hart to the court at Nonsuch. The next few moments are still something of a grey area as John Hart meets Walsingham for the very first time. In an account written long after the event, Robert Parsons submitted rather naively that the secretary was so impressed with his prisoner that he took pity on him. This does not sound at all like Walsingham. It seems more likely that Sir Francis saw clearly through the prisoner's bold exterior and detected certain signs of weakness in Hart which, with time, he felt he could exploit.

Whatever was said at that initial confrontation, Walsingham runs true to type by sending Hart to Oxford for a specified term of three months during which he is to be re-educated in religion by John Rainolds or Reynolds (1549-1607). The reader will find, time and again, that three months was considered sufficient time to teach and convert someone to the tenets of Protestantism.

At this stage, Hart is unaware that the three months will gradually extend themselves into four years and seven months in custody, during which he will exhibit alternating bouts of moral courage and weakness. The secret and illegal dossier he will compile during his time in prison reveals just a small part of those traumatic experiences. And now, after more than four hundred years, his Latin *Diarium Turris* finally enters the English language.

THE DIARY TRANSLATED

NOTES

1. Each entry of the Diary has been allocated a prefix number which did not feature in the original Latin *Diarium*. These numbers have only been appended to facilitate cross references to other notes.

2. Footnotes have been kept to a minimum by means of a number of appendices which are given after the translation. In their turn, where necessary, these appendices are back-referenced to certain entries or footnotes.

3. Name spellings tend to vary from one authority to another. In the translation, only one spelling will be cited; all other styles and aliases will be found in the biographical notes in Appendix 13.

4. Repeated mentions are given to *Tower Bills*. All of the available Bills for the period of the Diary are reproduced at Appendix 2. Unfortunately, the series is incomplete but, even allowing for these gaps, the Bills can often be the only authority for confirming or refuting entries from the Diary.

5. Unless otherwise stated, all executions were by hanging, drawing and quartering. In passing the sentence, the judge was required to spell out all the gory details of what would happen, thus:
   It is the judgement of this court that you ... name ... return to the prison from whence you came; from thence you must be drawn to the place of execution; when you come there, you must be hanged by the neck, but not until you are dead, for you must be cut down alive; then your bowels must be taken out and burned before your face; then your head must be severed from your body and your body divided into four quarters, and these must be at the queen's disposal. And God Almighty be merciful to your soul.

THINGS THAT HAPPENED IN THE TOWER OF LONDON FOR THE CATHOLIC FAITH FROM 1580 TO 1585.

INDEX or DIARY

FROM OBSERVATIONS AND RECOLLECTIONS THAT HAPPENED DURING ALL HIS TIME AS A CAPTIVE

PREFACE

Apart from those prisons in the City of London which are reserved for other purposes (among which is Ludgate which is only used to imprison freemen citizens for debt), there are eleven public and capacious prisons into which almost all types, sexes and ages are thrown these days because they confess the Catholic religion. Their names are: the Gatehouse, Westminster, the Fleet; Newgate, Bridewell, the two Compters, the King's Bench, the Marshalsea, the White Lion, the Clink, and the Tower or Fortress [see Appx 4]. In the last of which, as by the special grace of God, for the sole reason that I was a priest of the Catholic Church, I was detained for more than four years and underwent various vicissitudes of conditions, circumstances and sufferings and was even sentenced to death (which was later commuted to exile), it seemed to me that I would be doing something not unusual, nor hostile to the glory of God, if I were to write out what I had noted when I was in that prison, day by day. Here therefore the Christian reader, by comparing what happened in the one prison with what must have happened in the other ten in that city and then those with all the others which are in the rest of England, and comparing the happenings of four years with the twenty-seven that Elizabeth has reigned, can easily estimate how many and how great were the Catholics who have suffered for the faith in that kingdom and are still suffering.

In order that you may understand these things better, it is necessary to know that this prison which they call the Tower is different from the other prisons in that each prisoner has his own cell or prison-room and his own guard who always keeps him under observation, preventing him from seeing or speaking with others and making any communication, either by letter or messenger, impossible. From his cell, he is escorted to all other places, whether he is to undergo torture (which was inflicted on the Catholics at various times at the will of their persecutors) or to be examined or questioned.

Now, in this prison, there are seven different types of torture or particular forms of ill-treatment which can be inflicted on different people at different times for differing reasons. Of these, the first is the Pit, a certain subterranean hole twenty feet deep and entirely without light.

The second is a cell, or rather a very narrow cave, scarcely large enough for an upright man which, from the little rest it allows, they call 'Little Ease'.

The third is the Rack which, by means of rollers and other machinery, tears a man's limbs asunder.

The fourth they call 'The Scavenger's Daughter', a name derived from that of the inventor, I believe; it consists of an iron band which compresses the hands, feet and head into a single circle.

The fifth is the iron gauntlets, by which means the hands are excruciatingly crushed.

The sixth is the fetters (Manacles) which load the arms.

The seventh is irons which are fitted to the feet.

This information will facilitate the understanding of the record which follows [*see* Appx 5].

I should also point out that this record only includes those things which were inflicted on Catholics on account of their religion that came to my notice in spite of the fact that I was imprisoned separately from the others. Other could doubtless have been noted by others at the same time. In the meantime, Christian reader, these few should be enough to arouse your pity so that you pray to God for our afflicted country. Farewell.

DIARY OF THAT WHICH PASSED IN THE TOWER OF LONDON

—— 1580 ——

JUNE [1]

1. 15th. William Tirwhit, the eldest son of that famous man Robert Tirwhit, knight[2], was conveyed to the Tower on account of his Catholic religion, because he had heard Mass said on the occasion of his sister's wedding.
2. 18th. Robert Tirwhit, William's brother, was imprisoned for the same cause[3], even though he was very ill and no petition or guarantee of good behaviour was able to prevent his imprisonment in the Tower, for which reason he died soon after[4].
3. 19th. There were also at this same time in this same prison some important Irish Catholics; the Archbishop of Armagh, the Earls of Kildare and Clanricarde, Lord Devlin and Nugent and Miagh, gentlemen[5].

---

1 Being himself arrested in June 1580, John Hart did not enter his name into this month but used the above data as a vehicle to illustrate that he was in London, but not yet in the Tower, at the time. From the number of errors he has entered up in this month, it can be proved beyond doubt that he must have written them out at a much later date and certainly from poor hindsight or misinformation.

2 Sir Robert Tirwhit (Tirwight, Tiruit, Tyrrwhit, etc) was a wealthy landowner from Lincolnshire who had gained his knighthood in 1543. His major claim to fame is that of heading the embarrassing and scandalous enquiry into the alleged immoral conduct of Thomas Seymour, Lord Seymour of Sudely and Lord High Admiral in 1549. This was relevant to his relationships to the young Princess Elizabeth Tudor during the period when she had been his ward. In the course of this investigation, witnesses were called to show that his lordship had become far too familiar with his ward to the extent that 'the Princess is enceinte by the Lord Admiral'. Although the princess did not conceive a child, there were sufficient grounds for proving Seymour's guilt of the charge of aspiring to the throne particularly as he had been married to the dowager Queen Catherine Parr before this time.

Seymour was beheaded on Tower Hill on Wednesday 20th March 1549. Three days before, the privy council had consented that 'his head and body are to be buried in the Towre'. Historians suggest that the impressionable princess was so embarrassed by this enquiry that she became incapable of forming a sound relationship with any man from thence onwards, hence her remaining a spinster for life.

3 The actual warrant calling for Robert's committal is found in APC dated 26th June 1580. It incorporated a relevant clause to the effect that Sir Owen Hopton, Lieutenant of the Tower, was to 'further restrain William Tirwhit heretofore sent unto him more than it is reported heretofore he hath been'. Thus, even though the date given in the Diary is eight days earlier than that recorded by this state document, Hart was perfectly correct in saying that William preceded his brother Robert into the Tower.

4 Robert Tirwhit did not die in this manner. Due to the complicated and delicate nature of the cause for a Tirwhit martyr, the case is more closely examined at Appendix 10.

5 By giving this dated statement, John Hart has caused considerable confusion over these six Irish Catholics 'who were held at this same time in this same prison'. On the date he cited it will be shown (Appx 13) that only Richard Creagh, Archbishop of Armagh was in Tower custody. All of the others did not arrive until much later dates. Despite the many transactions involving these Irish prisoners, including the torture of some of their number, they gain no further mention in the Diary. It would appear that Hart had only placed their names here to show they were all held in the Tower during the period of his Diary.

DECEMBER[1]

4. 5th. Ralph Sherwin, Thomas Cottam, Robert Johnson, Luke Kirby, priests, Nicholas Roscarrock and Henry Orton, noted laymen, brought to the Tower from other prisons[2].
5. 10th. Thomas Cottam and Luke Kirby, priests, placed under compression in the Scavenger's Daughter for more than one hour. The former bled profusely from the nose [3].
6. 15th. Ralph Sherwin and Robert Johnson, priests, tortured on the rack and strongly shaken[4].
7. 16th[5]. Ralph Sherwin subjected to the rack for the second time.
8. 21st. George Peckham, knight[6], brought to the Tower from another prison[7].
9. 23rd. Jerome Stevens, layman, for the same reason, similarly dealt with[8].
10. 19th. 29th[9]. John Bosgrave, of the Society of Jesus, and John Hart, priest, and John Paschall, layman, were brought from other prisons to this one[10].
11. 31st. The said John Hart, after five days sleeping on the bare earth, led to be tortured on the rack[11]. Henry Orton received the same treatment[12].

---

1 There were no entries from July to November 1580 because John Hart was at Oxford for three months undergoing religious instruction under John Reynolds. When he returned at the end of that time and was seen to be as resolute in his Catholicism, Walsingham had him placed into the Marshalsea Prison.

2 Other than Roscarrock, who was classed as being able to pay his own prisoner fees, all other captives named in this entry were entered into *Tower Bills* from where it will be seen (Appx 2) that they all arrived the previous day, Sunday 4th December.

3 When Robert Parsons wrote this entry into his *Annals of the Schism*, he reversed the names and showed the 'latter' suffered the nose bleed. This minor alteration in layout might have been occasioned by the eventual order in which they were executed (see entry 51).

4 This entry from the *Diarium* was retained and worded exactly the same in Parsons' *Annals of the Schism*.

5 In the original *Diarium*, this entry was dated '19th' yet Bayley's reproduction (Appx 1) does tend to go slightly adrift at this stage.

6 In the original Latin, this prisoner was cited as *eques auratus* which should correctly be translated as 'Golden Knight'. This was the usual term to denote ordinary knighthood as opposed to a Knight of the Garter or of the Bath. At his accolade, a golden knight would be presented a pair of golden spurs.

7 Bayley omitted this entry entirely.

8 This entry was also missing from *Bayley's* reproduction of the *Diarium*.

9 In the original *Diarium*, this entry carried just the one date '29th'; the other figure actually belongs to entry 7 (see note 10 above). According to *Tower Bills*, these prisoners were committed to the Tower five days earlier. It can only be suggested that this 'slip of the pen' on Hart's part was purposely inserted to guarantee his own anonymity if his secret notes were ever discovered.

10 Bosgrave and Hart were brought from the Marshalsea whilst Paschall came from the Compter in the Poultry.

11 The peculiar turn of phrase that Hart uses for his third person description of his torture should be compared alongside entries 6 and 7 above. Whereas in those entries we find other prisoners being 'tortured on the

rack' or 'subjected to the rack', we notice in Hart's case that he was 'led to be tortured on the rack'.

This might at first appear to be trivial criticism but, if the letter he composed on 1st December 1581 is then examined (Appx 11), it will be appreciated that this entry has been composed in such a way as to reflect only a part of the truth whilst at the same time telling an outright lie. Within the framework of his letter, Hart admitted quite honestly that he had '...been at the rack (though I endured nothing thereon)...' In normal circumstances, the entries in a personal diary do not resort to such equivocation; but the fact that the *Diarium* was to be handed over and perused by his superiors, the editor of *de Schismate* and the printers at Rome would certainly have prompted Hart into usage of such terminology.

The warrant for Hart to be tortured, without naming the rack, was dated 24 December 1580 (APC 12:294-295) and included the names of Bosgrave and Pascall, of whom Hart was not aware due to the secrecy under which torture was administered.

12   No warrant survives in the name of Henry Orton and, because Hart has cited the same date, it is highly unlikely that Orton suffered torture on this occasion.

—— 1581 ——

JANUARY

12. 3rd[1]. Christopher Tomson, revered priest, brought to the Tower and subjected to the rack the same day.
13. 14th. Nicholas Roscarrock, noble layman, tortured on the rack.
14. 15th. John Paschall and Jerome Stevens, laymen, were led by fear of torture to make an open declaration against the faith and to declare their willingness to attend heretical services; the following day they were sent away to the seduction of others.
15. 16th[2]. The same day at the same public meeting, Owen Hopten, Lieutenant of the Tower, having dragged us by military force to church, declared openly that there was no one in his fortress who did not go willingly to the Protestant church[3].
16. 29th[4]. John Nichols, previously a Calvinist minister then a feigned Catholic, voluntarily risking himself in returning from Rome, taken by the heretics and thrown into the Tower. Ministers came to him and overcame him with arguments. He therefore, on a given day, abjured the Roman faith and assumed the role of preacher against us and was immediately set free.

---

1. From the *Tower Bills* it will be seen that Christopher Tomson was committed on 24 December 1580. Any warrant that might have authorised the use of the rack on that date or the one cited by Hart may no longer be found in State Papers.
2. This is a small typographical error on the part of *Bayley* or his printers. In the original pages of the *Diarium* this entry was also dated '15th' which thereby agrees with entry 14 as being the 'same day' which, in this case, was a Sunday.
3. It is of particular interest to find here how the chapel of St Peter ad Vincula was used not only for religious ceremonies but also to disseminate the news of the day. The mere fact that entries 14 and 15 above shows a dating known to be a Sunday leaves us wondering if this data was actually written up at the time or at a later date.
4. This is another of *Bayley's* errors where the original *Diarium* entry was dated '16th' (*see* footnote 2 above). There were no entries for 29 January.

FEBRUARY

17. 5th. The same Nichols mounted the pulpit to inveigh against the Roman Pontiff, at whose expense he boasted he had for some years lived in Rome. All the prisoners were carried by force to hear him but they interrupted him more than once in the midst of his raving and, when his sermon was finished, hooted him away.
18. 5th. 31st[1]. And from that time until the feast of Pentecost, every Sunday and feast day, we were taken by our guards and the soldiers to listen to the heretical sermons preached by ministers specially selected to do so. We always accused them of lying as they descended from the pulpit in the presence of the people and thus provoked them to dispute with us in spite of Hopton the Lieutenant's threats of torture if we did not keep silent[2].
19. 8th. Thomas Briscoe, layman, recently a pupil at the college of Rome, taken at the port and brought to the Tower; held five months in the Pit[3].
20. 10th. George Dutton, layman, transferred to the Tower from another prison[4]; for fear of torture, after forty six days, he agreed in part to the demands of the heretics; that he would go to their churches; and, even though he openly said he would never accept communion, was allowed his freedom on those conditions.

---

1   In the *Diarium* this entry carried just the one date, February 5th, which was also a Sunday. The additional figure '31st' is yet another of *Bayley's* errors. Pentecost or Whit Sunday of that year fell on 14th May.

2   Citing the same date, February 5th, Parsons inserted this information into his *Annals of the Schism* but reduced the wording to read:
    'From this till Whitsuntide, the lieutenant of the Tower forced the Catholics into the chapel that they might hear the heretics preach'.

3   Claims for Briscoe started in *Tower Bills* on December 24th of the previous year.

4   It was not possible to learn the other prison in which Dutton had been held prior to transfer to the Tower. The threat of torture must only have been a verbal one as there is no record of a warrant in his name. There is also an unusual irregularity over Dutton but this will be looked at in depth in Appendix 13.

MARCH

21. 19th[1]. John Nichols, having prepared an invective sermon, again mounted the pulpit, in whose honour several dignitaries and courtiers were present; but his speech was so inept that they were ashamed and Cottam the priest, with astonishing freedom of mind, gravely reminded them of his office, which was thought to be the reason why his death followed so soon after. Nichols however was held in contempt by everyone from that time on.
22. 20th[2]. After Nichols, several different ministers were introduced to us at different times, who insulted us, wished to persuade us to change by their curious sermons and called us seditious rebels, idolaters and public enemies[3].
23. 27th[4]. Alexander Briant, priest, brought to the Tower from another prison, where he had been tortured by thirst, and was burdened by heavy chains for two days. Then sharpened needles were forced under his nails[5] to make him confess where he had seen Father Parsons[6], which admission he steadfastly refused to make.
24. 6th[7]. The same Briant was thrown into the Pit; then, after eight days, was taken to the rack on which he suffered very severely, once that very day and twice the next day; after which last stretching of his body, as I heard from his own mouth (shortly before his death), he felt no pain at all even when the torturers were at their cruellest and inflicting the greatest tortures on him[8].

---

1   This was also a Sunday.

2   In the columns alongside this entry in the original *Diarium*, the figure '20th' came at the start of the entry and, unmentioned by *Bayley*, a figure '27th' came towards the end.

3   By this time, the reader will possibly have noticed how much John Hart holds back when writing of his co-prisoners yet how he then allows his ink to flow when describing the behaviour of Nichols and the other 'heretics'. There is no doubt that his Diary would have been of more value if he had been a little more accurate with his dates. The fact that he mentions other persons being brought to the Tower 'from other prisons' suffices to show he was not held completely incommunicado; it would therefore have been useful if he had given the names of the previous places of confinement. It would also have proved of immense value if he had named the building in which he was detained and those of his fellows; but the names of the various buildings might not have been as well advertised as is today the case. Chances are that certain prison towers were more commonly named after the occupant, e.g. 'Mr Smith's residence'.

These points of criticism do appear to debase the historical merits and value of the *Diarium*: but just imagine the impact it must have produced when first published in the sixteenth century. The readership would not have had opportunity to check the accuracy of dates, and the brevity of each entry was sufficient to shock. By being just that little more verbose in his writings of the heretics, Hart could achieve a much stronger propaganda effect.

4   This is a major fault by *Bayley*. In the original *Diarium* pages, this entry was undated, the figure '27th' actually belonging to the previous entry as explained under footnote 27.

5   The so-called 'torture' by thirst probably took place in the Wood Street Compter wherein Briant had previously been confined. There was no necessity for issuing a warrant for such treatment, simply a word

in the ear of the turnkey responsible for him. The employment of chains for confining prisoners was regular practice in all prisons and must never be regarded as 'torture'. In all such cases, the victim was at liberty to alleviate his distress by paying an agreed 'fee of irons', thereby enhancing the keeper's income; but the missionaries would not have had the wherewithal to pay such sums. The employment of sharpened needles is usually said to have occurred in the Tower; yet, in listing the 'seven forms of torture or ill treatment' in his preface, John Hart made no reference to them. Whereas their use was never mentioned in the warrants of this period, it illustrates that the commissioners to torture had certain leeway to exercise their own ideas for inflicting unimagined sufferings on their victims. The only other comparable example in recorded history is that of Cuthbert Simpson who was described in Foxe's *Actes and Monuments* as having arrows drawn through his bound fingers prior to confinement in the Scavenger's Daughter and stretching on the rack in 1557.

6   See Introductory Notes regarding Robert Parsons, the spiritual leader of the Jesuits in England.

7   Appearing exactly as shown in the *Diarium*, this entry for an event of 6th came immediately after that of 27th of the month. On closer inspection, there is a strong likelihood that the printers at Rome have omitted a month heading at the start of this entry. If a 'MAY' heading is inserted immediately above entry 24 – there were no entries from April to June in this year – then the contents would more closely tally with the committal and torture warrant issued in Briant's name on 3rd May 1581 (*APC 13: 37-38*).

8   If any further proof is needed to show this is Hart's Diary, then the wording of this entry is just such evidence. In the way he has compiled this entry, John Hart has quite literally placed his own signature to the *Diarium*.

   The only possible occasion on which anyone could have conversed with Briant about the use of needles and effects of the rack 'shortly before his death' and still live to tell the tale must have been the morning of December 1st, 1581 when Hart was removed from his cell to join Briant, Campion and Sherwin in readiness for the journey to Tyburn (see entry 39 and associated notes). The mere fact that he mentioned Briant's execution shows this entry must have been written out on a much later date.

JULY[1]

25. 14th[2]. John Paine, priest, who was betrayed by a certain Eliot, on whom he had bestowed many benefits, was captured; also on the same day, John Shert and George Godsalf, priests, were captured. All conducted to the Tower.
26. 22nd. Edmund Campion, Society of Jesus, priest, betrayed by the same Eliot, captured and brought to the Tower in grand procession; inscribed above his head 'Campion, Seditious Jesuit'[3].
27. 22nd. Together with Campion, there were conveyed to the same prison – Thomas Ford, William Filby, John Colleton, priests, Edward Yates, Edward Keynes, John Cotton, William Hildesley, Humphrey Keynes, Philip Loes, John Jacob, noble gentlemen, and finally William Weblin and John Mansfield, Catholic men of lower condition who had been converted by Campion's sermons[4].

---

1   No entries in the Diary for April, May or June (but cf. note 7 to entry 24 above); yet John Hart is named in the Tower Bill for the entire quarter ending 24th June 1581.

2   In the absence of the Michaelmas and Christmas 1581 *Tower Bills*, it was impossible to confirm the accuracy of this dating but most recusant historians, including Anstruther, accept the date Hart has given.

3   Eliot's own account of the events at Lyford (*see* Appx 3) confirmed the dates given for entries 26 and 27.

4   From Eliot's account it will be noticed that only eight laymen were taken with the priests at Lyford. From the contents of *Acts of the Privy Council* dated 26th July 1581 it was also proved that the Sheriff of Berkshire was paid a reward of £33 for his duties in conducting four priests and eight laymen to the Tower. However, if the reader checks off the names given above, he will see that nine laymen were entered by Hart. The odd one out is Philip Loes who, although not taken with the others at Lyford, was probably captured in London in the process of buying paper for use on the printing works at Stonor House and must have arrived in custody the same day.

AUGUST

28. 13th[1]. William Hartley, priest, together with John Stonor, Stephen Brinkley, lay gentlemen, with four of their household, printers of books, John Harris, John Harvey, John Tucker and John Compton arrested with their press in the house of the famous lady, Lady Stonor, were all brought to the Tower[2]. The last of whom, being of a more timid nature[3], when the prison guards with drawn swords threatened him with death unless he promised to attend the heretic church, gave in and thus obtained his liberty[4].
29. 31st[5]. Thomas Pound, a noble layman and notable confessor, who had passed many years of his life in other prisons on account of his faith, was brought to the Tower.
30. 31st. Edmund Campion, secretly tortured twice, together with the priests and laymen taken with him[6], although completely unprepared, was led forth to dispute with the heretics in the public chapel of the fortress; in that condition he could produce no reasoned arguments in favour of the Catholic faith; but he responded as best he could to the attacking ministers. Other disputations were held with Campion after this, twice or three times, I believe, by important ministers[7], but they were held in private, not in public as before, because the heretics realised that these first disputations had not damaged his cause enough.

---

1   Although John Hart delayed mention of Campion's torture until entry 30 below, the first official warrant for the torture was issued on 30th July 1581 (*APC 13: 144-155*). The outcome of that session of torture was to issue the order for a search to be made at Stonor Park on 4th August. These letters instructed the pursuivants to 'make diligent search and enquire for certain Latin books...which Edmund Campion, upon his examination, hath confessed to have been printed there in a wood...'

   In naming Stonor House during his examination, Campion was convinced that his printer friends and all of their equipment had moved to another safe location as was their usual routine; but, as this entry proves, they were all apprehended there and brought directly to the Tower. Campion was distressed that he had betrayed his trusted friends and never forgave himself for his own apparent weakness (cf. *Waugh*).

2   Stonor House, built over many centuries from 1190 to the 1930's, has been a recognised centre for Roman Catholicism since the period of recusancy. It has its own chapel wherein Mass is regularly celebrated. The room in which the printing press was found by the pursuivants, known as 'Mount Pleasant', may still be examined by visitors to this stately home.

3   The diarist's choice of words for the weakness of this captive makes a tragic contrast against Hart's own weaknesses when entry 39 is examined.

4   After making a comparison with the names shown below under entry 56, it would seem that Hart was correct in describing the circumstances surrounding Compton's rapid release.

5   This is yet another of those annoying errors that found their way into *Bayley's* reproduced pages. In the original *Diarium*, this entry was dated Agust 17th which, even so, is still three days remiss as the official warrant for Pound's committal (*APC*) was dated August 14th.

6   However, 'the laymen taken with him' do not appear to have undergone any form of torture. In his *Annals of the Schism*, Robert Parsons reworded this entry to show:

   'Aug 31st. Father Campian [sic], twice tortured on the rack, is made to dispute with the heretical ministers'.

7   One of the 'important ministers' who attended Campion's disputations in the chapel was Philip Howard, 17th Earl of Arundel (and Surrey) who, according to his many biographers, was so impressed with the prisoner's conduct that he soon afterwards sought reconciliation into the Catholic faith. The discovery of his secret conversion in 1585 resulted in Howard's committal to the Beauchamp Tower wherein many of his inscriptions still endure. Fated to spend as many as ten and a half years in custody, he died in captivity 'not without a suspicion of having been poisoned' and was canonised in 1970 (*see* Appx 8).

OCTOBER[1]

31. 31st[2]. Edmund Campion tortured for the third time on the rack after being questioned; this was altogether more severe[3].
32. 31st. John Paine, priest, tortured on the same rack and badly shaken[4].

---

1   There were no entries for September 1581.

2   The warrant for this session of torture was issued on October 29th (*APC 13:249*). Allowing time for delivery of instructions to the commissioners who were appointed to attend, Hart's dating cannot be too wide of the mark. The commissioners in this case were John Popham, the attorney-general; Sir Owen Hopton, Lieutenant of the Tower; John Hammond of the Doctors Commons and, as the rack was specified, Thomas Norton, the rack-master.

3   In the presence of so many officials, the strictly set out rules for the torture of prisoners would have been meticulously observed. After all, this was a prelude to the impending trials of the captured priests (see entries 33-36 below) but, in their aspirations of netting even more priests or recusants, the officials present might have been 'more severe' than usual. The success of capturing all of the men from Stonor was still fresh in their minds and, as Campion had been 'broken' before, they aspired to do so again.

   In his *Annals of the Schism*, Robert Parsons used the same date and recorded that Campion was tortured but did not specify the method employed. Whereas the warrant had also named Thomas Ford 'and others', they were unmentioned in either publication.

4   John Paine was not one of the priests named in the 29 October warrant (*APC 13:249*) but he might have been one of 'the others' whom the board wished to interrogate. Another known session of torture inflicted on Paine under authority of a warrant issued on 14th August (*APC 13:171-172*) was not mentioned by Hart or Parsons.

NOVEMBER

33. 14th. Edmund Campion, Ralph Sherwin, Thomas Cottam, Robert Johnson, Luke Kirby, James Bosgrave, Edward Rishton, priests, and Henry Orton, layman, were taken before the Royal tribunal and informed of the many crimes of which they stood accused, with no power to make any defence except to say in one word whether they were guilty or not guilty[1].
34. 16th. Thomas Ford, Alexander Briant, John Shert, William Filby, Laurence Richardson, John Colleton, John Hart, priests, brought before the judges in the same way and then returned to prison[2].
35. 20th. Edmund Campion and his seven companions aforesaid were again led to judgement and, even though they had hardly known each other beforehand and had never met together in the same place at the same time, were condemned on the evidence of suborned witnesses of the crimes of conspiracy which they were said to have concocted together in the same place at the same time; and they were sentenced to death.
36. 21st. The next day, Thomas Ford with his companions (except Colleton) were condemned to death in the same way[3]: Colleton, however, when he was due to be condemned, was saved by the testimony of a certain nobleman who claimed to have seen him in England at the very time when this conspiracy was supposed to have been hatched in Rome and Rheims; by which testimony the judge was compelled to clear him from sentence of death even though, against all English judicial precedents, he ordered him to be returned to prison.
37. 21st. Several others could have said the same for themselves as was said for Colleton, especially Ford, because he had been in England longer than Colleton; but these men of God did not wish to delay their own martyrdom.
38. 21st[4]. William Filby, who had been condemned to death, was tortured in the iron manacles until the day of his death because he seemed ever more joyful and constant in his faith[5]. Alexander Briant was put into iron shackles for two days after his condemnation because he had secretly shaved the top of his head so that he would look like a priest in court and made himself a wooden cross which he carried with him openly to judgement[6].

---

1   This arrangement of names is most remarkable in that the first five are those who were eventually executed – though not in that order – whereas the last three were exiled much later. This, combined with the arrangement of names in entry 34 below, is too much of a coincidence.

THE DIARY TRANSLATED

2   As with the previous entry, the first five named here were later sent to the gallows whilst the other two were numbered amongst the exiles of 1585. This would indicate that these entries were made out at a much later date after the executions were complete.

3   It should be noticed that, from this entry forward, John Hart was himself standing in the shadows of the gallows. No writer has ever been able to pin down the dramatic change in his character over the next ten days (*see* entry 39 and footnote). But William Allen, the superior at Douay and Rheims, must have expected something of the kind when he openly admitted that there were bound to be a few from within the ranks of his missionaries who would ultimately break down under the pressures, strains and severe interrogations they would face.

4   This entry was dated '22nd' in the original *Diarium*. The figure shown is yet another of *Bayley's* errors.

5   No warrant survives for this alleged 'torture' on Filby; but restraint in iron manacles or fetters was actually a form of punishment for which the Lieutenant required no official warrant from the council.

6   By his bold action in shaving his priest's tonsure and carrying a crucifix into the courtroom, Briant knew he would antagonise his judges and was almost pleading for a death sentence.

DECEMBER

39. 1st. Edmund Campion of the Society of Jesus, Ralph Sherwin of the College of Rome, Alexander Briant of the Seminary of Rheims[1], priests, by Royal command, taken from the Tower and dragged on wicker hurdles[2] to the pillory[3] to end their lives in glorious martyrdom[4].

— 1582 —

JANUARY

40. 11th. John Hart, priest, because he refused to co-operate with the heretics in any way after his condemnation, was sent to the Pit for nine days[5].
41. 23rd. Edward Yates, noted layman, who had been captured with Campion, removed from the Tower to another prison[6].

---

[1] Yet *Anstruther* claimed that Briant trained for the priesthood at Douay before the enforced move to Rheims. Briant was actually ordained from Cambrai in March 1578.

[2] As the name implies, the hurdles on which condemned men were dragged to the scaffold were very much like hurdle gates, being affixed to the horse's harness at the one end whilst the lower end trailed along the ground. This would have made for a most uncomfortable experience as the victims were dragged along the uneven road surfaces, being jolted by all obstacles met on the way. The traditional route from the Tower to Tyburn would have been by way of the populous roadway to the north of St. Paul's Cathedral, thence through Holborn and Newgate and straight along Oxford Street.

[3] The Latin patibulum translates this way; but the diarist could find no Latin equivalent to describe the infamous 'hanging tree' in the shape of a triangle that had been newly erected at Tyburn for the execution of Blessed John Story in 1571. It was claimed that as many as eight victims could be hanged from each branch of this framework making a total of twenty-four at a time, although there are no records of as many as this suffering at one stroke.

[4] This must have been the most difficult entry for John Hart to put to paper when it is realised that he himself was taken out of the Tower that morning and secured to the same hurdle as Edmund Campion. The other couple were secured to another hurdle. There is no doubt that Hart would have been dragged off to Tyburn to suffer a like fate (and probably merit, like the others, later canonisation) if he had not offered his conformity in exchange for his life at the last moment before the horses drew away. This plea was sufficient for the sheriffs to untie his bonds and send him back with his guards to his prison cell wherein he wrote his letter of submission to Walsingham (*see* Appx 11).

In the *Annals of the Schism*, Robert Parsons reworded this entry to show:

'Dec 1. Fathers Campian and Bryant and the Rev. Ralph Sherwin hanged, bowelled and quartered for the faith at Tyburn'.

[5] Having learned of John Hart's apostasy on 1st December 1581, here we find him reporting how he was punished rather than being rewarded or released. William Allen at Rheims later suggested this was caused by a visit from Hart's mother who 'spoke to him in such lofty terms of martyrdom that, if she found him hot with the desire of it, she left him on fire'.

The *DNB* suggested that, after receiving Hart's letter, Walsingham decided to send his prisoner to Oxford for three months religious re-education under John Reynolds; but this does not reflect in the *Tower*

Bills (Appx 2) in which claims for Hart's fees are continuous with no interruption. We have already seen that Hart had spent three months at Oxford after his capture in June 1580 and how this tuition came to nothing. Any subsequent meetings he might have had with Reynolds, more especially in 1582, must therefore have taken place at the Tower.

Walsingham's possession of Hart's letter was a trump card to be played whenever and however he chose. Whether Hart really was on fire with his wish for martyrdom was of no consequence to the secretary of state who, by threatening to reveal the contents of that letter, could induce full co-operation from the miserable prisoner.

It is interesting to find Hart's punishment in the Pit being mentioned by another co-prisoner, Luke Kirby, who recorded, 'This morning, 10th Januarie 1582, for not yielding to Reynolds of Oxford, Father Hart was committed to dungeon'. Yet again, John Hart preserves his anonymity by dating the event to the following day.

6   In his recusant prisoner returns, the keeper of the Gatehouse, Westminster recorded in March 1583, 'Yatte, a Barkeshyere man borne, and sent in by mr. Leefetenante of the Towewer by your honors ordere a yere since'.

Yate made a final appearance in the Gatehouse prisoner return of 8th April 1584 after which nothing more is known (*CRS Miscellanea, Vol 2*).

FEBRUARY

42. 7th. George Haydock and Arthur Pitt, arrested priests, were thrown into the Pit for five days[1].

MARCH

43. 5th[2]. Anthony Focatio[3], a Portuguese gentleman and devoted to the Catholic faith, after two years in prison and great sufferings on the rack, when he was near to death (for he was an old man and broken by torture) was carried out on a litter and a few days later gave up his soul to Christ[4].
44. 22nd[5]. Robert Copley, layman, sentenced to seven days in the Pit[6].
45. 30th. 31st[7]. John Paine, priest, taken to judgement and the next day convicted of a false crime, that he had wished to kill the queen, and condemned to death.

---

1 Claims for both these prisoners started two days earlier, on February 5th.

2 Yet another of *Bayley's* errors when this entry was originally dated '15th' March.

3 This is the spelling style most used for this man in *Tower Bills*, wherein he is occasionally shown as 'Fogaca' (*see* Appx 13).

4 The *Tower Bills* provide adequate proof that Fogaza had been in constant custody since September 30th, 1580 and probably before that time but the relevant bill is missing. The final claim for his fees was dated 25th March 1582. In this case we can be certain of the accuracy as the next bill in the series contains no demands for him. This final demand was not annotated 'Mort' as was Hopton's usual practice whenever a prisoner died or was executed and, without any further corroborative proof, we are compelled to accept that Fogaza died some time between 15th and 25th March 1582.

   The mere fact that he had conspired against the queen and might even have suffered at the rack at some earlier stage of his incarceration was unmentioned by the diarist. Hart was more concerned with the fact that a foreign Catholic had died the death of a martyr far away from his homeland. An official warrant for torture in Fogaza's name or in any similar spelling form was not found on record.

5 This particular entry was dated '23rd' in the original *Diarium*.

6 This was the only isolated instance in which a prisoner of this name was mentioned. He has not been found in any other documents of the period; nor is he named in *Tower Bills*, which would infer that he was financially capable of paying his own fees.

7 But the order for Paine to be delivered to the sheriff of Essex in order to be conducted to his trial at the Essex Assizes was dated 12th March 1581-2 (*APC*). It appears he left the Tower on 20th of the month and was condemned at Chelmsford on the 23rd (*Anstruther*).

APRIL

46. 2nd. John Paine, priest, led out from London and gained a martyr's crown[1].
47. 7th. William Hildesley, layman, having found men to guarantee his good behaviour, was released from prison[2]. John Stonor and John Cotton, noble laymen, were released on almost the same conditions[3]. Thomas Alfield, priest, captured[4].
48. 29th. Luke Kirby and Thomas Ford, priests under sentence of death, during the time they expected death were held in irons for thirty days.

MAY

49. 19th. Stephen Rowsham[5], priest, and Thomas Burns, layman[6], captured and brought to the Tower.
50. 22nd[7]. Thomas Ford, John Shert and Robert Johnson, priests, suffered martyrdom.
51. 30th. William Filby, Luke Kirby, Lawrence Richardson and Thomas Cottam, priests, likewise obtained the martyr's crown through death[8].

---

1   In his *Annals of the Schism*, Parsons reworded this entry to show:
    'April 2. John Paine, priest, martyred at Chelmsford'.

2   No further evidence came to hand to support or refute this suggestion that Hildesley was released on the given date.

3   In support for the theory that Hart wrote out some of his Diary from poor hindsight, it was noticed in this case that the Diary entry here is premature by as many as eighteen days. In fact, bonds were taken from Francis Stonor, John's brother, on April 25th, 1582 (*APC*) in which it was specified that John was to be liberated for the usual term of three months to undergo religious training. The order continued by stating, 'If he does not yield to conformity, he is to be returned to any prison nominated by the Council'. The absence of his name from all later prisoner lists suggests that he continued in his conformity.
    Yet again, in the case of John Cotton, another warrant of the same date as that for Stonor (*APC*) specified that he was to be delivered over to his brother Richard upon which they were both to travel 'direct to their grandmother's house and there remain for three months', no doubt for the religious re-education of the former prisoner.

4   Although Alfield might have been captured on this date – *Anstruther* quoted it verbatim – it is difficult to say where he might have been held from then until 29th April 1582 on which date order for his committal to the Tower and torture at the rack were issued (*APC, CSPD*). Being a priest, we may only wonder why no claims were made for him in *Tower Bills* and why he was liberated within a brief space of five months, which the diarist did not mention.

5   In the initial stages of researching the Diary, this particular prisoner was most difficult to locate due to his being indexed by Bayley as Stephen Ransom, a name which does not appear in any other archives.

6   Thomas Burns, Burnes or Barnes, the layman named here, should not be confused with the missionary priest whose committal is shown in entry 83. The layman who was apprehended with Stephen Rowsham would certainly have been named in the missing *Tower Bill* for Michaelmas 1582 (*see* Appx 2); he certainly appears with Rowsham in the next bills covering the period from 30 September 1582 to 29 December 1583. In the gap occasioned by the missing Lady Day 1584 Bill, it would appear that the layman was

removed and his place filled by the priest of similar name who, although named 'Thomas Barnes' in the bills, can only equate to the 'John Barnes' named in the Order for Exile (*see* Appx 6). It can only be imagined that the layman was allowed free on the usual terms some time between December 29th, 1583 and March 25th, 1584.

7   This has been wrongly dated by *Bayley*. The correct date given in the *Diarium* was May 28th which tallies with the claims for all three in *Tower Bills* which were finalised on the 27th of the month with the annotation 'Mort' (dead) alongside their names. The sequence in which their names are given – which was recorded in the same way by Parsons' *Annals* – is known to be the order in which they suffered death.

8   The *Diarium* and Parsons's *Annals of the Schism* both agreed to the same date and the order in which the martyrs died. For this and the previous entry, Parsons also cited the method of execution (hanging, bowelling and quartering) and the venue of their deaths (Tyburn).

JULY[1]

52. 19th. William Carter, layman, book printer, after several years of suffering in other prisons, brought to the Tower[2].
53. 23rd. Richard Slake[3], priest, was taken and loaded with fetters for twenty-three days and then confined for two months in the Pit.

AUGUST

54. 14th. John Jetter, a lay youth, was captured as he was returning from France[4]. Stephen Rowsham, priest, consigned to Little Ease, wherein he stayed for eighteen months and thirteen days[5].

---

1   There were no entries for June 1582.

2   In his *Annals* Robert Parsons amended this entry to read:
      'William Carter, printer, brought from another prison to the Tower'.

3   The *Tower Bill* for Michaelmas 1582 is lost from the series at Chancery Lane; but we should expect to find Richard Slake in the next Bill starting on September 30th. As he is not shown there, it must be assumed that the 'Richard Clarke' named therein must represent a misspelling of his name.

4   John Jetter or Getter was firstly located in a prisoner list from the Clink prison (*CRS Miscellanea, Vol II, p. 227*) where he was described as 'late servant unto one Mr. Higgins of London, Scryvener, committed ye 7th daye of Auguste 1582 and sente for from hence to the Towre by the Right Worshipfull Sir Owen Hopton and ther remaynethe'. It is most unusual for Hart to omit this mention of Jetter being brought in from another prison as he had done for many others.

5   Confinement in Little Ease (*see* Appx 5) for such a long period of time was not unusual (cf. John Baillie in *The Marvellous Chance*); but the peculiar figures cited for Rowsham give cause to doubt the diarist's accuracy. If we accept that Rowsham was committed on 19th May 1582 (entry 49) and then imagine him being cast immediately into Little Ease, he would not have emerged therefrom until the start of December 1583, long after the date quoted above. On the other hand, if he was cast into that evil dungeon on the date Hart has given, Rowsham could not have served out the specified period of 'eighteen months and thirteen days' as he was removed to another prison inside seventeen months (*see* Appx 13).

    These niggling points of criticism – just the kind that could be seized upon by Walsingham to refute the inaccuracy of the record – would qualify why Parsons chose to remove all mention of this event from his *Annals of the Schism*.

SEPTEMBER

55. 1st. The forenamed John Jetter, after suffering torture by the Scavenger's Daughter, was confined to the Pit for eight days. He was then led to the rack (1) and cruelly tortured until he nearly fainted; but, in the midst of his agony when ready as it were to expire, his countenance brightened with joy, he invoked the name of Jesus and laughed his persecutors to scorn (2).

56. 16th (3). William Hartley, priest, and John Jacobs, John Harvey, John Harris and John Tucker, laymen, sent from the Tower to other prisons (4).

57. 20th. Ralph Leatherborough (5), merchant from Rouen (6), because of his faith, placed into the Tower (7).

---

1   Ex-entry 54 and footnote. Any warrant for torturing Jetter on the rack is no longer found on record.

2   Following the final claim for Jetter on 23rd July 1583 (*Tower Bills*) and totally overlooked by the diarist, it was discovered that Jetter was removed to Newgate prison on 25th July 1583 (APC) wherein he is presumed to have died some time in 1585 (*CTS Pamphlet H 469, p. 47*). Because the circumstances surrounding his death are so poorly documented, he has been classed as *Dilatus* to denote that his cause for recognition as a martyr is still being pursued.

3   Here we find another of Hart's dating errors; but this time he is adrift by as many as thirteen months. It was impossible to determine how such a gross error could have been committed when the keeper of the Marshalsea, in all of his subsequent prisoner returns (*CRS, Miscellanea, Vol 2*), repeatedly averred he had received all of these prisoners in August 1581, solely a matter of days after they arrived at the Tower (*see entries 27 and 28*). This rapid transfer elsewhere also explains their absence from *Tower Bills*. Nonetheless, although we know Hart was kept in isolation from the other prisoners, we are still left wondering at the reason for these names cropping up at such a late date after their transfer.

4   It will be recalled from entry 28 that Harvey, Harris and Tucker had been among the printers brought to the Tower after the raid at Stonor House. The keeper of the Marshalsea repeatedly claimed he had received them with William Hartley on 23rd August 1581. John Jacob or Jacobs had been sent to the same prison slightly ahead of them, on 16th August.

    The three printers continued to appear in all later Marshalsea lists until April 8th, 1584. Harvey and Harris made no further appearances leaving Tucker in the Marshalsea until July 1586. There is every likelihood that he made a later return to the Tower as there is a mention of a prisoner named 'Tucker' who was removed from the Tower to Newgate on 18th October 1588 (*APC*) under instructions that he was to be 'proceeded against by law, in accordance with instructions issued to the Lieutenant'. Those instructions could not be found and so there was no method of learning if, after the move to Newgate, Tucker might have been executed in the wake of the Armada.

5   As a person of substance and property, Ralph or Rudolph Leatherborough would have paid his own fees and would not feature in *Tower Bills*.

6   In the Latin *Diarium* it was shown that the merchant came from 'Rothomago' which translates into the original name for Rouen which was 'Rotomagus'.

7   This foreign merchant must only have spent a brief time in custody as he was named in a list headed 'Prisoners Discharged Since June 1582...Uppon Bondes' (*CRS Miscellanea Vol 2, p. 228*) This document did not cite the release dates of those named therein and John Hart gave no mention of Leatherborough's release. From the propaganda value of his Diary, Hart could stir up considerable anger from his readers at this news of a foreign national, holding no allegiance to the queen, being placed into the country's most infamous prison complex.

DECEMBER[1]

58. 1st[2]. John Hart, priest already condemned to death, was punished with twenty days in irons because he refused to agree with the minister Reynolds.

—— 1583 ——

FEBRUARY[3]

59. 16th. John Mundin, priest, captured and held tight for twenty days in the iron fetters[4].

JUNE[5]

60. 19th. John Hart, beforenamed, by reason of the same offence, thrown into the Pit for forty days[6].
61. 24th. Stephen Brinkley, lay gentleman, as a result of the intercession of his friends and having found people to stand bail for his good behaviour, released after two years of imprisonment[7].

---

1. There were no entries for October and November 1582 but it is worth mentioning here a letter which John Hart wrote to William Allen on 15th November 1582 and which has been quoted by a number of recusant historians. In view of what we have learned thus far of the diarist, it would prove of particular interest to quote just a part of his letter to gain an insight into his later actions. The relevant paragraph reads:
    '...all of us by the Grace of God are in the faith, and there is not one of us who is not resolved to hold the faith and fight against heresy, though it were necessary to shed his blood for his religion...'
    We may only ponder over the circumstances that might have provoked such wording and wonder even more if Walsingham or Reynolds might have been at his elbow as he put pen to paper or if they read through the contents before it was allowed to leave the Tower.
2. The dating of this protest by Hart is remarkable in that it was the first anniversary of his personal escape from execution with Campion, Sherwin and Briant (entry 39 and notes). History stays silent over exactly what caused the disagreement with his religious mentor; but there was certainly something that must finally have stung his conscience.
3. No entries for January 1583.
4. Robert Parsons used precisely the same date and wording for this entry in his *Annals of the Schism*. Nonetheless, the *Tower Bills* prove that 'John Monden' was committed four days earlier, on 12th February 1582-3.
5. There were no entries for March, April or May 1583.
6. It should be noticed that the period of nothing to report is immediately followed by a third person account of Hart being punished. When this is compared alongside his previous punishment (entry 58), it will be seen that there is also a gap of slightly more than two months without any entries in his Diary.
7. Ex-entry 28. Unfortunately, the *Acts of the Privy Council* for 1582 to 1586, which might have contained the authority for Brinkley's release, are no longer to be found at the Record Office. We are therefore compelled to accept the dating Hart has entered here. Quite obviously, the 'good behaviour' which was stipulated would have meant his conformity to the established Anglican form of worship. Dates are uncertain but it is known that Brinkley fled the country some time in 1585 and later employed his expertise in helping Robert Parsons with the printing press at Rome. There is every likelihood that Brinkley assisted in the production of the 1586 and 1587 editions of *De Schismate*.

OCTOBER[1]

62. 3rd[2]. John Somerville, lay gentleman, son-in-law of that famous man Edward Arden, as he was a Catholic, was thrown into the Tower accused of plotting to kill the queen[3].

NOVEMBER

63. 4th[4]. Hugh Hall, priest and confessor to the Somervilles[5], and three days later, Edward Arden[6], his father-in-law, were arrested for the same reason.
64. 7th[7]. Francis Throgmorton, famous and richly endowed young man and eldest son of John Throgmorton, knight, being accused of plotting on behalf of the Queen of Scots, was apprehended and placed into Little Ease on the first day.
65. 16th. Mary Arden and Margaret, her daughter, wives of the previously named Edward Arden and John Somerville; Elizabeth Somerville, maid and true sister of the same John, thrown into the Tower.
66. 17th. George Throgmorton, brother of the above Francis, apprehended.
67. 23rd. D[8]. Francis Throgmorton severely tormented on the rack and cast into the Pit on the same day. Also on the same day, D. Edward Arden was also subjected to the rack[9].
68. 24th. Hugh Hall, priest, also tortured on the rack[10].

---

1 No entries for July, August or September 1583

2 Another mistake from *Bayley* when the original *Diarium* dated this event to '30th'.

3 Even though Somerville underwent an examination at the Tower on 6th October (*CSPD*), claims for his fees did not commence in *Tower Bills* until 29th of the month, proving John Hart once again to be a day late in recording the committal.

4 In the 1586 *Diarium*, this entry carried two dates, '4th' at the start and '7th' towards the end. *Bayley's* printers did not include the latter figure (but see footnote 7 below).

5 Quite surprisingly, Hugh Hall was not named in the Tower Bill for the Christmas 1583 quarter. In the absence of the next bill from the series (Appx 2) – which might have incorporated a back-dated claim for his fees – we only start to see the claims for Hall from 26th March, 1584.

6 Claims for one 'Edmonde Arden' began in *Tower Bills* on November 6th, making Hart a day late in recording the episode.

7 As explained in footnote 5 above, this figure '7th' actually belongs to the closing stages of entry 63. In the pages of the original *Diarium*, entry 64 was dated 13th November.

8 The insertion of the capital letter 'D' before some of the names from this point forward were not an error of *Bayley's* printers; they featured in exactly the same places in the *Diarium*. No footnote was added to indicate what these letter D's might signify. Admittedly, in most writings of the period the prefix 'D' before a name usually indicated 'Doctor'; but, as none of those bearing this prefix in the Diary were qualified Doctors, it is needful to conjecture what meaning was implied by the diarist.

Considering that Francis Throgmorton and Edward Arden were the only prisoners marked with the letter 'D' in entries 67, 69, 70 and 72, and in view of the crimes they were alleged to have committed against the queen, it is considered that John Hart had second thoughts about including their cases in his Diary and therefore made this small hieroglyphic to signify he wanted them 'Deleted', despite the fact that they were Catholics who were executed.

9. Given the circumstances that the Throgmorton Plot was allegedly aimed at taking away the queen's life, there is every chance that Francis Throgmorton and Edward Arden were subject to torture on the rack; but the warrants of authority may no longer be found due to the absence of *Acts of the Privy Council* for 1582-1586.

10. Although most historians agree that Edward Arden could not have been party to the Throgmorton Plot, it has usually been intimated that the condemnatory evidence against him was elicited from the family priest. Here we find Father Hart alluding to the torture of Hugh Hall, even though the official warrant is no longer on record.

DECEMBER

69. 2nd. D. Francis Throgmorton again subjected to the rack, twice in the same day[1].
70. 16th. D. Edward Arden and John Somerville, noted laymen, Hugh Hall, priest, and Mary Arden, Edward's wife, condemned to death[2].
71. 22nd[3]. John Somerville, who was hardly of sane mind, was transferred to another prison and the following night was found strangled (hanged) in his prison cell whether by his own hand or by others was not established.
72. 26th[4]. D. Edward Arden led to the scaffold and there hanged, protesting his innocence of that of which he was accused and claiming that his real crime was the profession of the Catholic faith.

---

1   This was probably a continuance of the torture alluded to in entry 67 and footnote.

2   This particular entry also gained mention in Stow's *Annals* in which he recorded:
    '[On 16th December] Edward Arden, Mary, his wife, Hugh Hall and others, being indicted at Warwick, were arraigned at the Guildhall where they were all condemned of high treason'.

3   *Bayley's* printers have committed yet another error here when the original entry was dated 21st December; but even this date is at fault, Hart being yet again a day late in recording the incident. From the evidence of the *Tower Bills* (Appx 2), it will be seen that claims for John Somerville (and Edward Arden) came to an end on 19th December 1583. Both were removed to Newgate prison that same day and placed into separate cells. Within a space of two hours after their arrival, Somerville was found strangled in his cell but the case has never been explained unless the unsoundness of his mind caused him to commit suicide. On the following day, 20th December, Somerville's head was crudely hacked off and placed on London Bridge alongside that of Edward Arden who had been executed earlier that day.

4   Here we find yet another entry wherein both Hart and *Bayley* have committed mistakes. Although the latter had shown '26th' at the start of this entry, John Hart dated Arden's execution to 22nd December. Yet in his *Annals of the Schism*, Robert Parsons corrected and reworded the entry to show,
    'Dec 20. Edward Arden, layman, hanged, bowelled and quartered at Smithfield for the faith'.
    Thus, not only is John Hart proven to be two days late in reporting the execution but, in the one instance in which he showed the style of execution, he managed to get this wrong. In an age when most traitors were executed by the accepted form at Tyburn, Robert Parsons' allusion to the execution at Smithfield is most extraordinary. It would be difficult to confirm if this really was the venue of Arden's death or if Parsons had committed a small mistake in his *Annals*.

— 1584 —

JANUARY

73. 11th. William Carter, layman, made a martyr for the printing of Catholic books[1].
74. 18th. William Shelley, a bright and noble layman, and Gervase Pierpoint, noble man, brought to the Tower[2].

FEBRUARY

75. 2nd. 3rd[3]. Robert Nutter, priest, taken and, after two days, put in the Pit for forty-three days and suffered in the Scavenger's Daughter on the fourth and sixth days after his arrest[4].

---

[1] In his *Annals of the Schism*, Robert Parsons changed the words of this entry to show,
  'Jan 10. William Carter, printer, hanged, bowelled and quartered at Tyburn'.
  In this case, however, it was not the diarist who had entered the wrong date but Parsons who is a day early in showing when Carter was put to death. It is quite possible that Parsons, having proved John Hart to be a day late with so many other episodes, decided to deduct a day for this entry as a matter of course. All other accounts of Carter's execution agree with Hart's dating of Saturday 11th January.

[2] Hart failed to mention here that both of these prisoners were brought to the Tower from another prison. Before this transfer they were confined to the Marshalsea Prison, Southwark whence a list headed 'Mass Hearers in the Marshalsea, 24th August 1582' (*SPD vol. 155, n27*) incorporated their names.

[3] An error from *Bayley* where the *Diarium* showed three dates in the column, '2nd, 3rd, 4th'.

[4] But in the *Annals of the Schism* this entry reads:
  'Feb 2nd. Robert Nutter, priest, taken and laid in the pit of the Tower for forty-seven days, twice underwent the torture of the scavenger's daughter'.

MARCH[1]

76. 4th. 5th. 10th[2]. George Haydock, John Mundin, James Fenn, Thomas Hemerford and John Nutter, priests, received sentence of death, of whom the last three lay in the Pit for six days after their condemnation and were loaded with leg irons until they suffered martyrdom[3].
77. 13th. Thomas Stephenson[4], priest, arrested and made to lie down on the ground without a bed for twenty-seven days and wore leg irons for thirty-nine days.
78. 13th. George Godshall and Stephen Rowsham, priests, removed from the Tower to other prisons[5].
79. 22nd. 23rd. William Brumlum[6] and Francis Arden, noted laymen, seized[7].

---

1   This MARCH heading was inserted in *Bayley's* reproduced Diary; yet it did not feature in the original *Diarium*. It should be completely ignored as all subsequent entries relate to incidents that occurred in February. There were no entries for March 1583-4.

2   The first of these figures actually belongs alongside entry 75 as explained in footnote 3 to entry 75 above. Entry 77 was dated '5th' near the start and '10th' towards the end.

3   In the *Annals of the Schism*, Robert Parsons broke this entry down into two separate entities as follows:
      Feb 7. George Haddock, John Munden, John Nutter, James Fenn, Thomas Hemerford, arraigned at Westminster and found guilty of high treason, because they had been made priests abroad.
      Feb 12. The priests tried on the 7th hanged, bowelled and quartered at Tyburn.
      These dates, two days later than those cited by the *Diarium*, have proved to be correct and are the ones usually cited in records of martyrology. It was impossible to ascertain the order in which they suffered because each account arranges them into a different order. No doubt the reader has noticed how Parsons has removed all mention of the Pit and leg irons.

4   Following all the points of criticism over Hart's dating of certain events, it comes as a pleasant surprise to find the date given above agrees with the claims for Thomas Stephenson or Stevenson which started in *Tower Bills* on '13th ffebruarie'.

5   The Marshalsea prisoner list (*SPD, vol 169, n25*) clearly stated that 'George Godsalf and Stephen Rusham' were sent there from the Tower on 12th February 1583-4, thus highlighting yet another instance when Hart was a day late in recording the incident.

6   Of all the entries in his Diary, this one stands out as certain proof that John Hart must have been gleaning his information from someone in a position of trust. In this case, his Latin entry for this name 'Brumlumnus' which tends to agree with the entry of William Brumlum who, according to the *Tower Bill*, was committed on 23rd February 1583-4.
      Moreover, in the next available Bill and in all subsequent claims, the prisoner's name has been changed to 'Crumlum' or 'Cromlome'. Even more remarkable is the alteration of name spelling that John Hart used in entries 88 and 90 wherein it will be seen that the same prisoner was called 'Crumlumnus' and 'Crumlumno' respectively. Even allowing for the missing Michaelmas 1584 Bill, it would be too much of a coincidence to suggest that the man named Brumlum was removed elsewhere to be replaced at a later date before the end of the quarter by someone called Crumlum.
      We must therefore acknowledge that these entries in the Diary and *Tower Bills* allude to the same person.
      Nevertheless, no two writers – one a prisoner 'prevented from seeing or speaking with others' and the other the Lieutenant's clerk sat in his office diligently tabulating his master's expenses for caring for those in his keeping – would ever make the same sudden change to a name spelling at virtually the same time.

There had to be a link of some kind between the two and the most likely candidate would be someone who could wander into the clerk's office at will before carrying news of any new committals back to the prisoner. Such a man would have been Hart's guard 'who always keeps him under observation'.

7   Francis Arden, who might have been related to Edward Arden (ex-entry 63, etc), should not be confused with the more famous prisoner John Ardent or Arden who earned himself a place in the Tower's hall of fame by escaping with John Gerard in 1597.

In the handwritten notes entitled *Prisoners of the Tower*, former Chief Yeoman Warder A.H. Cook, DCM, MM, BEM erroneously linked the two men together under the one name 'Francis John Arden'; but it has now been proved that they were two entirely separate individuals.

The Francis Arden named above was, according to *Tower Bills* (Appx 2), committed on 23rd February 1583-4, which tends to agree with John Hart's dating which suggests that Brumlum/Crumlum and Arden were 'seized' on 22nd and committed next day.

JUNE[1]

80. 10th. D. Francis Throgmorton, noble layman, punished with death. On the same day, a disgraceful libel was circulated about him[2].
81. 13th. Thomas Layton, noted layman, captured and cast into the Pit[3].
82. 19th. Thomas Worthington, priest, captured and detained in the Pit for two months and three days[4].

AUGUST

83. 24th. Thomas Barnes, priest, captured[5].
84. 27th. William Aprice, noted layman, conducted to the Tower and immediately thrown into the Pit for twenty-three days.

---

1 This is yet another of *Bayley's* errors of printing. In the Latin *Diarium* the heading shown here was 'JULY'. There were, in fact, no entries for April, May or June 1584.

2 In the *Annals of the Schism*, this entry was amended by Parsons to show:
   'July 10. Francis Throgmorton, layman, hanged, bowelled and quartered at Tyburn'.

3 In the absence of a claim for Thomas Layton in the *Tower Bill* covering 24 June to 24 September 1584, we have to accept Hart's dating for his arrival in the Tower.

4 Yet again, we have to accept Hart's dating of 19th July 1584 as being that on which Worthington arrived.

5 See also entry 49 and associated footnote. The only priest with any marked similarity must be John Barnes who was presumably committed at this time. Due to a missing *Tower Bill*, we are compelled to accept Hart's dating; yet in the next available Bill starting on 1st October 1584 we begin to notice the claims for 'Thomas Barnes'. *Anstruther* appears to have confused the priest who arrived in August 1584 with the layman who had been in custody since 30 September 1582.

As further proof that Hart really meant John Barnes the priest, we need only look at the final entry of his Diary in which he recounted that Thomas Barnes was one of the twenty-one religious exiles whereas the Order for Exile (Appx 6) clearly showed the priest was named John Barnes. Yet again, the reader will notice, no doubt, the collusion between the diarist and the man who compiled the *Tower Bills*.

SEPTEMBER

85. 13th. Gervase Pierpoint, layman, having found a guarantor for his good behaviour, was released but arrested again the following month[1].
86. 16th. William Creighton, of the Society of Jesus, and Patrick Addy, priest, who were in transit to Scotland, against all international laws, were taken at sea and thrown into prison[2].
87. 24th. William Aprice was for the second time placed into the Pit for forty-eight days.

OCTOBER

88. 16th. William Crumlum[3] imprisoned in the Pit for two months and twenty-four days.

NOVEMBER

89. 10th. Robert Nutter for the second time assigned to the Pit for two months and fourteen days[4].

---

1 Ex-entry 74. It was not possible to check out Hart's suggestion that this prisoner was allowed free and then returned to prison as the Michaelmas 1584 *Tower Bill* has been lost from the series. As a result we can only find the claims ending 24 June and re-commencing on 1st October 1584.

2 Here we find John Hart being accurate in recording a committal that agrees with the *Tower Bills* which started to show claims for Creighton and Addy on 16th September.

3 Regarding the change of name spelling of Brumlum and Crumlum, see footnote 6 to entry 79.

4 In the *Annals of the Schism* Parsons recorded of this incident:
    'Nov 10. Robert Nutter laid in the Pit again where he was kept for more than two months.'

— 1585 —

JUN[1]

90. 4th. Patrick Addy, Scots priest, cast into the Pit for four days and William Crumlum again for seven days.
91. 7th. 21st[2]. Jasper Haywood, James Bosgrave and John Hart of the Society of Jesus[3], priests, Christopher Tomson, Arthur Pitts, Robert Nutter, Thomas Stephenson, Richard Slack, Thomas Barnes, Thomas Worthington and ten other priests and one layman (making twenty-one in number)[4], when we expected nothing of the sort, were by order of the queen, placed in a boat and put ashore on the coast of Normandy; and, not long after, fifty others followed us into the same exile, all of us condemned to death if we ever returned to our country. PRAISE BE TO GOD.

---

1   There were no entries for December 1584. This 'JUN' heading, however, is a major printing error from Rome because this is exactly how it appeared in the 1586 *Diarium*. By rights the heading should have been 'JAN'; but, as anyone with experience of transcribing handwritten documents from the archives will agree, it is a simple matter to misconstrue some lower case letters which look alike such as 'a' and 'u'. Even though *Bayley* entered wrong numerals at the start of entry 91, the event is known to have taken place in January 1584-5.

2   This is another printer's error from *Bayley* where the Latin original actually carried just the one date, 21st. The same information was recorded in Parsons' *Annals* as: 1585. Jan 21. Deportation of twenty-one prisoners against their will, twenty priests and one layman. This also coincides with the Order For Exile (Appx 6) in which the names of all twenty-one deportees are given.

3   This entry must have been compiled some time after November 1585 when Hart entered the Society of Jesus (*see* Appx 13).

4   The ten other priests were Edward Rishton, William Tedder, Samuel Coniers, William Warmington, William Hartley, William Dean, Richard Norris, William Bishop, William Smith and John Colleton. The unnamed layman was Henry Orton.

CONFLICT OF EVIDENCE

During the initial stages of this project it was noticed that the contemporaneous State documents often had an annoying tendency to throw up evidence that clashed with certain entries in the Diary; but, as any research student will admit, this is just one of the annoying aspects of his work that he is compelled to accept whenever the writings of two authorities are brought together. The researcher soon becomes acclimatised to the fact that his humble writing must, at the very least, form a 'compromise of lies'.

These discrepancies bring to mind the oft-quoted tale of Sir Walter Ralegh's later imprisonment from 1603 to 1616 during which time he occupied many idle hours in compiling his *History of the World*, a copy of which may still be seen in his former cell in the Bloody Tower.

Whilst sat at his desk, poring over his beloved books and ruminating over some event long past, he was distracted by the noise of two men outside on Tower Green having a rather fierce interchange of words. From the remoteness of his prison chamber, Ralegh could not make out what had caused the trouble but, being somewhat curious, he later found an opportunity to question some of the witnesses he had noticed on the sidelines of the affair. He was astounded at the replies which all tended to give an entirely different slant on exactly what might have happened. The would-be historical author later commented on the irony of the situation in which he had been trying to make sense of something that had happened hundreds of years ago and yet could not discover the truth of an event that had happened as many minutes before. This might explain why his work comes to an abrupt conclusion in the year BC 130.

The footnotes used throughout the pages of the Diary translation have tended to criticise and disprove much of what our poor diarist had to record by his pen; but how are we to say, at this distance in time, which writer was the more accurate in his literary endeavours? On the one hand, we find the writings of a priest confined in the most appalling conditions imaginable due to his opposition to the order of the day; on the other we find, more often incomplete than not, the official records of those authorities who were set upon a course to discredit and weaken the power of those who dared oppose their regimen. On both sides we can find sufficient bigotry to twist the meaning of certain phrases they employed to their own advantage.

On those occasions when two or more accounts were brought together alongside the Diary, it was occasionally possible to point a finger at whosoever had not told 'the whole truth and nothing but the truth'; but, in the absence of certain archives, this was not always practicable. Nonetheless, we have been able to survey and assess a number of events and fascinating personalities in an honest endeavour to learn exactly what might have transpired during this all-too-brief period of the history of the Tower of London.

It is considered that the inspection has been neutral, fair and unbiased in an honest desire that those five years will be better understood and more clearly catalogued. After all, a lapse of more than four hundred years to wait for the *Diarium* to be translated and analysed is far too long. In an age that has seen the virtual abandonment of the Latin Mass and a steady decline in the number of experts in that tongue, there should no longer be a necessity for the reader to thumb through those pages in *Bayley* wondering exactly what they could mean.

By means of Sarah Barter-Bailey's accurate translation and the editor's associated notes and additions, we have now disclosed the answers to many hitherto unsolved mysteries of the Tower of London and have seen the way some of the Elizabethan prisoners were treated.

ANALYSIS

To all intents and purposes, the Diary can be subdivided into two basic constituents. Firstly, the preface that must only have been committed to paper after John Hart had been ejected from England as an undesirable. It was there that we saw his allusion to 'the twenty-seven years that Elizabeth has reigned' as a clear indication that he was writing in 1585. From the haven of security at his seminary college, the diarist could finally give full vent to all his emotions against the injustices he and his co-religionists had endured during their time at the Tower. The style he employs – invoking the anger, pity and support of his readers – reads very much like a propaganda leaflet comparable with those produced by underground presses against oppressive regimes in recent years. This was his sole intent. In Hart's opinion, in common with most Catholics of his day, the country was literally being forced to live under the heel of the jackboot and would only find salvation by returning to the 'true faith'.

The second part comprises the miscellaneous collection of ninety-one dated entries of which, it must be stressed, only eighteen were deemed worthy of retention in Robert Parsons' *Annals of the Schism*. Copious footnotes beneath those entries have pinpointed certain errors and equivocations that were committed by Hart and the changes that Parsons introduced;

ANALYSIS

but an understanding of Hart's 'slips of the pen' may be easily qualified if we just pause for a moment to recall that the imprisoned priest could not have been witness to all the events he recorded. As he admitted in his preface, he was 'imprisoned separately from the others'; so how did he secure his information or disinformation?

It was noticed that many of his errors had the annoying tendency to be a day later than those given by other independant authorities. Admittedly, some of his irregularities are even more distantly misdated; but the evidence tends to suggest that there was someone – probably in a high position of trust or authority – who kept Hart informed on quite a regular basis on events taking place outside his prison cell. The most obvious candidate must be 'his own guard who always keeps him under observation' but there was no method of learning which of the thirty Yeoman Warders (*see*Appx 12) had the responsibility for the diarist.

It is fascinating to learn that at least one Yeoman Warder, Samuel Kennet *or* Kent was converted to Catholicism by Hart shortly after he arrived in prison at the Tower (*Anstruther*). Because Kennet's name was not cited in the 1580 listing, we may only assume he joined the Tower staff shortly after that list was complied as it is known that Kennet left the country in the summer months of 1582 and was ordained seven years later. The conversion alone suffices to show that prisoner and guard did not sit idly staring at one another across the prison chamber. A close rapport, often verging on deep respect, admiration and friendship, could be built up over the months they spent alone. As an example, when Henry 'Tower' Laurens was committed to the home of Yeoman James Futterell on 'The Parade' (i.e. Tower Green) on 6th October 1780, he formed such a lasting bond with his keeper and his family over the next fourteen months that they maintained their friendship for many years after (*Life of Henry Laurens* by David Duncan Wallace Ph.D. (Knickerbocker Press, New York and London, 1915)).

More recently, Kapitänleutnant Werner Lott, commander of U-boat 35, was interviewed in the Tower by the commander of HMS *Kelly* after he and his crew had been captured on 29th November 1939. Having spent the rest of the War in various places of confinement in England and Canada, Mr Lott renewed his friendship with this gallant British officer and continued a lasting correspondence with him until Lord Louis Mountbatten was assassinated by an illegal terrorist organisation in August 1979.

Even though the Warders were compelled to obey the orders of a very severe regimen, it is patently obvious that snippets of news would crop up in their daily conversations probably a day or so after the event. Such items of news might need to be drawn out by guile but, as they were by then in the past, they were no longer of any import. Even the other prisons from which newcomers arrived do not appear to have been mentioned otherwise Hart would surely have alluded to them.

By the same token, it must now be manifest that the imprisoned priest did not begin compiling the diary immediately after his arrest. Small yet nonetheless egregious errors in the earlier entries indicate he could only have written them out at a much later date and certainly from poor hindsight. It might just be possible that the entire contents were never committed to paper until he reached his seminary in 1585; the mental exercise of memorising ninety-one very simple episodes cannot be classed a heavy task for a man of Hart's calibre with so little else to occupy his time. It might even have helped him to retain his sanity during the long hours of his imprisonment.

However, after his recantation from the hurdle on 1st December 1581 (*see* entry 39 and footnotes), John Hart acquired those important commodities denied all other prisoners – pen, ink and paper – with which Sir Francis Walsingham employed him in refuting Catholic writings. These precious assets must have provided the impetus to putting together a secret journal, the early episodes from memory and later ones as they came to his notice.

The entire contents of *Diarium Turris* do not qualify as a unique milestone of literary achievement; anyone with a smattering of Latin could certainly have improved on the wording of most entries, especially those eight which dealt with the executions of martyrs. Robert Parsons certainly did so and often with fewer words. He did at least define the method and venue of most executions. Only a few of Hart's entries act as testimonials to the religious devotion of those named in his notes. Occasionally the clergyman in Hart comes to the surface to sermonise against the 'heretics'; yet never once in praise of his own Church. The sheer brevity of his notes leaves us wondering if this might just have been a preparatory phase in readiness for a more definitive work that had to be curtailed by the diarist's untimely death in the momentous year that finally saw his basic work published at the rear of *De Schismate*.

With all these major points of criticism, there still remains one overriding question at the end of it all that requires careful consideration. We have conjectured how and when the Diary might have been composed but we must surely consider the most obvious question of all, 'Why did he write it?' In vindication, Hart proudly boasted in his preface that he was 'doing something not unuseful nor hostile to the glory of God'; but can it honestly be admitted he achieved such criteria? In view of his many errors, his constant equivocations and the way it was virtually spurned by Parsons, the reply must be a resounding 'NO'.

Looking though the entire spectrum of his writings, let us just stand back for a moment and try to read between the lines. We saw that Hart faced trial as a traitor (entry 34) and was condemned to death (entry 36) and yet, unlike many of his co-prisoners, he escaped his appointment with the executioner. Firstly (entry 39 and footnotes), we saw him being actually tied to the hurdle and then pleading for his life in return for conformity. Later in these pages we shall read the actual letter he composed moments after his bonds had been untied (Appx 11). Whereas he might then have made the proper outward signs and worked for Walsingham in refuting Catholic dogma, his protest against Reynolds exactly one year later (entry 48) suffices to prove he had not conformed with his inner man. It was later proposed that he should suffer with those named in entry 50; but was again granted a last minute reprieve by Walsingham. It might have been very soon after this event that he resigned himself to the fact that he was never fated to be a martyr of Tyburn and stood a fairly good chance of securing a release from the Tower in appreciation of the services he had rendered for the queen's secretary of state.

The fact that he was eventually banished with the other twenty Catholics (entry 91) would not, and could not, have entered his thoughts until much nearer the time. Even so, it must have been patently clear to him that, in one way or the other, he would eventually be confronted by his superiors and have to give them an account of his time in prison. What better way of ingratiating himself with them than to produce a fully written up record as a *fait accompli* on reaching Rheims? By doing so, he might hopefully avoid a deep searching inquisition and thereby conceal from them his little-known failings and weaknesses during his absence.

In all sincerity, there can be no other logical explanation for writing the *Diarium*. It was purely intended to provide John Hart with a personal insurance policy, the small print of which would take more than four hundred years to decipher. By his rejection of as many as seventy-three of those entries, Parsons had eventually shown that he had penetrated the secret but, out of loyalty to a fellow priest and Catholic, never qualified the reasons for such drastic amendment action when compiling his *Annals of the Schism*.

SUMMARY

Despite the abandonment of the Latin Mass in favour of the English Book of Common Prayer, publication of *De Schismate* and its associated parts, including the *Diarium*, in Latin presented little or no problem in Protestant England. Any scholar with a formal education would have been competent enough to read the contents. In schools, colleges and universities, Latin was still very much on the curriculum, being probably studied in greater depth than the mother tongue if the English spelling mistakes in some of the State Papers are any indication.

Far from being a 'dead language', Latin was the equivalent of Esperanto for the Christian world, most legal documents being drawn up in that tongue. The classics could only be studied in Latin and, whilst Englishmen have always been loath to study other foreign languages, Latin was a necessity. For example, when the English statesman, Sir Thomas More, met the Dutch scholar, Desiderius Erasmus, it came quite naturally for them both to converse quite animatedly in Latin, even to the point of exchanging rather bawdy and risqué jokes.

Printing presses were being set up around the country and many were the Latin publications available for anyone to read. Those produced on secret presses for the Catholic cause highlighted the latest tyranny being forced upon their community and pleaded for toleration, sympathy and support for the oppressed. Not only in Latin but often in the strongest possible English terms, the queen and her ministers often came in for criticism.

On occasion, pamphlets and tracts were printed on underground presses in England (cf. Edmund Campion's *Rationes Decem*) but many more, in common with *De Schismate*, were published abroad and then smuggled across the Channel or North Sea, possibly secreted in waterproof wrappings beneath a fisherman's catch or in hidden compartments in passengers' luggage. It was explained earlier that this study could not determine whence Bayley discovered the pages for his reproduced *Diarium*, whether it might have been a handwritten document or an extract from the relevant edition of *De Schismate*; but this does not matter. What is more important is that Bayley, as assistant Keeper of Tower Records, did find one or the other on his shelves in the Tower Records Office as proof that the authorities had obtained a copy of some kind.

The 1586 copy of *De Schismate* that was perused at the British Library for this present work was intriguing and a mystery in itself, bearing as it did the embossed imprint of the name and coat of arms of one of the greatest heroes of Elizabethan England, Sir Richard Grenville. Considering the limited number that might have found their way onto the English market, we may only pause and wonder how much the hero of the *Revenge* might have paid for the illegal purchase and what opinion he might have formed of the contents.

The queen and her council would not have been overly pleased with any publication that even dared to suggest Elizabeth was an illegitimate child of an incestuous love affair. After all, it was common knowledge that the offspring of incest could be mentally retarded or complete imbeciles. With the added bonus of the *Diarium Turris* in the second edition of the same book, the readership was now able to learn the intimate and macabre secrets of the Tower and its torture chamber. There was no way to ban the book in any of its three editions; but possession of such 'popish frumpery' would be penalised with the harshest of measures. No doubt, Sir Richard Grenville kept his copy well concealed!!!

Other similar tracts were finding their way onto the black market and were being purposely planted on the pews in churches or scattered on benches in inns, taverns and other public places; or just dropped in the street to be avidly gathered up and taken away for covert reading by eager sympathisers or handed over as quickly as possible to law enforcement agencies in a desperate bid to learn who had dispersed such 'slanderous material'. Without let up, this paper campaign would continue throughout Elizabeth's reign and long afterwards.

By the time we reach the end of the *Diarium*, of the eighty-five persons named therein, twenty-four had been liberated on the usual conditions of conforming in religion; nineteen had been executed; fourteen were in exile on the continent; nine had been transferred to other gaols; three had died in custody; and twelve others remained in their Tower cells awaiting a decision on their fate. This leaves just four whose eventual fates have still not been unearthed from documents consulted in this study.

A number of those who had offered conformity later had a change of heart, re-embraced the Catholic faith and suffered further hardships; most of the martyrs have now been beatified or canonised and studies of their causes still continue; some of the exiles, including Hart and Rishton, died in their exile having never seen their homeland again whilst others of their number elected to defy the order for banishment and returned to these shores in the full knowledge that, if captured, they were condemned out of hand; those remaining in custody both at the Tower and in the other prisons eventually gained release of one kind or another.

The Tower of London would never again witness as much barbarity as had taken place there during the four years and seven months of Hart's Diary. Admittedly, the persecution of the Catholics would still continue unabated for many a long year; but, by then, the Tower of London was considered too noble an edifice to cater for the likes of such persons who could adequately be held in the less important prisons.

APPENDIX 1

THE LATIN DIARY
AS PRINTED IN
BAYLEY'S
HISTORY AND ANTIQUITIES OF
THE TOWER OF LONDON

(Pagination and font slightly altered, and omissions inserted)

Rerum pro Religione Catholica ac in Turri Londinensi gestarum. Ab Anno Domini 1580, ad Annum usque 1585. Indiculis seu diarium. Ab eo observatum atque collectum qui toto illo tempore captivus interfuit.

PRÆFATIO

<small>Carceres Londinenses et eorum nomina.</small>

PRÆTER eos carceres in civitate Londinensi, qui alios in usus reservantur (cujusmodi est Ludgatum honestioribus tantum civibus ob debita assignatum) undecim sunt omnino publici et capaces; in quos omnis fere generis, sexus et ætatis homines, his diebus ob fidei catholicæ confessionem conjiciuntur, horum nomina sunt, porta Westmonasteriensis, Flitum, Neugatum, Briduelum, Contoria duo, Bancus regius, Mariscalcaum, Virloinum, Clincum, et Turris sive Castrum. In quorum postremo, cum ipse singulari Dei benificio, eo solo nomine quod ecclesiæ catholicæ sacerdos essem, quatuor annis et amplius detentus fuerim, variasque rerum, temporum, afflictionum vicissitudines subierim, mortisque sententiam tandem acceperim (quam tamen postea exilio commutarunt) existimavi, rem me facturum non inutilem, nec a Dei gloria servitioque alienam, si quæ

<small>Huius Dio coni</small>

præsens in illo carcere notaveram, per dies distincta, literis traderem. Hinc enim Christianus lector, comparatione facta unius hujus carceris cum reliquis decem illius civitatis; et illorum deinde, cum cæteris omnibus quæ sunt in universa Anglia; quatuor etiam annorum quibus hæc contigerunt, cum viginti et septem quibus Elizabetha regnavit; conjecturam facile inire poterit, quot et quanta catholici pro fide in illo regno passi sint et patiantur.

<small>Quæ sunt peculiariæ Turris Londinensis</small>

Ut autem res melius intelligatur, sciendum est illud huic carceri quem Turrim appellant, præ cæteris esse peculiare, vt captivus quisque suum habeat cubiculum seu carcerem proprium, propriumque custodem, qui illum obseratum semper teneat, cæterorumque a conspectu et colloquio arceat, omneque commercium tam per literas, quam per nuncios intercludat. Ex hoc deinde cubiculo ad alia loca omnia educitur, sive supplicia adeunda sunt (quæ varijs temporibus pro persecutorum libidine catholicis infliguntur) sive vt examinetur aut quæstioni subjiciatur.

<small>Septem suppliciorum genera</small>

Suppliciorum autem, sive afflictionum particularium, quæ modo huic, modo illi adhibentur, septem in hoc carcere numerantur genera: quorum primum est, Lacus, sive spelunca quædam subterranea, viginti pedum altitudine profunda, sine lumine.

Secundum est cubilicum quoddam seu antrum arctissimum vix hominem erectum capiens, quod ab exigua requie quam præstat, Litilesium appellarunt.

Tertium est equuleus, quo, machinis quibusdam rotisque ligneis, hominus membra in diversa distrahuntur.

Quartum vocant Scavingeri filiam, ab inventore opinor deducto nomine; constat autem ex circulo ferreo, qui manus pedesque, et caput in unum orbem compingit.

Quintum est ferrearum chirothrecarum, quibus manus gravissimo cruciatu involvuntur.

Sextum est vinculorum, quæ branchijs gestantur.

Septimum denique compendum ferreorum qui aptantur pedibus, his cognitis facile intelligentur cætera quæ in diario sequuntur.

Admonitio Illud tantum admonendum est me hoc indiculo ea solum complexum esse, quæ religionis causa, catholicis inflicta fuerunt; quæque ad meam notitiam (qui separatim a cæteris custodiebar) pervenire potuerunt; cætera suo tempore ab alijs annotata prodibunt. Interim, Christiane lector, hæc pauca sufficiant ad charitatem tuam excitandam, vt pro patria nostra tam afflicta Deum roges. Vale.

Diarium Rerum Gestarum in Turri Londinensi, Anno Domini, 1580.

Jun.

15. Gulielmus Tiruitus, clarissimi viri Roberti Tiruiti equitis aurati filius primogenitus, religionis Catholicæ causa comprehensus, quod in sororis nuptijs missam audivisse dicerrtur, in Turrim subjestus est.

18. Robertus Tiruitus, Gulielmi frater, eadem de causa captus; et licet vehementer agrotaret, nulla tamen intercessione aut fidei sponsione obtinere potuit, vt in Turrim non conjiceretur, vnde paulo post mortuus est.

19. Erant hoc ipso tempore in hoc eodem carcere Hiberni proceres catholici archiepiscopus Armacanus, comites Kildarensis, et Clanricardensis, baro Deluinus, Nugetus item, Meuusque nobiles.

Decemb.

5. Rodolphus Cervinus, Thomas Cotomus, Robertus Jonsonius, Lucas Kirbæus, presbyteri, Nicolaus etiam Roscarocus, et Henricus Ortonus, laici nobiles, ex alijs carceribus in Turrim perductu.

10. Thomas Cotamus et Lucas Kirbæus, Presbyteri, Scavengeri filiam ad unam horam et amplius passi; ex quo prior copiosum sanguinem e naribus emisit.

15. Rodolphus Cervinus, et Robertus Jonsonus, presbyteri, equulei tormento gravissime vexati.

16. Rodolphus Cervinus iterum equuleo subjicitur.

19. 29. Joannes Posgravius Soc. Jesu et Joan. Hartus, presbyteri, Joan etiam Paschalis, nobilis laicus, ex alijs carceribus in hunc commutantur.

21. Georgius Peckamus, eques auratus, ex alio carcere in Turrim deductus.

23. Harramus Stevenus, laicus, eadem cause, Eodem pertractus.

31. Idem Joannes Hartus postquam dies quinque in terra decubuisset, ad equulei cruciatum deductus est, idem factum Henrico Ortono.

ANNO DOMINI 1581.

Jan.

3. Christophorus Tomsonus, presbyter gravis, in Turrim deductus, eodem ipso die equuleo subjectus est.

14. Nicolaus Roscarocus, nobilis laicus, equuleo tortus.

15. Joan. Paschalis, et Harramus Stevenus, laicus, tormentorum metu adducti, ut in publico conventu; nonnulla contra fidem profiterentur, et nominatim se hæreticorum sacra adire velle; in sequente die ad aliorum allectationem liberi dimittuntur.

16. Eodem die eodemque in conventu, Odoeus Hoptonus, Turris præfectus, cum nos militum vi, ad ecclesiam pertraxisset, publice protestatus est, se neminem in suo castro habere, qui libenter ecclesiam protestantum non adiret.

29. Joannes Nicolaus minister antea Calvinianus postea catholicus Roma rediens, vltro se offerens ab hæreticis capitur et in Turrim conjicitur, ad quem ministri statim tanquam cum eo argumentis acturi, accedunt; ille autem ad diem statutum fidem Romanam abjurat, et concionatoris munus contra nos assumit, liberque dimittitur.

Feb.

5. Idem Nicolaus suggestum conscendit, in Rom. Pontif (cujus expensis se aliquot annis Romæ vixisse jactitabat) invecturus, omnes captivi ad eum audiendum vi pertrahebantur, quem tamen debacchantem aliquoties interruperunt, et finita concione communibus vocibus exagitatum, exploserunt.

5. 31. Atque ab hoc tempore ad festum usque Pentecostes sequentis, singulis Dominicis ac festis diebus, custodum nostrorum ac militum manibus, abrepti fuimus ad conciones hæreticas, quæ a ministris ad hoc designatis fiebant audiendas, quos semper e suggestu descentes præsente populo, mendaciorum convincebamus, et ad disputationem provocabamus, exclamante interim et tormenta minitante Hoptono præfecto, ni taceremus.

8. Thomas Briscous, laicus, collegij Romani paulo ante alumnus, in porta captus et ad Turrim adductus in lacu ad menses 5 detinetur.

10. Georg. Duttonus, laicus, ex alio carcere in Turrim perlatus, cruciatuum metu post 46 dies hæreticorum postulatis ex parte consensit, ut adiret eorem sacra, licet aperte profitereur, se ipsorum communionem nunquam accepturum, ea tamen conditione liberate donatur.

Mar.

19. Joan. Nicolaus iterum parata concione invectiva pulpitum conscendit, cujus honestandi causa nonnulli proceres aliique nobiles aulici, affuerunt, sed ille tam inepte se gessit, ut eos puduerit et Cotamus presbyter mire spiritus libertate, gravissime eos officij sui admonuit quæ res mortis suæ, deinde accelerandæ causa fuisse putatur. Nicolaum tamen omnes ex eo die contempserunt.

20. Post Nicolaum diversi ministri varijs temporibus inducti fuerunt, qui nobis vicissitudine quadam coram conviciarentur, singulis enim concionibus dum persuadere nobis volebant, seditiosos rebelles, idololatras, ac perduelles appellabant.

27. Alexander Briantus presb. ex alio carcere, ubi siti fere enectus fuerat, in Turrim conjicitur, compedibusque gravissimis per duos dies oneratur. Tunc aciculi acutissimi sub ungues ei immissi fuerunt vt confiteretur quo in loco P. Personium vidisset, quod fateri tamen constantissime recusavit.

6. Idem Briantus in lacum conjicitur, indeque post octo dies retractus est ad equuleum, quem passus est omnium graviss. hoc ipso die semel, et die postero bis ex ipsius tamen ore post (paulo ante martyr) audivi, se nihil quicquam doloris sensisse in vltima hæc corporis sui distensione, cum maxime sævirent tortores, ut ingentes ei afflictiones inferrent.

Jul.

14. Joannes Paynus, presbyter, proditione cujusdam Elioti, quem illi plurimus beneficijs affecerat, capitur; eadem etiam die Joannes Shirtus et Georgius Godsalvus, Presbyteri, comprehensi; omnes in Turrim conjiciuntur.

22. Edmundus Campianus Societas Jesu, presbyter, ejusdem Elioti proditione captus, magna celebritate ad Turrim perducitur, inscriptione hac majusculis literis in galero posita, Campianus Jesuita seditiosus.

22. Vna cum Campiano perducti sunt ad eondem carcerent Thomas Fordus, Gulielmus Filbæus, Joannes Conlintonus, presbyteri, Edouardus etiam Yatus, Edouardus Kaines, Joannes Cottonus, Gulielmus Hildesleus, Homfredus Kaines, Philippus Lous, Joannes Jacobus, nobiles laici, et denique Gulielmus Valbinus, et Joannes Manfeldus, inferioris conditiois homines catholici, qui Campiani concionibus interfuerant.

Aug.

13. Gulielmus Hartlæus, presbyter, et vna cum eo, Joannes Stonerus et Stephanus Brinklerus, nobiles laici: quatuor etiam famuli, librorum impressores, Joannes Harrisius, Joannes Harreus, Joannes Tukerus, et Joannes Comptonus vna cum prælo comprehesi, in domo clarissimæ foeminæ, dominæ de Stonar, in Turrim perducti fureunt; quorum postremus natura timidior, cum carceris custos educto gladiolo mortem ei mineratur, nisi ecclesiam hereticam aditurum se promitteret, cassit, et ea ratione libertatem obtinuit.

31. Thomas Poundus, nobilis laicus, insignis confessor, qui multos annos propter fidei confessionem in alijs carceribus vitam egerat, ad Turrim deducitur.

31. Campoianus bis clam equuleo tortus, vna cum presbyteris concaptivis et laicis catholicis, imparatus omnino producitur ad disputandum cum hæreticis, in publico castri sacello; ea conditione, vt nullum argumentum ipse pro fide catholica adduceret, sed respondere tantummodo ministris impugnantibus.

Habitæ sunt postea aliæ cum Campiano disputationes bis opinor seu ter, postulantibus ita proceribus sed privatim omnino, et non publice vt antea; eo quod non parum suæ causæ nocuisse primas illas disputationes hæretici intellexerant.

Octob.

31. Edmundus Campianus tertio equuleo torquetur post disputationes, hocque omnium gravissime.

31. Joannes Faynes, presbyter, ejusdem equuleo cruciatu vehementissime exagitatus.

Novemb.

14. Edmundus Campianus, Rodolphus Ceruinus, Thomas Cotamus, Robertus Jonsonus, Lucas Chirbæus, Jacobus Bosgravius, Edouardus Risthonus, presbyteri, et Henricus Ortonus, laicus, ad tribunal regium sistuntur et conceptis verbis de multorum criminum fictis capitibus accsantur, nulla alia defensionis potestate facta, quam ut uno verbo vel reos vel non reos se esse dicerent.

16. Thomas Fordus, Alexander Briantus, Joannes Shertus, Gulielmus Filbæus, Laurentius Richardsonus, Joannes Colintonus, Joannes Hartus, presbyteri, eodem plane modo judicibus præsentati, in carceres reducuntur.

20. Edmundus Campianus cum prædictus septem socijs iterum ad judicium perductus, licet nunquam antea se invicem cognovissent, nec vnquam omnes in eodem se vidissent, de eisdem tamen conspirationum criminibus, qui eodem in loco eodemque tempore facta fuisse fingebantur, subornatis testibus omnes condemnabantur, mortisque sententiam acceperunt.

21. Postero die Thomas Fordus cum omnibus socijs (excepto Colintono) eodem modo morti fuerunt adjudicati: Colintonus vero cum esset condemnandus, nobilis quidam in Anglia illum se vidisse testabatur eodem illo tempore quo hæc conspiratio Romæ et Rhemis facta dicebatur, quo testimonio judex coactus est mortis eum sententia liberare, licet contra omnem judicij Anglicani forman, eundem iterum carceribus mancipandum adjudicaverit.

21. Poterant alij nonnulli idem pro se, quod Colintonus, dixisse; præsertim Fordus, quia diutius in Anglia quam Colintonus fuerat, sed noluerunt homines Dei martyrium suum impedire.

21. Gulielmum Filbæm ad mortem condemnatum, quod hilarior ac constantior videretur, manicis ferreis, ad diem usque transitus afflixerunt. Alexander vero Brianto, quod coronam sibi secreto rasisset, ut more sacerdotis compareret in judicio crucemque ligneam sibi composuisset, quam secum palam ad judicium ferret, post condemnationem, compedes ferreos ad biduum injecerunt.

Dec.

1. Edmundus Campianus societis Jesu, Rodolphus Cervinus, collegij Romani, Alexander Briantus, seminarij Rhemensis, presbyteri, reginæ jussu e turri eductu, et vimineis cratibus ad patibulum pertracti, glorioso martyrio vitam finierunt.

ANNO DOMINI 1582

Jan.

11. Joanes Hartus, presbyter, quod ne post condemnationem hæreticis vlla in re accommodare se vellet, in Lacum dimissus est ad novem dies.

23. Edouardus Yatus, nobilis laicus, qui cum Campiano captus fuerat, e Turri in alium carcerem dimittitur.

Febr.

7. Georgius Haddocus et Arturus Pittus, presbyteri comprehensi, quorum posterior in Lacum conjectus est ad quinque dies.

Mar.

5. Antonius Fugatius, Lusitanus nobilis, insignis pro fide catholica zelator post dourum annorum in carcerationem et gravissimos equulei toleratos cruciatus, cum morti esset propinquus (senex enim erat tormentis diffractus) lectica clam emissus, paucissimis post diebus animam Christo reddidit.

22. Robertus Coplæus, laicus, in Lacum ad dies 7 constitutus.

30. 31. Joannes Paynus, presbyter, judicibus exhibitus et postero item die mendacissima quadam criminatione convictus, quod reginam occidere voluisset, mortis damnationem accepit.

April.

2. Joannes Paynus, presbyter, Londino eductus præclaro martyrio coronatur.

7. Gulielmus Hildesleus, laicus, fidei jussoribus datis e carcere dimittitur.

    Eisdem fere conditionibus, Joannes Stonerus, et Joannes Cottonus, nobiles laici, liberantur. Thomas Alfildus, presbyter, capitur.

29. Lucas Kirbæus, et Thomas Fordus, presbyteri, ad mortem condemnati, dum mortem expectant, compendibus ferreis per triginta dies vinciuntur.

Maij.

19. Stephanus Rausamus, presbyter, et Thomas Burnus, laicus, comprehenduntur, et in Turrim adducuntur.

22. Thomas Fordus, Joannes Shirtus, et Robertus Johsonus, presbyteri, martyrio afficiuntur.

30. Gulielmus Filbæus, Lucas Kirbæus, Laurentius Richardsonus, presbyteri, eandem martyrij palmam morte consecuti sunt.

Jul.

19. Gulielmus Corterus, laicus, librorum impressor post aliquot annorum afflictiones in alijs carceribus in Turrim deducitur.

23. Richardus Slackus, presbyter, capitur, et compedibus per dies 23, oneratur; deinde in Lacum ad duos menses compingitur.

Aug.

14. Joannes Getterus, juvenis laicus, ex Gallia rediens capitur.

Stephanus Rausamus, presbyter, in Litilesium compingitur, ubi mansit decem et octo mensibus ac diebus 13.

Sept.

1. Prædictus Joannes Getterus, postquam Scavengeri filia cruciatus fuisset, in Lacum ad dies octo demittitur; deinde eductus ad equuleum, gravissime torquetur ad deliquium fere animæ, in quo summo cruciatu cum jam animam efflaturus videbatur, insigni vultus lætitia Jesu nomen invocabat et tortoribus illudebat.

16. Gulielmus Hartleius, presbyter, et Joannes Jacobus, Joannes Harvæus, Joannes Harrisius, et Joannes Tukerus, Laici, ex Turri in alios carceres dimittuntur.

20. Rodolphus Letherborus, mercator Rothomago veniens, propter fidem in Turrim conjicitur.

Decemb.

1. Joannes Hartus, presbyter, ad mortem comdemnatus, viginti dierum compedibus castigatur, eo quod cuidam Reinaldo ministro consentire nollet.

ANNO DOMINI 1583, MENS. FEBR.

16. Joannes Mundinus, presbyter, capitur, et compedibus ferreis ad dies viginti stringitur.

Jun.

19. Johannes Hartus, prædictus, propter eandem offensionem per quadraginta quatuor dies in Lacum conjicitur.

24. Stephanus Brinklæus, nobilis laicus, intercessione amicorum et fide jussoribus datis, post duorum annorum incarcerationem dimittitur.

Octob.

3. Joannes Somervilus, nobilis laicus, Edouardi Ardeni clari viri gener, cum esset catholicus, ea criminatione in Turrim conjicitur, quod animum habuisset occidendi Reginam.

Novemb.

4. Hugo Hallus, presbyter, Somervili confessarius, triduo post et idem Edouardus Ardenus socer eadem de causa comprehenduntur.
7. Franciscus Trogmortonus, præclarissimarum dotum juvenis, et Joannis Trogmortoni, equitis aurati primogenitus, accusatus quod pro regina Scotiæ nonnulla tractasset comprehenditur, et primo die in Litilesio custodiebatur.
16. Maria Ardena, et Margarita ejusdem filia, uxores prænominatorum Edouardi Ardeni et Joannis Somervili, Elizabetha etiam Somervila virgo, soror germana ejusdem Joannis, in Turrim conjiciuntur.
17. Georg. Trogmortonus, præicti domini Francisci frater, comprehenditur.
23. D. Franciscus Trogmortonus equuleo gravissime torquetur, et eodem die in Lacum dimittitur, eodem etiam die D. Edouardus Ardenus eidem equulei cruciatui subjicitur.
24. Hugo Hallus, presbyter, equuleo etiam torquetur.

Decemb.

2. D. Franciscus Trogmortonus iterum equuleo subjicitur, bis eodem die.
16. D. Edouardus Ardenus et Joannes Somervilus, nobiles laici, Hugo Hallus, presbyter, Maria etiam Ardena, Edouardi vxor, ad mortem condemnatur.
22. Joannes Somervilus cum vix sane mentis esset e Turri in alium carcerem traducitur, nocteque senquenti in carcere strangulatus inventus est, an a se vel alijs non ita constat.
26. D. Edouardus Ardenus ad patibulum eductus, suspendio interemptus est, protestatus se innocentissimum esse in ijs omnibus quorum insimulabatur, præterquam quatenus religionis catholicæ professio crimen eset.

ANNO DOMINI 1584.

Jan.

11. Gulielm. Carterus, laicus, ob libri catholici impressionem martyrio affectus.

18. Gulliel. Shelleius, vir clarus et nobilis, Gervasius item Perpointus, nobilis, ad Turrim perducti.

Febr.

2.3. Robertus Nutterus, presbyter, capitur, et post biduum in Lacum ad dies 47 conjectus, compedes ad dies 43 gessit, die autem quarto et sexto post apprehensionem Scavengeri filiam bis passus est.

Mar.

4.5.10. Georg. Haddocus, Joannes Mundinus, Jacobus Fennus, Thomas Hemerfordus, et Joannes Nutterus, presbyteri, sententiam mortis acceperunt, quorum posteriores tres in Lacu post condemnationem ad dies sex compedibus ferreis onerati jacuerunt quousque omnes martyrio afficerentur.

13. Thomas Stevensonus, presbyter, comprehenditur et humi cubans sine lecto dies 27 compedes etiam gessit ad dies 39.

13. Georgius Godsalvus et Stephanus Rausamus, presbyteri, ex Turri in alios carceres mittuntur.

22.23. Gulielmus Brumlumnus et Franciscus Ardenus, nobiles laici, capiuntur.

Jun.

10. D. Franciscus Trogmortonus, nobilis laicus, morte afficitur, eodem ipso die sparso contra illum per ignominioso libello.

13. Thomas Laytonus, nobilis laicus, capitur, in hac Lacum traducitur.

19. Thomas Worthingtonus, presbyter, capitur, et in Lacu detinetur ad menses duos, dies tres.

Aug.

24. Thomas Barnus, presbyter, comprehensus.

27. Guliel. Apricius, nobilis laicus, in Turrim conjicitur, et statim post in Lacum ad dies 23.

Mens. die Sep.

13. Gervasius Perpointus, nobilis laicus, fide jussoribus datis dimittitur, sed mense sequente iterum comprehenditur.

16. Gulielmus Critonus, Societatis Jesu, et Patricius Abdæus, presbyter, Scoti, cum in Scotiam proficiscerentur, contra omne jus gentium ex mari in Angliam trahuntur ad carceres.

24. Gulielmus Apricius iterum in Lacum conjicitur ad dies 48.

Oct.

16. Gulielmus Crumlummus in Lacum traditur ad menses duos, dies vero 24.

No.

10. Robertus Nutterus iterum in Lacum compingintur mensibus duobus et diebus 14.

ANNO DOMINI 1585.

Jun.

4. Patricius Addæus, presbyter, Scotus, in Lacum dimittitur ad dies 4. item fit Gulielmo Crumlummo iterum ad dies 7.

7. 31.   Gaspar Haynodus, Jacobus Bosgravius, et Joannes Hartus, Soc. Jesu presb. Christophorus etiam Tonsonus, Arturus Bittus, Robertus Nutterus, Thomas Stevensonus, Sichard Slackus, Thomas Barnus, Thomas Worthingtonus dece'que alij sacerdotes, et unus laicus (eramus enim numero viginti et unus) cum nihil tale expectaremus præcepto reginæ in navim impositi inniti plane in littus Normannicum ejecti fuimus, et non longe post quinquaginta alij, eodem exilij genere consecuti nos sunt, imposita nobis omnibus expressa capitis poena, si unquam patriam reverteremur.

LAUS DEO.

APPENDIX 2

THE TOWER BILLS
1580–1585

These accounts, submitted quarterly by the Lieutenant of the Tower to claim his fees for those prisoners he had to maintain at the expense of the Crown, are mostly held at the Public Record Office under *E407-56*. Unfortunately, the series – ranging from 1575 through to 1765 – is not complete, many of the 'missing' documents being located in Calendars of Treasury Bills. On the plus side, it is fortunate for those who might not be able to transcribe the Tudor and Stuart handwriting styles that the bills covering the important period from 1575 to 1681 have been painstakingly transcribed by John Hungerford Pollen in *CRS, Miscellanea, Vols 3 & 4*. However, a few of these have been found to contain a number of minor errors of which the discerning reader should be warned. Corrections for the Bills covering the period of the Diary are incorporated into this appendix.

As previously mentioned, the earliest Bill in the PRO file dates from 1575. However, it was noticed that two earlier Bills, covering a period from 1551-2 and another from 1571-2, were reproduced in *Bayley Part 2, pp lii & lv-lvi;* but neither of these could be located in the PRO file, despite an insistence from the PRO, as a result of a request from the Resident Governor on behalf of Mr Harrison, that all records perused by Bayley were passed on to them at the time of the transfer to the Central Record Office, Chancery Lane in the 1850s. For further information see *Tower Bills* in Bibliography.

Even with the filling of many gaps, the series is still incomplete; nor do the Bills list each and every person in custody during each quarter. The monarch and privy council insisted that persons of substance and wealth should pay their own fees during the period of their captivity.

As we are solely concerned with the time span embraced by the *Diarium*, this appendix only contains those Bills relevant to 1580 to 1585. To facilitate their understanding, the Roman numerals given in the originals have all been transcribed into Arabic numbers, viz, a claim for the sum of vj^{li} xij^{s} iij^{d} will herein appear as £6.12s.3d.

The financial year was divided into four quarters for which the Lieutenant's clerk drew up neatly collated demands in copperplate lettering on large sheets of heavy paper. These quarters were, unless otherwise stated:

- Midsummer – covering the period from 25th March until 24th June. It should be remembered that each year actually started on Lady Day, 25th March, viz, 24 March 1580 was immediately followed by 25 March 1581.
- Michaelmas – 25th June to 24th September.
- Christmas – 25th September to 24th December.
- Lady Day – 25th December to 24th March.

Because the heading at the start of each bill followed the same basic format, it has been shown in full at the beginning of the first bill but is thereafter abbreviated to avoid undue repetition.

LADY DAY 1580

The demaunds of Sr Owen Hopton, knyght, Lieutenant of the Tower of London, for the dietts and chardges of certein prisoners there remaynynge, as hereafter are particulerlye declared.

Richard Craighe. In primis for the Diett and chardges of Richard Craighe beginninge the 25th of December and ending the 27th March 1580, then next folowinge being 13 wicks at 13s.4d. the wicke for himselfe – £8.13s.4d. One keeper at 5s. the wicke – £3.5s. Fewell and candell at 4s. the wicke – £2.12s. Amountinge to the some of...
£14.10s.4d.

Thomas Hardinge. Item, etc... 13 wicks [dates and rates as above]... £14.10s.4d.

John Prestall. Item, etc... 13 wicks [dates and rates as above]... £14.10s.4d.

Francis Brewninge. Item, etc... 13 wicks [dates and rates as above]... £14.10s.4d.

Hugh Singleton. Item, etc... 26th December to 22nd January... 4 wickes [rates as above] Amountinge to the Some of... £4.9s.4d.

William Padge. Item, etc... 23rd December to 24th March... 13 wickes [rates as above]... Amountinge to the Some of... £14.10s.4d.

Peter Duglas. Item, etc... 26th December to 27th March... 13 wicks at 6s.8d. for hym selfe – £4.6s.8d. Fewell and candell at 2s.6d. the wicke – £1.12s.6d. Amountinge to the Some of... £5.19s.2d.

Sm – £83.0s.2d.

[signed] Owyn Hopton

MIDSUMMER 1580. Not available.
MICHAELMAS 1580. Not available.

CHRISTMAS 1580

The demaunds, etc...

Richard Craighe. In primis for the diett and chardgs of Richard Craighe begynynge the 30th September 1580 and ending the 23rd December then next folowinge beinge 12 wickes at 13s.4d. the wicke for hym selfe – £8. One keeper at 5s. the wicke – £3. Fewell and candell at 4s. the wicke – 48s. Amountinge to the Some of... £13.8s.0d.

John Prestall. Item, etc... 12 wickes [dates and rates as above]... £13.8s.0d.

Thomas Hardinge. Item, etc... 12 wickes [dates and rates as above]... £13.8s.0d.

William Padge. Item, etc... 12 wickes [dates and rates as above]... £13.8s.0d.

Frauncis Brewninge. Item, etc... 12 wickes [dates and rates as above]... £13.8s.0d.

Anthonie Focatio. Item, etc... 12 wickes [dates and rates as above]... £13.8s.0d.

David Williamson. Item, etc... begynynge the 29th November and ending the 23rd December then next folowinge beinge four wickes at 6s.8d. the wicke for hym selfe – £1.6s.8d. Fewell and candell at 2s.6d the wicke – 10s. Amountinge to the Some of... £1.16s.8d.

The Earle of Kilricarde [sic in Ms for Clanricarde]. Item, etc... begynynge the 4th December 1580 and endinge the 24th of the Same then folowinge, beinge three wickes at £3. the wicke – £9. Amountinge to the Some of... £9.0s.0d.

Robert Johnson. Item, etc...4th December to 24th of the Same... three wickes at 6s.8d. the wicke – 20s. Fewell and candell at 2s.6d. the wicke – 7s.6d. Amountinge to the Some of... 27s.6d.

Thomas Cotham. Item, etc... three wickes [dates and rates as above]... 27s.6d.

Luke Kyrbie. Item, etc... 4th December to 25th of the Same... three wickes [rates as above]... 27s.6d.

Ralfe Sheringe. Item, etc... three wickes [dates and rates as above]... 27s.6d.

Henrie Orton. Item, etc... three wickes [dates and rates as above]... 27s.6d.

Summa Totalis – £98.2s.2d.

[signed] Owyn Hopton

LADY DAY 1581

The demaunds, etc...

Therle of Clenricarde. In primis for the dyett and chardgs of the Earle of Clenricarde begynynge the 24th December and endinge the 25th of Marche then next folowinge, beinge 13 wicks at £3. the wicke. Amountinge to the Some of... £39.0s.0d.

Richard Craighe. Item, etc... 13 wickes [dates as above]... at 13s.4d. the wicke for hym selfe – £8.13s.4d. One keaper at 5s. the wicke – £3.5s. Fewell and candell at 4s. the wicke – 52s. Amountinge to the Some of... £14.10s.4d.

John Prestall. Item, etc... 13 wickes [dates and rates as above]... £14.10s.4d.

Thomas Hardinge. Item, etc... 13 wickes [dates and rates as above]... £14.10s.4d.

William Padge. Item, etc... 13 wickes [dates and rates as above]... £14.10s.4d.

Francis Brewninge. Item, etc... 13 wickes [dates and rates as above]... £14.10s.4d.

Anthony Fogaca. Item, etc... 13 wickes [dates and rates as above]... £14.10s.4d.

William Johnson. Item, etc... [same term]... 13 wickes at 6s.8d. for hym selfe – £4.6s.8d. Fewell and candell at 2s.6d. the wicke – 32s.6d. Amountinge to the Some of... £5.19s.2d.

Thomas Cotham. Item, etc... 13 wickes [dates and rates as above]... £5.19s.2d.

Luke Kirbie. Item, etc... 13 wickes [dates and rates as above]... £5.19s.2d.

Henrie Orton. Item, etc... 13 wickes [dates and rates as above]... £5.19s.2d.

Ralph Sheringe. Item, etc... 13 wickes [dates and rates as above]... £5.19s.2d.

John Hartt. Item, etc... 13 wickes [dates and rates as above]... £5.19s.2d.

Christopher Tomson. Item, etc... 13 wickes [dates and rates as above]... £5.19s.2d.

James Bosgrave. Item, etc... 13 wickes [dates and rates as above]... £5.19s.2d.

Thomas Briscoe. Item, etc... 13 wickes [dates and rates as above]... £5.19s.2d.

John Nicolls. Item, etc... 13 wickes [dates and rates as above]... £5.19s.2d.

George Dutton. Item, etc... 13 wickes [dates and rates as above]... £5.19s.2d.

Summa totalis – £191.12s.10d.

[signed] Owyn Hopton

MIDSUMMER 1581

The demaunds, etc...

The Earle of Clenricarde. Imprimis, etc... begynnynge the 25th of Marche 1581 and endinge the 24th of June then next folowinge... 13 wickes at £3 the wicke – Amountinge to the Some of... £39.0s.0d.

Richarde Craygh. Item, etc... 13 wickes [dates as above]... 13s.4d. for hym selfe – £8.13s.4d. One keaper at 5s, the wicke – £3.5s. Fewell and candell at 4s. the wicke – 52s. Amountinge to the Some of... £14.10s.4d.

John Prestall. Item, etc... 13 wickes [dates and rates as above]... £14.10s.4d.

Thomas Hardinge. Item, etc... 13 wickes [dates and rates as above]... £14.10s.4d.

Anthony Focatio. Item, etc... 13 wickes [dates and rates as above]... £14.10s.4d.

John Dutton. Item, etc... 20th ffebruarie 1580 and endinge the second of June then next folowinge, beinge 14 wicks at 13s.4d. the wicke for hym selfe – £9.6s.8d. One keaper at 5s.0d. the wicke – £3.5s.0d. Fewell and candell at 4s. the wicke – 56s.0d. Amountinge to the Some of... £15.12s.8d.

William Padge. Item, etc... 25th Marche and endinge 8th Marche [*sic* for April] then next folowinge, beynge too wickes at 13s.4d. the wicke for hym selfe – 26s.8d. One keaper at 5s. the wicke – 10s.0d. Fewell and candell at 4s. the wicke – 8s.0d. Amountinge to the Some of... 44s.8d.

Mrs. Hyde. Item, etc... 20th Marche 1580 and endynge the 10th June 1580 [*sic* for 1581] beinge 11 wickes at 26s.8d. the wicke. Amountinge to the Some of... £14.13s.4d.

Robert Johnson. Item, etc... 25th of Marche, 1581, and endinge the 24th of June then next folowinge, beinge 13 wicks at 6s.8d. the wicke – £4,6s.8d. Fewell and candell at 2s.6d. the wicke – 32s.6d. Amountinge to the Some of... £5.19s.2d.

Thomas Cotham. Item, etc... 13 wickes [dates and rates as above]... £5.19s.2d.

Luke Kirbie. Item, etc... 13 wickes [dates and rates as above]... £5.19s.2d.

Ralfe Sheringe. Item, etc... 13 wickes [dates and rates as above]... £5.19s.2d.

Henrie Orton. Item, etc... 13 wickes [dates and rates as above]... £5.19s.2d.

Christopher Tomson. Item, etc... 13 wickes [dates and rates as above]... £5.19s.2d.

James Bosgrave. Item, etc... 13 wickes [dates and rates as above]... £5.19s.2d.

Thomas Briscoe. Item, etc... 13 wickes [dates and rates as above]... £5.19s.2d.

John Harte. Item, etc... 13 wickes [dates and rates as above]... £5.19s.2d.

Alexander Bryan. Item, etc... 13 wickes [dates and rates as above]... £5.19s.2d.

Thomas Mehoe. Item, etc... 7th Marche 1580 and endinge the 25th June 1581 beinge 16 wickes at 6s.8d. the wicke – £5.6s.8d. Fewell and candell at 2s.6d. the wicke – 40s. Amountinge to the Some of... £7.6s.8d.

Summa – £196.10s.4d.

[signed] Owyn Hopton

MICHAELMAS 1581. Not available.
CHRISTMAS 1581. Not available.

LADY DAY 1582.

The demaunds, etc...

Richarde Craighe. In primis, etc... 24 December 1581 to 25 Marche 1582... 13 wicks [rates as before]... £14.10s.4d.

John Prestall. Item, etc... 13 wickes [dates and rates as above]... £14.10s.4d.

Anthonie Focatio. Item, etc... 13 wickes [dates and rates as above]... £14.10s.4d.

Thomas Mehoe. Item, etc... 13 wickes [dates and rates as above]... £14.10s.4d.

George Godshalle. Item, etc... 13 wickes [dates and rates as above]... £14.10s.4d.

mort. *John Shorte*. Item, etc... 13 wickes [dates and rates as above]... £14.10s.4d.

mort. *John Paine*. Item, etc... 13 wickes [dates and rates as above]... £14.10s.4d.

John Collington. Item, etc... 13 wickes [dates and rates as above]... £14.10s.4d.

Thomas Foorde. mort. Item, etc... 13 wickes [dates and rates as above]... £14.10s.4d.

Robert Johnson. mort. Item, etc... 13 wickes at 6s.8d. the wicke – £4.6s.8d. Fewell and candell at 2s.6d. the wicke – 32s.6d. Amountinge to the Some of... £5.19s.2d.

Lucke Kirbie. mort. Item, etc... 13 wickes [dates and rates as above]... £5.19s.2d.

William Philbie. mort. Item, etc... 13 wickes [dates and rates as above]... £5.19s.2d.

Henrie Orton. mort. Item, etc... 13 wickes [dates and rates as above]... £5.19s.2d.

Christopher Tomeson. mort. Item, etc... 13 wickes [dates and rates as above]... £5.19s.2d.

James Bosgrave. Item, etc... 13 wickes [dates and rates as above]... £5.19s.2d.

Thomas Briscoe. Item, etc... 13 wickes [dates and rates as above]... £5.19s.2d.

John Hartt. Item, etc... 13 wickes [dates and rates as above]... £5.19s.2d.

Phillipp Loes. Item, etc... 13 wickes [dates and rates as above]... £5.19s.2d.

Lawrence Richardson. mort. Item, etc... 13 wickes [dates and rates as above]... £5.19s.2d.

James Negent. Item, etc... 5th February 1581 and endinge the 25th March 1582 then next folowinge, beinge 7 wicks, at 13s. 4d. for hymselfe – £4.13s.4d. One keap. at 5s. ye wicke – 35s. Fewell and candell at 4s. ye wicke – 28s. Amountinge to the Some of... £7.16s.4d.

Arthur Petts. Item, etc... 7 wicks [dates and rates as above]... £7.16s.4d.

George Haddocke. Item, etc... 7 wicks [dates and rates as above]... £7.16s.4d.

Thomas Cotham. mort. Item, etc... beginninge the 24th December 1581 and endinge 25th Marche 1582 then next folowinge, beinge 13 wicks at 6s.4d. the wicke – £4.6s.8d. Fewell and candell at 2s.6d. the wicke – 32s.6d. Amountinge to the Some of...
£5.19s.2d.

Summa totalis – £219.12s.10d

[signed] Owyn Hopton

THE TOWER BILLS 1580-1585

MIDSUMMER 1582.

The demaunds etc...

Richarde Crayghe. In primis... from 25 Marche to 24 June 1582... 13 wicks at 13s.4d. for hym selfe – £8.13s.4d. One keap at 5s. ye wicke – £3.5s. Fewell and candell at 4s. the wicke – 52s. Amountinge to the Some of... £14.10s.4d.

John Prestall. Item etc... 13 wicks [dates and rates as above]... £14.10s.4d.

Thomas Mehoe. Item, etc... 13 wicks [dates and rates as above]... £14.10s.4d.

George Godshalle. Item, etc... 13 wicks [dates and rates as above]... £14.10s.4d.

James Newgent. Item, etc... 13 wicks [dates and rates as above]... £14.10s.4d.

Arthur Petts. Item, etc... 13 wicks [dates and rates as above]... £14.10s.4d.

George Haddocke. Item, etc... 13 wicks [dates and rates as above]... £14.10s.4d.

ex. *John Shorte*, mort. Item, etc... 25th Marche, 1582, and endinge the 27th Maye... nyne wicks at 13s.4d. for hym selfe – £6. One keap at 5s. ye wicke – 45s. Fewell and candell at 4s. the wick [- 28s.]. Amountinge to the Some of... £10.12d [*sic*]

ex. *Thomas Forde*. mort. Item, etc... 9 wicks [rates as Shorte]... £10.12d.

John Collington. Item, etc... 13 wicks [rates as before]... £14.10s.4d.

mort. *John Payne*. Item, etc... the 25th Marche and endinge the laste daye of the same, beinge one wicke, at 13s.4d. for hym selfe. One keap at 5s. the wicke. Fewell and candell at 4s. the wicke. Amountinge to the Some of... 22s.4d.

mort. *Thomas Cotham*. Item, etc... the 25th Marche and endinge the 27th Maye, beinge nyne wicks, at 6s.8d. the wicke – £3. Fewell and candell at 2s.6d. the wicke [- £1.2s.6d.] Amountinge to the Some of... £4.2s.6d.

Robert Johnson. mort. Item, etc... 9 wicks [dates and rates as above]... £4.2s.6d.

Luke Kyrbie. mort. Item, etc... the 25th Marche and endinge 30 Maye... 9 wicks [rates as above]... £4.2s.6d.

William Philbie, mort. Item, etc... 9 wicks [dates and rates as Kyrbie]... £4.2s.6d.

Lawrence Richardson. mort. Item, etc... [dates and rates as Kyrbie]... £4.2s.6d.

John Harte. Item, etc...the 25th Marche 1582 and endinge the 24th June... 13 wicks at 6s.8d. the wick – £4.6s.8d. Fewell and candell at 2s.6d. the wick – 32s.6d. Amountinge to the Some of... £5.19s.2d.

mort. *Christopher Tomson*. Item, etc... 13 wicks [dates and rates as above]...
£5.19s.2d.

mort. *Henrie Orton*. Item, etc... 13 wicks [dates and rates as above]... £5.19s.2d.

James Bosgrave. Item, etc... 13 wicks [dates and rates as above]... £5.19s.2d.

Thomas Briscoe. Item, etc... 13 wicks [dates and rates as above]... £5.19s.2d.

Phillipp Loes. Item, etc... 13 wicks [dates and rates as above]... £5.19s.2d.

Summa totalis – £193.14s.6d.

[signed] Owyn Hopton.

MICHAELMAS 1582 – Not available.

CHRISTMAS 1582.

The demaunds...

Richard Craiyghe. Imprimis, etc... 30 September to 23th [sic] December... 12 wicks [rates as before]... £13.8s.0d.

John Prestall. Item, etc... 12 wicks [dates and rates as above]... £13.8s.0d.

Thomas Mehoe. Item,etc... 12 wicks [dates and rates as above]... £13.8s.0d.

Geordge Godshall. Item, etc... 12 wicks [dates and rates as above]... £13.8s.0d.

James Newgent. Item, etc... 12 wicks [dates and rates as above]... £13.8s.0d.

Arthur Petts. Item, etc... 12 wicks [dates and rates as above]... £13.8s.0d.

Geordge Haddocke. Item, etc... 12 wicks [dates and rates as above]... £13.8s.0d.

John Collington. Item, etc... 12 wicks [dates and rates as above]... £13.8s.0d.

Stephine Rowsham. Item, etc... 12 wicks [dates and rates as above]... £13.8s.0d.

Thomas Barnes. Item, etc... 12 wicks [dates and rates as above]... £13.8s.0d.

Richard Clarke [sic for Slacke]. Item, etc... 12 wicks [dates and rates as above]... £13.8s.0d.

Christopher Tomson. Item, etc... 12 wicks [dates and rates as above]... £13.8s.0d.

John Harte. Item, etc... 12 wickes at 6s.8d. ye wicke – £4. Fewell and candell at 2s.6d. ye wicke – 30s. Amountinge to the Some of... £5.10s.0d.

Henrie Orton. Item, etc... 12 wickes [dates and rates as above]... £5.10s.0d.

James Bosgrove. Item, etc... 12 wickes [dates and rates as above]... £5.10s.0d.

Thomas Briscoe. Item, etc... 12 wickes [dates and rates as above]... £5.10s.0d.

John Jetter. Item, etc... 12 wickes [dates and rates as above]... £5.10s.0d.

Phillipp Loes. Item, etc... 30th September to 4th November... 5 wickes [rates as above]... Amountinge to the Some of... 45s. 10d.

Summa Totalis – £190. 11s.10d.

[signed] Owyn Hopton.

LADY DAY 1583.

The demaunds...

Richard Craighe. In primis, etc... 24th December 1582 to 25 March 1583... 13 wicks [rates as before]... £14.10s.4d.

John Prestall. Item, etc... 13 wickes [dates and rates as above]... £14.10s.4d.

THE TOWER BILLS 1580-1585 95

Thomas Mehoe. Item, etc... 13 wickes [dates and rates as above]... £14.10s.4d.

Geordge Godshall. Item, etc... 13 wickes [dates and rates as above]... £14.10s.4d.

James Newgent. Item, etc... 13 wickes [dates and rates as above]... £14.10s.4d.

Arthur Petts. Item, etc... 13 wickes [dates and rates as above]... £14.10s.4d.

Geordge Haddocke. Item, etc... 13 wickes [dates and rates as above]... £14.10s.4d.

John Collington. Item, etc... 13 wickes [dates and rates as above]... £14.10s.4d.

Stephine Rowsham. Item, etc... 13 wickes [dates and rates as above]... £14.10s.4d.

Thomas Barnes. Item, etc... 13 wickes [dates and rates as above]... £14.10s.4d.

Richard Slake. Item, etc... 13 wickes [dates and rates as above]... £14.10s.4d.

Christopher Tomson. Item, etc... 13 wickes [dates and rates as above]... £14.10s.4d.

John Monden. Item, etc... 12th ffebruarie 1582 and endinge the 25th of Marche 1583, beinge syx wickes at 13s.4d. for hym selfe – £4. One keap. at 5s. ye wicke – 30s. Fewell and candell at 4s. ye wicke – 24s. Amountinge to the Some of... £6.14s.0d.

John Harte. Item, etc... 13 wickes [rates as before]... £5.19s.2d.

Henrie Orton. Item, etc... 13 wickes [rates as before]... £5.19s.2d.

James Bosgrove. Item, etc... 13 wickes [rates as before]... £5.19s.2d.

Thomas Brisco. Item, etc... 13 wickes [rates as before]... £5.19s.2d.

John Jetter. Item, etc... 13 wickes [rates as before]... £5.19s.2d.

Summa totalis – £210.13s.10d.

[signed] Owyn Hopton

MIDSUMMER 1583 – Not available.

MICHAELMAS 1583

The demaunds...

Richard Craighe. Imprimis, etc... beginninge 24th of June, 1583 and endinge the 29th of September, beinge 14 wickes [rates as before]. Amountinge to the Some of...
£15.12s.8d.

John Prestall. Item, etc... 14 wickes [dates and rates as above]... £15.12s.8d.

Thomas Mehoe. Item, etc... 14 wickes [dates and rates as above]... £15.12s.8d.

Geordge Godshall. Item, etc... 14 wickes [dates and rates as above]... £15.12s.8d.

James Newgent. Item, etc... 14 wickes [dates and rates as above]... £15.12s.8d.

Arthur Petts. Item, etc... 14 wickes [dates and rates as above]... £15.12s.8d.

Geordge Haddocke. Item, etc... 14 wickes [dates and rates as above]... £15.12s.8d.

John Collington. Item, etc... 14 wickes [dates and rates as above]... £15.12s.8d.

Stephine Rowsham. Item, etc... 14 wickes [dates and rates as above]... £15.12s.8d.

Thomas Barnes. Item, etc... 14 wickes [dates and rates as above]... £15.12s.8d.

Richard Slake. Item, etc... 14 wickes [dates and rates as above]... £15.12s.8d.

Christopher Tomson. Item, etc... 14 wickes [dates and rates as above]... £15.12s.8d.

John Monden. Item, etc... 14 wickes [dates and rates as before] £6.14s.0d.

John Harte. Item, etc... [dates as above] 14 wickes at 6s.8d. ye wicke – £4.13s.4d. Fewell and candell at 2s.6d. – 35s. Amountinge to the Some of... £6.8s.4d.

Henrie Orton. Item, etc... 14 wickes [dates and rates as above]... £6.8s.4d.

James Bosgrave. Item, etc... 14 wickes [dates and rates as above]... £6.8s.4d.

Thomas Briscoe. Item, etc... 14 wickes [dates and rates as above]... £6.8s.4d.

John Jetter. Item, etc... 24th of June, 1583, and endinge the 23rd of Julie then next folowinge, beinge fowre wicks at 6s.8d. the wicke – 26s.8d. Fewell and candell at 2s.6d. the wicke – 10s. Amountinge to the Some of... 36s.8d.

Summa totalis – £215. 4s. 0d.

[signed] Owyn Hopton

CHRISTMAS 1583

The demaunds...

Richard Craighe. Item, etc... beginninge the 29th of September and endinge the 29th of December, beinge 13 wickes [rates as before]... £14.10s.4d.

John Prestall. Item, etc... 13 wickes [dates and rates as above]... £14.10s.4d.

Geordge Godshall. Item, etc... 13 wickes [dates and rates as above]... £14.10s.4d.

Arthure Petts. Item, etc... 13 wickes [dates and rates as above]... £14.10s.4d.

George Haddocke. Item, etc... 13 wickes [dates and rates as above]... £14.10s.4d.

John Collington. Item, etc... 13 wickes [dates and rates as above]... £14.10s.4d.

Stephine Rowsham. Item, etc... 13 wickes [dates and rates as above]... £14.10s.4d.

Thomas Barnes. Item, etc... 13 wickes [dates and rates as above]... £14.10s.4d.

Richard Slake. Item, etc... 13 wickes [dates and rates as above]... £14.10s.4d.

Christopher Tomson. Item, etc... 13 wickes [dates and rates as above]... £14.10s.4d.

ex. *John Monden*. Item, etc... 13 wickes [dates and rates as above]... £14.10s.4d.

ex. *William Carter*. Item, etc... 29th of September 1583 and endinge the 5th of Januarie then next folowinge, beinge 14 wicks, at 13s.4d. for hym selfe – £9.6s.8d. One keaper at 5s. the wicke – £3.10s. Fewell and candell at 4s. ye wicke – 56s. Amountinge to the Some of... £15.13s.4d.

John Hartte. Item, etc... 29th September 1583 and endinge the 29th December, beinge 13 wicks [rates as before]... £5.19s.2d.

Henrie Orton. Item, etc... 13 wicks [dates and rates as above]... £5.19s.2d.

James Bosgrave. Item, etc... 13 wicks [dates and rates as above]... £5.19s.2d.

Thomas Briscoe. Item, etc... 13 wicks [dates and rates as above]... £5.19s.2d.

Item for the dyett and chardgs of *John Somervile*, esquier, beginninge the 29th of October 1583, and endinge the 19th of December then next folowinge, beinge seven wicks at 26s.8d the wicke for hym selfe – £9.6s.8d. One keaper at 6s.8d. the wicke – 46s.8d. Fewell and candell at 6s. 8d. ye wicke – 46s.8d. Amountinge to the Some of... £14.0s.0d.

Item for the dyett and chardgs of *Edmonde Arden* beginninge the 6th of November 1583, and endinge the 19th of December then next folowinge, beinge 6 wicks at 26s.8d. the wicke for hym selfe – £8. One keaper at 6s.8d. the wicke – 40s. Fewell and candell at 6s.8d. the wicke – 40s. Amountinge to the Some of... £12.0s.0d.

Summa totalis – £228. 3s. 8d.

[signed] Owyn Hopton

LADY DAY 1584 – Not available.

MIDSUMMER 1584
[heavily torn]

The demaunds...

Richard Craighe. Inprimis, etc... beginninge the 25th Marche 1584 and endinge the 25th of June then next folowinge, beinge thirtine wicks at [13]s.4d. the wicke for hym selfe – £8.13s.4d. One keaper at 5s. ye wicke – £3.5s.0d. Fewell and candell at 4s. ye wicke – 52s. Amountinge to the Some of... £14.10s.4d.

John Prestall. Item, etc... 13 wicks [dates and rates as above]... £14.10s.4d.

Arthur Petts. Item, etc... 13 wicks [dates and rates as above]... £14.10s.4d.

John Collington. Item, etc... 13 wicks [dates and rates as above]... £14.10s.4d.

Thomas Barnes. Item, etc... 13 wicks [dates and rates as above]... £14.10s.4d.

Richard Slacke. Item, etc... 13 wicks [dates and rates as above]... £14.10s.4d.

Christopher Tomson. Item, etc... 13 wicks [dates and rates as above]... £14.10s.4d.

Hughe Halle. Item, etc... 13 wicks [dates and rates as above]... £14.10s.4d.

Robert Nutter. Item, etc... 13 wicks [dates and rates as above]... £14.10s.4d.

Jervice Parpoynte. Item, etc... ye 19th of Januarie 1583, and endinge the 23th [sic] of June 1584, next folowinge, beinge 22 wicks at [13s].4d. for hym selfe – £14.13s.4d. One keaper at 5s. the wicke – £5.10s. Fewell and candell at 4s. ye wicke – 42s. [corrected to £4.8s.]. Amountinge to the Some of... £24.11s.4d.

Edwarde More. Item, etc... the fyrst of Januarie, 1583, and endinge the 24th of June next folowinge, 1584, beinge 25 wicks at 13s.4d. ye wicke for hym selfe – £16.13s.4d. One keaper at 5s. ye wicke – £6.5s. Fewell and candell at 4s. ye wicke – £5. Amountinge to the Some of... £21.14s.4d.
[corrected to £27.18s.4d.]

Jasper Haywoode. Item, etc... the 7th ffebruarie, 1583, and endinge the 21st June, 1584, next folowinge, beinge 19 wicks at 13s.4d. the wicke for hym selfe – £12.13s.4d. One keaper at 5s. the wicke – £4.15s. Fewell and candell at 4s. ye wicke – £3.16s. Amountinge to the Some of... £27.18s.4d.
[corrected to £21.4s.4d.]

Thomas Stephenson. Item, etc... 23rd ffebruarie, 1583, and endinge the 25th of June, 1584 beinge 19 wicks [rates as above]... £21.4s.4d.

Frauncis Arden. Item, etc... 23rd ffebruarie, 1583, and endinge the 21th [sic] of June 1584 beinge 17 wicks [rates as above]... £18.19s.8d.

William Bromlum. Item, etc... 23rd of ffebruarie 1583, and endinge the 21th [sic] of June next folowinge, beinge 17 wicks at 6s.8d. ye wicke – £5.13s.4d. Fewell and candell at 2s.6d. ye wicke – 32s.6d. Amountinge to the Some of... £7.15s.10d.

John Hartte. Item, etc... 26th of Marche, 1584, and endinge the 25th of June next folowinge, beinge 13 wicks [rates as before]... £5.19s.2d.

Henrie Orton. Item, etc... 13 wicks [dates and rates as above]... £5.19s.2d.

James Bosgrove. Item, etc... 13 wicks [dates and rates as above]... £5.19s.2d.

Marie Arden. Item, etc... 26th of Marche, 1584, and endinge the 25th of June next folowinge, beinge 13 wicks at 26s.3d. the wicke for her selfe – £17.6s.8d. Her keaper at 6s.8d. ye wicke – £4.6s.8d. Fewell and candell at 6s.8d. ye wicke – £4.6s.8d. Amountinge to the Some of... £26.0s.0d.

Margarett Somervylle. Item, etc... 13 wicks [dates and rates as above]... £26.0s.0d.

Elizabethe Somervile. Item, etc... 13 wicks [dates and rates as above]... £26.0s.0d.

Summa totalis – £348. 4s. 4d.

[signed] Owyn Hopton.

THE TOWER BILLS 1580-1585   99

MICHAELMAS 1584 – not available.

CHRISTMAS 1584

The demaunds...

Richarde Craighe. Item, etc... fyrst of October, 1584, and endinge the 24th of December next folowinge, beinge 12 wicks [rates as before]... £13.8s.0d.

John Prestall. Item, etc... 12 wicks [dates and rates as above]... £13.8s.0d.

Hughe Halle. Item, etc... 12 wicks [dates and rates as above]... £13.8s.0d.

Edwarde Moore. Item, etc... 12 wicks [dates and rates as above]... £13.8s.0d.

Frauncis Arden. Item, etc... 12 wicks [dates and rates as above]... £13.8s.0d.

William Cromlome. Item, etc... 12 wicks [dates and rates as above]... £13.8s.0d.

William Aprice. Item, etc... 12 wicks [dates and rates as above]... £13.8s.0d.

Jarvice Parpoynte. Item, etc... 12 wicks [dates and rates as above]... £13.8s.0d.

Thomas Layton. Item, etc... 12 wicks [dates and rates as above]... £13.8s.0d.

Thomas Bryscoe. Item, etc... 12 wicks [dates and rates as above]... £13.8s.0d.

Patricke Addie. Item, etc... 26th of September, 1584, and endinge the 24th of December next folowinge, beinge 14 wicks at 26s.8d. ye wicke for hym selfe – £9.6s.8d. One keaper at 5s. ye wicke – £3.10s.0d. Fewell and candell at 4s. ye wicke – 54s. [*sic* for 56s.]. Amountinge to the Some of... £15.10s.8d.
[*sic* for £15.12s.8d.]

William Critton. Item, etc... 14 wicks [dates and rates as above]... £15.10s.8d
[*sic* for £15.12s.8d.]

Margarett Somervylle. Item, etc... fyrste of October, 1584, and endinge the 24th of December next folowinge, beinge 12 wicks at 26s.8d. ye wicke for her selfe – £16. One keaper at 6s.8d. ye wycke – £4. Fewell and candell at 6s.8d. ye wicke – £4. Amountinge to the Some of... £24.0s.0d.

Arthur Petts. dismyssed. Item, etc... fyrst of October, 1584 and endinge ye 21st of Januarie next folowinge, beinge 16 wicks at 13s.4d. for hym selfe – £14.13s.4d. [*sic in Ms* for £10.13s.4d.]. One keaper at 5s. ye wicke – £4. Fewell and candell at 4s. ye wicke – £3.4s.0d. Amountinge to the Some of...... £21.17s.4d.

[**Editor's Note** – *Due to the £4 error in calculating the personal allowances for this and the following eight men, the resulting totals also reflect an additional £4.00 when all totals should have read £17.17s.4d. Whether this was a fraudulent claim for £36.00 or an error in calculation cannot be classified; but, as the figures were not always subject to scrutiny, it would seem that the Bill was settled by the Privy Council without question. If the extra £4.00 per prisoner had been for expenses incurred in moving them into exile, it would surely have been shown as a separate entity and would also have been claimed in respect of the last three exiles in the Bill; but, because the exiles had only to be escorted from their cells onto Tower Wharf* where their ship was waiting, the only expense was that of paying off the captain and crew of the ship once they returned from Normandy, with no reference to the Lieutenant].

John Collington. dismyssed. Item, etc... 16 wicks [dates and rates as above]... £21.17s.4d.

Richard Slake. dismyssed. Item, etc... 16 wicks [dates and rates as above]... £21.17s.4d.

Christopher Tomson. dismyssed. Item, etc... 16 wicks [dates and rates as above]... £21.17s.4d.

Robert Nutter. dismyssed. Item, etc... 16 wicks [dates and rates as above]... £21.17s.4d.

Jasper Haywoode. dismyssed. Item, etc... 16 wicks [dates and rates as above]... £21.17s.4d.

Thomas Stephinson. dismyssed. Item, etc... 16 wicks [dates and rates as above]... £21.17s.4d.

Thomas Worthington. dismyssed. Item, etc... 16 wicks [dates and rates as above]... £21.17s.4d.

Thomas Barnes. dismyssed. Item, etc... 16 wicks [dates and rates as above]... £21.17s.4d.

John Hartte. dismyssed. Item, etc... [dates as above] 16 wicks at 6s.8d. ye wicke for hym selfe – £5.6s.8d. Fewell and candell at 2s.6d. ye wicke – [£2.0s.0d.]. Amountinge to the Some of... £7.6s.8d.

Henrie Orton. dismyssed. Item, etc... 16 wicks [dates and rates as above]... £7.6s.8d.

James Bosgrove. dismyssed. Item, etc... 16 wicks [dates and rates as above]... £7.6s.8d.

Summa totalis – £402. 17s. 4d.(*)

[signed] Owyn Hopton

[(*) **Editor's Note** – *Whilst this sum total is correct for the figures cited, the small error of 2s. each for Patrick Addie and William Criton and the £4 errors in respect of nine prisoners would actually bring the sum total to £367.1s.4d.*].

LADY DAY 1585 – Not available.

[**Editor's Note** – *Although this Bill is not available, the next one in the series – Midsummer 1585 – continued to show claims for all of those named in the Christmas 1584 Bill less those marked 'dismyssed' and Gervase Pierpoint, who had been moved to another prison between 24 December 1584 and 24 March 1584-5. Other names have been appended but these fall outside the scope of this study.*]

APPENDIX 3

A very true Report of the apprehension and taking of that arch-Papist EDMUND CAMPION, the Pope his right hand; with three other lewd Jesuit Priests, and divers other Lay people, most seditious persons of like sort.

Containing also a controlment of a most untrue former book set out by one A.M. *alias* ANTHONY MUNDAY concerning the same: as is to be proved and justified by GEORGE ELLIOT, one of the Ordinary Yeomen of Her Majesty's Chamber.

Author of this Book, and chiefest cause of the finding of the said lewd and seditious people, great enemies to GOD, their loving Prince, and country.

Veritas non quaerit angulos

Imprinted at London at the *Three Cranes* in the Vintry by THOMAS DAWSON
1581

ANTHONY MUNDAY, in his Discovery of Edmund Campion and his Confederates, &c published on 29th January 1582, in giving an account of CAMPION's trial, states:

GEORGE ELLIOT, one of the ordinary Yeomen of Her Majesty's Chamber, upon his oath, gave forth in evidence as followeth:

That he living here in England among certain of that sect, fell in acquaintance with one Payne, a priest; who gave him to understand of a horrible treason intended against Her Majesty and the State, which he did expect shortly to happen.

The order how, and after what manner in brief is thus:

That there should be levied a certain company of armed men; which on a sudden should enterprise a most monstrous attempt. A certain company of these armed men should be prepared against Her Majesty, as many against my L(ord) of L(eicester), as many against my L(ord) T(reasurer), as many against Sir F(rancis) W(alsingham), and divers others whose names he doth not well remember.

The deaths of these noble personages should be presently fulfilled and Her Majesty used in such sort as [neither] modesty nor duty will suffer me to rehearse. But this should be the general cry everywhere, "Queen Mary, Queen Mary".

It was also appointed and agreed upon, Who should have this Man of Honour's room, and who should have that office. Everything was determined. There wanted nothing but the coming over of such Priests and others as were long looked for.

Upon this report, the aforenamed GEORGE ELLIOT took occasion to question with this PAYNE, How they could find in their hearts to attempt an act of so great cruelty; considering how high an offence it should be to GOD, besides great danger might arise thereby.

Whereunto PAYNE made answer, that the killing [of] Her Majesty was no offence to GOD, nor the uttermost cruelty they could use to her, nor [to] any that took her part; but that they might as lawfully do it to a brute beast. And himself would be one of the foremost in the executing [of] this villainous and most traitorous action.

(A most traitorous and villainous answer. Of every true subject to be read with due reverence of the person. A.M.)

To the Christian Reader,
GEORGE ELLIOT wisheth
all due reverence.

Some experience, Christian reader, that I have gathered by keeping company with such seditious people as CAMPION and his associates are, partly moveth me to write this book; and partly I am urged thereunto (although my wisdom and skill be very slender to set down and pen matter of less moment than this) for that I (being one of the Two in commission at that time from Her Highness's most honourable Privy Council for the apprehending of the said seditious CAMPION and such like; and the chiefest cause of the finding out of the said lewd people, as hereafter more at large appeareth) do think it a great abuse that the most part of Her Majesty's loving subjects shall be seduced to believe an untruth; and myself and he which was in commission with me (whose name is DAVID JENKINS, one of the messengers of Her Majesty's Chamber) very vilely slandered with a book set out by one ANTHONY MUNDAY concerning the apprehension of the said lewd people – which for the truth thereof, is almost as far different from truth as darkness from light; and as contrary to truth as an egg is contrary in likeness to an oyster.

And therefore considering I am able to report a truth for the manner of the finding and taking of the said seditious persons; although fine skill be far from me to paint it out; hoping the wise will bear with my want therein, and esteem a true tale, be it never so bluntly told, rather than a lie, be it never so finely handled – I have emboldened myself to take this treatise in hand; wherein God willing, I will describe nothing but truth; as by the sequel shall appear. Which is this:

That about four years past [1578], the Devil (being a crafty fox and chief Patron doubtless of the Pope's Prelacy; having divers and many officers and inferior substitutes to the Pope, his chief Vicar; and intending by them to increase the kingdom of this Antichrist) dispersed his said Officers in divers places of this realm; where, like vagrant persons (refusing to live within the lawful government of their country) they lead a loose life; wandering and running hither and thither, from shire to shire and country [county] to country, with such store of Romish relics, Popish pelf, trifles and trash as were able to make any Christian heart, that hath seen the trial of such practices as I have done, even for sorrow to bleed. Only thereby to draw the Queen's Majesty's subjects their hearts and faiths both from GOD and Her Highness; as namely, by delivering unto them Bulls from Rome, pardons, Indulgences, Medals, Agnus DEI, hallowed grains and beads, crucifixes, painted pictures and such other paltry; every part whereof they will not let [stop] to say to be matters very necessary for salvation.

BY reason whereof, most Loving Reader, I myself, about that time (1578), by the space of one quarter of a year together, was deeply bewitched and drawn into their darkness, as the blindest bayard of them all. But at the last, even then (by GOD's great goodness, mighty providence and especial grace) all their enchantments, witchcrafts, sorceries, devilish devices and practices were so broken and untied in me; and the brightness of GOD's divine majesty shining so surely in my heart and conscience: that I perceived all their doings to be, as they are indeed, only shows without substance, manifest errors and deceitful juggling casts, and none others.

Notwithstanding, I determined with myself, for certain causes which I omit, to sound the depth of their devilish drifts, if I might; and rather therefore used and frequented their company: whereby appeared unto me not a few of their ungracious and villainous false hearts, faiths and disloyal minds, slanderous words, and most vile treasons towards my most execllent and noble mistress, the Queen's Majesty, and towards divers of her most honourable privy Council; in such sort as many times did make mine eyes to gush out with tears for very sorrow and fear to think of it.

Wherefore, lately (about 14 May 1581), I made my humble submission unto the Right Honourable Her Highness's Privy Council, for my lawful living as aforesaid. At whose hands I found such honourable dealing, and by their means such mercy from Her Majesty, that I wish with all my heart all the Papists, which are subjects born to Her Highness, to run the same course that I have done; and then should they easily see what difference there is between the good and merciful dealing of our most gracious loving and natural Prince; and the great treacheries of that great enemy to our country, the Pope. For Her Highness freely forgiveth offenders; but the Pope pardoneth for money. Her Grace's hands are continuously full of mercy, ready to deliver enough freely to any that will desire and deserve it: and the Pope his great clutches and fists are ready to deliver nothing but devilish devices and paltry stuff of his own making, to set country and country together by the ears; and yet for these hath he money.

Truly it is a most lamentable case that every Christian should be seduced and drawn from the true worshipping of GOD, and their duty to their Prince and their country; as many are by the Pope and his Satanical crew. I beseech GOD to turn their hearts, and grant us all amendment; which can neither be too timely, if it were presently; nor never too late, whensoever it shall happen; unless willfully they proceed in their dealings, which GOD forbid. For humanum est errare, perseverare belluinum.

Shortly after my submission and reconciliation, as aforesaid, it pleased my Lords of Her Highness's most honourable Privy Council to grant the commission that I before spake of, to myself and to the said DAVID JENKINS, for the apprehension of certain lewd Jesuit priests and other seditious persons of like sort, wherever we should happen to find them within England. Whereupon we determined a certain voyage (journey): in which EDMUND CAMPION the aforesaid Jesuit and others were by us taken and brought to the Tower of London, in manner as hereafter followeth.

THE TRUE MANNER
OF TAKING OF EDMUND CAMPION
AND HIS ASSOCIATES

It happened that after receipt of our commission aforesaid, we consulted between ourselves, What way were best to take first? For we were utterly ignorant where, or in what place, certainly to find out the said CAMPION, or his compeers. And our consultation was shortly determined: for the greatest part of our travail and dealings in this service did lie chiefly upon mine own determination, by reason of my acquaintance and knowledge of divers of [the] like sect.

It then presently came to my remembrance of certain acquaintance which I once had with one THOMAS COOPER, a Cook, who, in November was two years, served Master THOMAS ROPER of (Orpington in) Kent; where, at that time, I in like manner served: and both of us about the same month departed the said Master Roper his service; I into Essex, and the said COOPER to Lyford in Berkshire, to one Master YATE. From whence, within one half year after, I was advertised in Essex, that the said Cook was placed in service; and that the said Master YATE was a very earnest Papist, and one that gave great entertainment to any of that sect.

Which tale being told to me in Essex two years before we entered [on] this journey, by GOD's great goodness, came to my memory but even the day before (13 July 1581) we set forth. Hereof I informed the said DAVID JENKINS, being my fellow in Commission, and told him it would be our best way to go thither first: for that it was not meant that we should go to any place but where indeed I either had acquaintance: or by some means possible in our journey, could get acquaintance. And told him we would dispose of our journey in such sort as we might come to the said Master YATE's upon the Sunday about eight of the clock in the morning; "where", said I, "if we find the said Cook, and that there be any Mass to be said there that day, or any massing Priest in the house; the Cook for old acquaintance and for that he supposeth me to be a Papist, will bring me to the sight thereof".

And upon this determination, we set from London (on Friday) the 14th day of July last; and came to the said Master YATE's house, the 16th of the same month, being Sunday, about the hour aforesaid.

Where without the gates of the same house, we espied one of the servants of the house, who most likely seemed, by reason of his lying aloof, to be as it were a Scout Watcher, that they might within accomplish their secret matters more safely.

I called the said servant, and enquired for him the said THOMAS COOPER the Cook.

Who answered, that he could not well tell, whether he were within or not.

I prayed him that he would friend me so much as to see; and told him my name.

The said servant did so, it seemed; for the Cook came forth presently unto us where we sat still on horseback. And after a few such speeches, as betwixt friend and friend when they have been long asunder, were passed; and still sitting upon our horses, I told him that I had longed to see him; and that I was then travelling into Derbyshire to see my friends, and came so far [out] of my way to see him. And said I, "Now I have seen you my mind is well satisfied; and so fare you well".

"No", saith he, "That shall you not do before dinner".

I made the matter very earnest to be gone; and he more earnest and importune to stay me. But in truth I was as willing to stay as he to have me.

And so, perforce, there was no remedy but stay we must. And having lighted from horseback; and being by him brought into the house and so into the buttery, and there caused to drink; presently after, the said Cook came and whispered with me, and asked, Whether my friend (meaning the said JENKINS) were with the church or not? Therein meaning, Whether he were a Papist or no?

To which I answered, "He was not; but yet", said I, "he is a very honest man, and one that wisheth well that way".

Then said the Cook to me, "Will you go up?" By which speech, I knew he would bring me to a Mass.

And I answered him and said, "Yea, for God's sake, that let me do: for seeing I must needs tarry, let me take something with me that is good."

And so we left JENKINS in the buttery; and I was brought by the Cook through the hall, the dining parlour, and two or three other old rooms, and then into a fair large chamber: where there was, at the same instant, one Priest called Satwell saying Mass; two other Priests kneeling by, whereof one was CAMPION, and the other called PETERS alias COLLINGTON (or rather COLLETON); three nuns and thirty seven other people.

When SATWELL had finished his Mass; then CAMPION invested himself to say Mass, and so he did; and at the end thereof, made holy bread and delivered it to the people there, to every one some, together with holy water; whereof he gave me part also.

And then there was a chair set in the chamber something beneath the Altar, wherein the said CAMPION did sit down; and there made a Sermon very nigh an hour long; the effect of his text being, as I remember, "That Christ wept over Jerusalem, &c". And so applied the same to this our country of England for that the Pope his authority and doctrine did not so flourish here as the same CAMPION desired.

At the end of which Sermon, I gat down unto the said JENKINS as soon as I could. For during the time that the Masses and the Sermon were made, JENKINS remained still beneath in the buttery or hall; not knowing of any such matter until I gave him some intelligence [of] what I had seen.

And so we departed, with as convenient expedition as we might, and came to one Master FETTIPLACE, a Justice of the Peace in the said country [county]; whom we made privy of our doings therein; and required him that, according to the tenour of our Commission, we would take sufficient Power, and with us thither.

Whereupon the said Justice of the Peace, within one quarter of an hour, put himself in a readiness, with forty or fifty men very well weaponed; who went in great haste, together with the said Master FETTIPLACE and us, to the said Master YATE his house.

Where, at our coming upon the sudden, being about one of the clock in the afternoon of the same day, before we knocked at the gates which were then (as before they were continually accustomed to be) fast shut (the house being moated round about; within which moat was great store of fruit trees and other trees, with thick hedge rows: so that the danger for fear of losing the said CAMPION and his associates was the more doubted); we beset the house with our men round about the moat in the best sort we could devise: and then knocked at the gates, and were presently heard and espied; but kept out by the space of half an hour.

In which time, as it seemeth, they had hidden CAMPION and the other two Priests in a very secret place within the said house; and had made reasonable purveyance for him as hereafter is mentioned: and then they let us into the house.

Where came presently to our sight, Mrs, YATE, the good wife of the house; five Gentlemen, one Gentlewoman, and three Nuns: the Nuns then being disguised in Gentlewomen's apparel, not like unto that they had heard Mass in. All which I well remembered to have seen, the same morning, at the Masses and Sermon aforesaid: yet every one of them a great while denied it. And especially the said Mistress YATE; who would not be content only to make a plain denial of the said Masses and the Priests: but with great and horrible oaths, forsware the same, betaking herself to the Devil if any such there were; in such sort as, if I had not seen them with mine own eyes, I should have believed her.

But knowingly certain that these were but bare excuses, and that we should find the said CAMPION and his compeers if we made narrow search; I eftsoons put Master FETTIPLACE in remembrance of our Commission:

and so he, myself and the said JENKINS Her Majesty's Messenger, went to searching the house; where we found many secret corners.

Continuing the search, although with no small toil, in the orchards, hedges and ditches, within the moat and divers other places; at the last [we] found out Master EDWARD YATE, brother to the good man of the house, and two countrymen called WEBLIN and MANSFIELD, fast locked together in a pigeon house; but we could not find, at that time, CAMPION and the other two Priests whom we especially sought for.

It drew then something towards evening, and doubting lest we were not strong enough; we sent our Commission to one Master FOSTER, High Sheriff of Berkshire; and to one Master WISEMAN, a Justice of Peace within the same County; for some further aid at their hands.

The said Master WISEMAN came with very good speed unto us the same evening, with ten or twelve of his own men, very able men and well appointed; but the said Master FOSTER could not be found, as the messenger that went for him returned us answer.

And so the said house was beset the same night with at least three score men well weaponed; who watched the same very diligently.

And the next day, being Monday (17th July 1581), in the morning very early, came one Master CHRISTOPHER LYDCOT, a Justice of Peace of the same shire, with a great sort of his own men, all very well appointed: who, together with his men, shewed such earnest, loyal and forward service in those affairs as was no small comfort to all those which were present, and did bear true hearts and good wills to Her Majesty.

The same morning began a fresh search for the said Priests; which continued with very great labour until about ten of the clock in the forenoon of the same day: but the said Priests could not be found, and every man [was] almost persuaded that they were not there.

Yet still searching, although in effect clean void of any hope of finding them, the said DAVID JENKINS, by GOD's great goodness, espied a certain secret place, which he quickly found to be hollow; and with a pin of iron which he had in his hand much like unto a harrow tine, he forthwith did break a hole into the said place: where then presently he perceived the said Priests lying all close together upon a bed, of purpose there laid for them: where they had bread, meat and drink sufficient to have relieved them for three or four days together.

The said JENKINS then called very loudly, and said, ""I have found the traitors!"; and presently company enough was with him: who there saw the said Priests [that], when there was no remedy for them but nolens volens, courteously yielded themselves.

Shortly after came one Master READE, another Justice of the Peace of the said shire, to be assistant in these affairs.

Of all which matters, news was immediately carried in great haste to the Lords of the Privy Council: who gave further Commission that the said Priests and certain others their associates should be brought to the Court under the Conduction of myself and the said JENKINS; with commandment to the Sheriff to deliver us sufficient aid forth of his shire, for the safe bringing up of the said people.

After that the rumour and noise for the finding out of the said CAMPION, SATWELL and PETERS alias COLLINGTON, was in the said house something assuaged; and that the sight of them was to the people there no great novelty: then was the said High Sheriff sent for once again; who all that while had not been seen in this service. But then came, and received into his charge the said Priests and certain others from that day until Thursday following.

The fourth Priest which was by us brought to the Tower, whose name is WILLIAM FILBIE, was not taken with the said CAMPION and the rest in the said house; but was apprehended and taken in our watch (on the 17th), by chance, in coming to the said house to speak with the said PETERS (or COLLINGTON), as he said; and thereupon [was] delivered likewise in charge to the Sheriff with the rest.

Upon Thursday, the twentieth day of July last, we set forwards from the said Master YATE his house towards the Court, with our said charges; being assisted by the said Master LYDCOT and Master WISEMAN, and a great sort of their men; who never left us until we came to the Tower of London. There were besides, that guarded us thither, 50 or 60 horsemen; very able men and well appointed: which we received by the said Sheriff his appointment.

We went that day to Henley upon Thames, where we lodged that night.

And about midnight we were put into great fear by reason of a very great cry and noise that the said FILBIE made in his sleep; which wakened the most that were that night in the house, and that in such sort that every man almost thought that some of the prisoners had been broken from us and escaped; although there was in and about the same house a very strong watch appointed and charged for the same. The aforesaid Master LYDCOT was the first that came unto them: and when the matter was examined, it was found no more but that the said FILBIE was in a dream; and, as he said, he verily thought one to be ripping down his body and taking out his bowels.

The next day, being Friday (21st July), we set forward from Henley. And by the way received commandment by a Pursuivant from the Lords of the Privy Council, that we should stay that night at Colebrook; and the next day after, being Saturday, to bring them through the City of London unto the Tower, and there to deliver them unto the charge of Sir OWEN HOPTON, Knight, Her Majesty's Lieutenant of the same; which accordingly we did.

And this is, in effect, the true discourse [of] that was used in the apprehension of the said CAMPION and his associates.

Some men may marvel that I would be silent so long for the setting out of the manner of their taking; considering I find myself aggrieved with the same untrue report set out by the said A. M[UNDAY]. In good faith I mean nothing less than to take any such matter in hand, if so great an untruth had not been published against us that were doers in those affairs; and besides hitherto divers other weightier business has partly hindered me therein.

But now at the last, although very late, I have rudely set down the verity in this matter: thinking it better to tell a true tale by leisure, than a lie in haste; as the said A.M., by his former book, hath done to his own discredit, the deluding of Her Majesty's liege people, and the slander of some which have intermeddled in the said cause.

The names of those that were taken and brought up to the Tower of London as aforesaid (22 July 1581)

1. Edward Campion	Jesuit and Priest
2. Thomas Satwell (Alias Foord) 3. John Peters (Alias Collington) [more properly Colleton] 4. William Filbie	Priests
5. Edward Yate 6. Edward Keynes 7. Humphrey Keynes 8. John Cotton 9. William Ilsley (Hildesley) 10. John Jacob (or James)	Gentlemen
11. John Mansfield 12. William Weblin (or Webley)	Husbandmen and Neighbours thereby

APPENDIX 4

PRISONS OF LONDON

In listing the eleven 'public and capacious prisons' of London in the Preface of his *Diarium*, it will be noticed from the accompanying map that John Hart listed them from west to east almost in exact geographical order. (cf. *Byrne* under Bibliography).

Porta Westmonasteriensis at the extreme western limit was the Gatehouse, Westminster. Standing to the west of the sanctuary in Tothill Street, this prison was actually two separate gates, each of two stories. To the east was 'the Bishop of London's prison for clerks' convict', whilst the other gate, adjoined to the first but to its west, was described as 'a jail or prison for offenders thither committed'. Whereas both sides were employed for the detention of recusants in Elizabeth's reign, the vast majority were held in the former easternmost gate.

Both gates date from the reign of Edward III (1327-1377), the reputed builder being Walter de Warfield, cellarer of the abbey. Evidence shows that it was in use as a prison as early as 1512. For the better part of the Elizabethan era, the keeper of the Gatehouse was Maurice Pickering. During the time span of the *Diarium*, he was entrusted with many religious offenders causing him to complain that he feared his inmates would starve because their friends were so poor and he was granted no allowances to care for them. He was severely reprimanded in a letter from Lord Burleigh and was compelled to write his 'most humble and sorrowful petition' in which he apologised to the Lord Chancellor for bemoaning his lot. His letter sufficed to ensure he retained the office until 1597.

Sir Walter Ralegh spent his last night in the Gatehouse before his execution in 1618. During Richard Lovelace's term of imprisonment in the same prison in 1642, he composed his immortal lines, 'Stone walls do not a prison make, nor iron bars a cage'. Although held here briefly in 1689, Samuel Pepys was released for reasons of health. The prison was demolished by an order in chapter in 1776, following complaints against its disgrace to the magnificence of the City, and never rebuilt, although one wall was left standing until 1836. Those in custody at the time of the demolition were removed to Tothill Fields Bridewell that had been expanded to accept them.

The site is simple to find as it was conveniently and purposely built close to Westminster Abbey. Make your way to the Abbey bookstall in Broad Sanctuary, in front of which there is a memorial to the old students of Westminster School who were killed in the Crimean War. The prison ran northwards from this spot towards Central Hall.

———— • ————

Flitum or the Fleet Prison, which was sited in Fleet Lane off Fleet Street, took its name from the river or stream of the same name. Fleet Street itself had originated as an ancient track running along the river bank just above high water mark. Fleet Lane led out of Fleet Street and down to the important river bridge. Although this provided the main landward approach towards Ludgate, much more importance was laid on the various landing stages for boats on the River Thames.

The entire district abounded in numerous wells around Clerkenwell which were accredited with miraculous healing powers. As such, the district was a virtual health resort under the protection of the church.

Records give proof of a gaol on the site as early as 1170-1, the very first of its kind to be designed and built for that one purpose. It was rebuilt in the reign of Edward III (1327-43) but had to be rebuilt once more at the end of the fourteenth century after the peasants under Wat Tyler burned it down in 1381.

From the reign of Henry VIII (1509-47) until 1641, the Fleet prison was used by the infamous Star Chamber for the detention of those persons considered not great enough to be held at the Tower. From 1197 through to 1558, the office of keeper had been an hereditary one held by the Leveland family, two of the earliest of whom were ladies, being the widows of keepers who had inherited the title. By the time we reach the *Diarium* era, John Calton was the keeper. Most of the evils practised there arose from the fact that the keeper was paid no salary as such but was expected to earn his living from his prisoners and their visitors. As can be imagined, such legislation threw the keeper and his staff wide open to bribes by which prisoners could obtain certain privileges.

Destroyed during the Great Fire, it was rebuilt very much the same as before, the inmates returning from temporary confinement at Lambeth. It boasted extensive grounds and yards and an imposing rackets ground that could be used by prisoners and public alike, one of the former called Robert Mackay becoming World Rackets Champion. One of the smaller yards was known as 'The Painted Ground' on account of a wall covered by one of the inmates with an imposing mural of galleons and other designs.

Official rules for the administration of the Fleet were introduced in 1727; but these merely acted to confirm the former abuses. There were two sections in the prison. Firstly, 'The Master's Side' which held those who were financially capable of paying their way; then there was 'The Common Side', consisting mostly of poor debtors with absolutely no means of support, who were compelled to beg for subsistence from the charity of passers-by.

Although appertaining to a later period of history, it would be remiss to leave the Fleet prison at this point without making brief mention of the peculiar practice of 'Fleet Marriages' that flourished here from as early as 1613 to well into the eighteenth century. It was accepted that the state of marriage could only be legally recognised by celebration in a church; but any other contract of marriage, wherever celebrated, was also legally binding, even if the celebrants were outside the law. This loophole led to various rituals being conducted in inns or taverns by pseudo-clergymen lining their pockets by undercutting the church. Society ladies found this most convenient at times. Wishing to evade gambling debts or any other peccadilloes, they would enlist the assistance of a Fleet prisoner who, for a small fee, would gladly offer his service as a 'husband'. By going through a form of marriage, the lady's debts, etc would automatically become her new husband's responsibility. For the groom, who was probably in prison for his own financial problems, this would have made little or no difference.

The prison was burned, the inmates released therefrom and one rioter shot on the roof during the Gordon 'No Popery' riots in 1780; but rebuilding started in the following year. Various committees in subsequent years introduced certain changes to regulations but most were ignored by the prison keeper and his staff. A frighteningly graphic description of the prison in the early part of the nineteenth century was provided by Charles Dickens in his *Pickwick Papers*. As such the prison was closed down in 1842 and demolished four years later, the site being sold to the London, Chatham and Dover Railway soon after.

———————— • ————————

As the name infers, *Neugatum* or Newgate was a prison built into a gateway. Dating back to as early as the twelfth century, it immediately adjoined the law courts of the Old Bailey. Tradition later ordained that any person destined for execution at Tyburn would spend his or her last night in the condemned cell at Newgate in company with their coffin and the 'Ordinary' or chaplain of the prison. During that final fateful evening, the parish clerk from nearby St Sepulchre's church was charged with ringing a hand bell beneath the window of the condemned cell whilst calling on the occupant to repent of all his sins. Next morning, the cart carrying the victim, his coffin, guards and the executioner would make a point of pausing outside the same church whilst nosegays were handed to them all.

Although the prison was 're-edified' by the executors of Richard Whittington in 1423, it had fallen into a ruinous condition by the time of the *Diarium* period. Known commonly as 'The Whit' or 'Whittington's Palace', the keeper of Newgate during John Hart's time was William Dyos or Deyos who, according to tradition, had purchased the office from the Sheriff of London. Built in five storeys and measuring some eighty-five feet by fifty, prisoners were not held in individual cells but at least had a unique provision of a purpose-built dining room.

The most notable and unique feature of Newgate prison was the 'pressing room' which was employed for application of *peine forte et dure* or pressing to death of such persons who refused to enter a plea at their trials. Provision was made by law by which the accused could refuse to enter a plea of 'guilty' or 'not guilty' on the strict understanding that his silence would lead him to the pressing room. For some classes of prisoners this refusal to plead had its advantages; but, once decided, it could not be revoked by a change of heart.

Once in the Press Yard or pressing room, the appellant would be laid out spreadeagled upon the floor and secured by chains. A board was then laid upon his chest onto which weights were added daily. A strict diet of 'three morsels of the coarsest bread on the first day and three draughts of stagnant water from the pool nearest the prison door on the second' and so on could only add to the strain of a slow and protracted death. Such victims would count themselves fortunate if, when an opportunity arose, a sympathetic guard or a friend threw his own weight onto the board thereby speeding up the moment of death, which must have been a blessed relief.

By dying this way, the estates belonging to the deceased victim remained intact for passing down to the next of kin – which might not have been the case if a formal trial had taken place – and thus this style of self-sacrifice carried the full force of the law. Whilst this might nowadays seem a brutal method of treating anyone, it must be surprising to learn that it was allowed to continue for so long, only being removed from the statute books in 1828.

Destroyed in the Great Fire of London, the newly built third Newgate prison opened in 1672. Most of the cost of £10,000 was wasted in designs of figures of 'great magnificence' on the outside, including one of Richard Whittington and his cat. It was later claimed that the beauty of the exterior 'aggravated the misery of the wretches within'.

In gradual stages, starting in 1770, a fourth and final Newgate prison was erected near and around the site with a view to removing the inconvenient gateway, from which the name was derived, that was becoming a cause for so much traffic congestion as the City developed. Built to a design by George Dancer the Younger, it was finally completed in 1779.

This building was severely damaged by fire and the prisoners released during the Gordon riots on 6th June 1780. Any prisoners recaptured by the army, who had turned out to assist, were thrown into wooden cages erected in the open areas around St Paul's Cathedral. With few modifications, the ruined shell was soon repaired and ready for business once more.

The Fleet river had by now dried up and was nothing more than an open sewer causing the death of many prisoners and their guests from gaol fever. A few improvements and modernisations were made to Newgate in the middle of the nineteenth century. The prison population was gradually thinned down by sending inmates elsewhere to newly built prisons and, on December 31st, 1881, Newgate ceased to function as a prison, being employed only as a temporary place of detention for those awaiting trial or execution. It was finally closed completely in September 1901 and was demolished the following year. The site was developed into The Central Criminal Court.

Briduelum or the Bridewell prison, which stood in Bride Lane, had originally been built as a royal residence during the reign of Henry III (1216-1272). Dedicated to St Bride, the palace was lavishly improved by Henry VIII from 1515 to 1520 and was sufficiently impressive as to serve as the venue for entertaining Charles V, Holy Roman Emperor, with pageants and music during his state visit in 1522. Three years later, Henry Blount, Earl of Nottingham, Duke of Richmond and illegitimate son of the king, was granted the Bridewell palace as his private residence. It was leased to the French ambassador from 1531 to 1539.

In 1553, this splendid residence was handed over to the Lord Mayor of London as a gift from King Edward VI, who died later that year. The former palace was to serve for the reception of vagrants and homeless children and as a house of correction of petty offenders, the very first of its kind ever seen in England. In exchange for their upkeep, petty criminals of both sexes were required to perform simple menial tasks such as baking, milling and spinning. Although this was something of a revolutionary and plausible ideal for its day, the keepers thus employed soon brought an end to these good intentions which accrued no benefit to themselves; and so the Bridewell rapidly reverted to the same low standards as all other prisons.

Despite many brave attempts to save the building by pulling down adjoining sheds and outhouses and throwing them into the Fleet river close by, the Bridewell was utterly destroyed in the Great Fire in 1666. Planning for a new prison on the same site began only ten days later and work was completed the following year.

The New Bridewell became one of the leading lights of prison reform. In 1675, it was the first to employ a teacher who was engaged to teach young men how to read and write; it was the first to have its own doctor (1700); and the first to issue prisoners free straw for their bedding (1788).

One particularly harsh aspect, however, still continued. This was the regular twice-weekly spectacle of public floggings outside Bridewell. Every Wednesday and Friday, crowds would begin to gather from early morning in anticipation to watch as the gaoler or junior beadle flogged petty offenders across the bare back until such time as the president of the court brought the ordeal to an end by rapping his table with a gavel. The flogging of females was abolished in 1791.

In 1832, Bridewell was brought under state control after all staff on the male side were dismissed. By January 1853, only a small handful of prisoners remained whilst Holloway had been further expanded. In April 1855, all of the chief officers were pensioned off and Bridewell finally closed down and the few remaining prisoners transferred to Holloway. Except for the Gateway, built in 1802, all buildings were demolished in 1863-4. The site is now occupied, since 1931, by the Unilever Building.

———— • ————

There have been many Compter or Counter prisons over the ages but the two *(Contoria duo)* to which the diarist referred must have been the Compter in the Poultry and the Wood Street Compter.

The latter, sited on the eastern side of Wood Street, was brought into use as a prison in 1555 after 'all the prisoners that lay in the Compter in Bread Street were removed to this Compter'. After this mass transfer of prisoners, the abandoned Compter, sited virtually where the Great Fire began, seems never to have been used as a prison again.

The prison to which the inmates were moved was firstly commanded by one William Blunte or Blount whose relationship to the two Lieutenants of the Tower of the same surname (Sir Richard Blount was Lieutenant of the Tower in 1558; and Sir Michael, son of the former, held the same office from 1590 to 1595) could not be discovered. Blount was later replaced by Walter Brown who held sway at Wood Street during the *Diarium* era. The main purpose of this compter was to serve as a debtors' prison and as an overflow when Newgate could not accomodate any more, even though overcrowding was the norm.

In Wood Street, there was sufficient space to pack in as many as seventy prisoners into its three sections; the wealthy were held in 'The Master's Side'; those with limited means of support went to 'The Knight's Side'; and the lowlier classes were thrown into 'The Hole'.

Although completely gutted in the Great Fire in 1666, the Wood Street

Compter was soon back in business, the office of keeper being considered so lucrative that it could only be acquired by purchase until 1766. All inmates were moved out to the Giltspur Compter in 1897 and the empty prison was demolished soon afterwards. Whilst all evidence of the prison above ground has disappeared, the surviving underground vaults are now owned by a wine merchant and may be hired for private functions, the entrance being down an alley off the eastern side of Wood Street, between Gresham Street and Cheapside.

Still continuing our journey eastwards, we then come upon the Compter in the Poultry standing on the northern side of the street – it is remarkable to note that there are no 'Roads' as such in the City of London – that still carries this unusual name. During Hart's term of imprisonment, this filthy prison was commanded by one Robert Gittyns. It was the oldest of all compter prisons and was mainly reserved for prisoners committed on order from the Lord Mayor.

Rebuilt following total destruction after the Great Fire, the Compter in the Poultry was still flourishing at a time when Elizabeth Fry (1780-1845) was dwelling in a house close by. It therefore seems likely that some of the scenes this lady witnessed as she passed the Compter inspired her to dedicate her life to prison reforms in favour of transporting wrongdoers to New South Wales. The Compter in the Poultry was demolished in 1817, the site now occupied by a branch of the Midland Bank.

———•———

The next four prisons named by Hart were all located to the south of the River Thames in the ancient burgh of Southwark which protected the approach roads to the important and only river crossing at London Bridge. The burgh or stronghold of Southwark has been dated back to A.D. 910 and was always looked upon as a safe haven for the criminal classes who could seek and find safety from prosecution there. In 1327, a royal charter was drawn up by means of which the City of London to the north was granted certain rights over this notorious district, thereby bringing to an end the common practice of criminals fleeing across the bridge to avoid arrest. Although Southwark had its own Compter prison, it was not mentioned by Hart as it had no part to play in the history of recusancy.

Furthest south was *Bancus Regius* or the King's Bench prison which derived its name from the close proximity of the Court of the King's Bench. After this law court was moved elsewhere, the prison still retained the original name, even during the reign of Elizabeth, although occasional mention was found to it being called the Queen's Bench or Her Majesty's Bench. The majority of the inmates were debtors, it being assessed in 1653 that there were 399 prisoners with a collective debt of £900,000.

During the period of the Diary, the keeper was one John Catisbye or Catesby. Recusant prisoners who came under his keeping were subject to extortion at every turn if only to survive.

The King's Bench originally stood close to the modern junction of Borough Road and Borough High Street (*see* map); but when it closed down in 1758, the prisoners were removed to the New King's Bench in Saint George's Fields. Containing as many as 224 rooms, the prison was obviously much larger and was surrounded by a tall wall. This prison was destroyed during Gordon's 'No Popery' riots in 1780 but rapidly rebuilt.

By the turn of the century, the prison had gained some notoriety for the laxity of its rules and was referred to in 1828 as 'the most desirable place of incarceration in London', boasting, among other luxuries, as many as thirty gin shops with a weekly turnover of 120 gallons. During the 1840s, it was amalgamated with the Fleet and Marshalsea and renamed the Queen's Bench prison. In the middle years of Victoria's reign, imprisonment for debt was abolished and for a time the buildings served as a military prison. It was demolished in 1880.

———•———

Moving northwards, the next prison of note was the Marshalsea *(Mariscalceum)* which, as the name implies, was commanded by the Knight Marshal who held the privilege of selling the keepership for an attractive fee. It had been in constant use as a prison since 1374 when King Edward III had granted 'the good men of Southwark' their right to build 'a certain house for the safe custody of prisoners'.

Rating second in importance only to the Tower of London, this prison held a most fearsome reputation grounded on the sadism of the keepers. Although attacked by Wat Tyler and the peasants in 1381, it suffered little damage and was soon able to function again. It had also been broken open to set the inmates free during Cade's rebellion in 1450. Further protests by the inmates in 1504 provoked a riot and resulted in many recaptured men being hanged.

The older Marshalsea, known all too well by Father Hart before his transfer to the Tower, boasted a dank dungeon known as 'The Hole' or 'Bonner's Cole Hole'. By virtue of his priesthood, it seems likely that Hart might well have spent a time confined therein as many of his contemporaries had done.

It originally stood in a space between Mermaid Court and Newcomen Road and should not be confused with the New Marshalsea prison that opened in 1811. It was this latter prison and not the former which Charles Dickens described in his *Little Dorrit*. The New Marshalsea was abolished as a prison in 1849 and later demolished, leaving a portion of the wall still enduring alongside the John Harvard and Local Studies Library in Borough Road.

———•———

During the years covered in the Diary, the White Lion *(Virlionum)* stood on the site that was utilised in 1811 for the building of the New Marshalsea. John Stow mentioned the White Lion standing in Suffolk Place. The unusual name was derived from 'a hostelry for the receipt of travellers' by the same sign. Its conversion from inn to prison has been dated to 1558.

Mention was found to its being abandoned for a time in favour of the Newtown Compter but, by the time John Hart was putting pen to paper, the White Lion was back in use once more as 'the appointed gaol for the County of Surrey'. As such, the keeper, Thomas Lewis, had the charge of many recusant prisoners.

As mentioned above, the site was later developed into the New Marshalsea which, in later years, was the place of confinement of Charles Dickens' father who was charged as a debtor. In the description of this prison by his immortal son, we can glean a vivid insight into the appearance of the buildings that might once have comprised part of the White Lion:

> It was an oblong pile of barrack buildings, partitioned into squalid houses standing back to back, so that there were no back rooms; environed by a narrow paved yard, hemmed in by high walls duly spiked at the top. It had a blind alley some yard and a half wide which formed the mysterious termination of the very limited skittle ground in which the debtors bowled away their troubles...

———•———

Nearest London Bridge was the Clink *(Clincum)* that has passed its name down into modern jargon as a term for any prison. The whole area around this prison, known as the 'Liberty of the Clink', fell outside local jurisdiction, it being subject to the Bishop of Winchester whose London residence had been close by since building started in 1107. In the Peasants' Revolt of 1381, a number of officials were killed near the adjoining London Bridge, the bishop's house was burnt down and a number of brothels pulled down. This probably explains why the Lord Mayor of London, William Walworth, – owner of *The Rose* brothel that had been destroyed – killed Wat Tyler during the confrontation with the boy-King Richard II.

In the reconstruction of the Bishop of Winchester's Palace, the Great Hall was extended by the famous architect Henry de Yeovil or Yevele

(d. 1400). Below ground were storage vaults, with gratings at street level to provide ventilation. At a later stage, some of these vaults became convenient places of confinement for 'erring and fractious monks or friars' secured in fetters, chains and bolts giving rise to a great deal of 'clinking and clanking', which might have been the origin of the title. However, in Medieval English, a clench or clinch denoted a rivet or nail that was driven home by a clinching-iron.

Due to an epidemic of syphilis in Europe reaching England in 1504, Henry VII gave order for all brothels in Southwark to close down. Within the space of a year, ten had reopened and the remainder by 1506. A further sweep by Cardinal Wolsey in 1519 netted fifty-four persons including the king's own footman.

First mentioned as a common prison in 1509, the Clink was used 'for such as should brabble, fray or break the peace on the said [river] bank or in the brothel houses'. Nonetheless, in Elizabeth's reign, a number of recusants were cast into the Clink to be held under the keeping of John Sheppard.

When Winchester House and park were sold after the English Civil War, the Clink fell out of use for a time. It was only occasionally used from then onwards until 1745 when abandoned in favour of a dwelling house in Bankside. This dwelling and the deserted Clink were utterly destroyed by the Gordon Anti-Popery Riots in 1780 leaving only the south wall with a great arch spanning Stoney Street, and the oriel window. Most of the site was cleared and developed into warehouses but these were burned down in the great conflagration of August 1814 when all of Clink Street was reduced to rubble.

———— • ————

Of all the prisons John Hart recorded, only the Tower of London still stands virtually intact. From 1570 to 1590, the Lieutenant of the Tower was Sir Owen Hopton who gained a number of mentions in the *Diarium*. He was not restricted to any 'speciality of the house' as were the other ten prisons when punishing or torturing prisoners (*see* Appx 5).

Hopton, as expected of his office, was required to attend each and every occasion when his charges were questioned under torture. Ruthless in implementing the queen's religious policies, Sir Owen's career suffered a serious setback in 1584 when his daughter, Cicely, was charged with carrying prisoners' messages from the Tower to the Marshalsea and back. It was not possible to learn if John Hart was implicated in this scandal; nor was there any method of learning if the young lady held a genuine sympathy with the imprisoned priests or if she was acting as a government agent. It suffices to say that a plan was advanced to remove Sir Owen from office soon afterwards *(CRS Miscellanea Vol 2, p. 239)* but he weathered the storm and continued to hold office until 6th July 1590 on which day he handed over the duties to Michael Blount (later Sir Michael).

A number of those named in the Diary have left reminders of their imprisonments by carving inscriptions into the stone walls. These will be described under the biographical notes at Appendix 13. The ground plan of the Tower will assist in locating the buildings in which they were held, if known.

In all cases wherein torture gains mention, it would be safe to say that this took place in the cellars of the Norman Keep or White Tower in the centre of the complex. Despite the suggestion of their existence, no traces have ever been found of any underground passages that led from other buildings into this basement. In his translation from Latin of *John Gerard, the Autobiography of an Elizabethan*, Philip Caraman appears to have misconstrued the portent of Father Gerard's description which related:

> We went to the torture room in a kind of solemn procession, the attendants walking ahead with lighted candles. The chamber was underground and dark, particularly near the entrance...

From this account, Caraman suggested, 'There is said to be an underground passage from the Lieutenant's lodgings...to the vaults under the White Tower, where he was tortured'; yet the above wording only mentioned the *chamber* being dark. On the assumption that the procession made their way across the open courtyard on that April evening, the absence of street lighting would have necessitated the lighted candles to find their way to the dark entrance.

APPENDIX 5

TORTURE AND PUNISHMENT

Before going into detail of the 'seven types of torture or particular forms of ill-treatment' which Hart mentioned in his preface, it will be necessary to enlarge on the subtle differences between 'torture' and 'punishment' as they are entirely separate and individual entities.

Although often harsh and painful, *punishment* of a prisoner could be inflicted without any recourse to a privy council warrant. The Lieutenant had full and independent powers to punish his charges for any minor infringement of prison rules and could use these punishments at any time, before or after trial and condemnation. No attendant commissioners need be present while the punishment took place and they could extend over a protracted period of time, eg, twenty days in the pit.

On the other hand, there were very strict rules which had to be observed for the *torture* of suspects and woe betide anyone who infringed these regulations. For a start, it could only be applied for investigating a crime which carried the death penalty; it could not be used until all other methods of gathering evidence had been exhausted; and certain classes were exempted. These included pregnant women, children under the age of twelve, aristocrats, clergymen of the established Church, doctors at law and the aged and infirm. Torture could never take place on a Sunday and there had to be reasonable grounds for suspecting that the victim had committed a capital crime. On the outside chance that the suspect would offer a voluntary confession of his crime prior to undergoing his ordeal, a warning or threat had firstly to be administered by the commissioners. Finally, any confession that had been obtained by use of the tortures had to be repeated, without coercion, within a space of twenty-four hours (*see Langbein* under bibliography).

Whilst it was accepted that an accused person who had withstood the pains of torture without giving a confession was deemed to have purged himself of all guilt and should be liberated, this aspect was often subject to abuse.

THE PIT

From Father Hart's description, this might have been the place that was described elsewhere as 'the dungeon among the ratts' (*APC 10:94* dated 17th November 1577 in reference to Thomas Sherwood). The mere fact that Hart wrote of it being 'twenty feet deep' would infer that it was the disused well shaft which may still be seen in the cellar of the White Tower to this day, despite the fact that no mention is given on the descriptive plaque of its alternative use.

The pit has often been confused with the oubliettes which were in the Well and Cradle Towers. Being close to the river and moat, these were probably nothing more than convenient methods for the residents to draw water from the moat outside; there is no evidence of prisoners being placed in them to be drowned by tidal movement as the river water flooded the moat. Such forms of executions were reserved for those accused of piracy and usually took place at Execution Dock in Wapping.

Confinement in the pit, with its resulting deprivation of light and the company of others, could drastically reduce a prisoner's morale. After the specified number of days, the victim might have been only too pleased to conform with his gaoler's orders. The seminary priests, however, may not have found these conditions too severe due to the spartan training they had undergone and the comfort they gained from prayer in solitude.

―――― • ――――

LITTLE EASE

This might almost be classed as the Tudor forerunner of 'the box' that was used to great effect on prisoners of war during the Korean War in the 1950's and, more recently, in Vietnam. It held all the terror of the pit but with the additional torment of being unable to stand at full height or lie down at full length.

It has always been accepted that Little Ease was situated somewhere in the cellar of the White Tower; but all traces have been erased, probably in the first half of the nineteenth century, either by being bricked up or by being converted into a passageway. It is therefore impossible to quote any dimensions for this cramped space into which the occupant was forced. Some idea of Little Ease might be formed from two inscriptions – numbers 15 and 62 – which still endure in the Beauchamp Tower. The latter carries the part signature of Thomas Peverel, a possible prisoner of 1570. Although the former inscription is not signed, it bears all of Peverel's hallmarks except that the crude figure is facing the opposite direction. Even so, in both cases, the figure of a man is depicted in what has been described

TORTURE AND PUNISHMENT

as 'an attitude of prayer', yet each is confined within an arched recess just a little larger than the figure. Number 15 even shows what appears to be a passage leading into the vaulted chamber.

From entry number 54, it was seen that Stephen Rowsham was placed into Little Ease for eighteen months, starting some time in August 1582. And yet, only three months later, entry 64 showed how Francis Throgmorton was placed into Little Ease, leaving cause to wonder if the small cell was capable of holding two prisoners at the same time or if there might have been more than one of these cells.

———— • ————

THE RACK

This particular instrument of torture is traditionally said to have been introduced into the Tower by John Holand, 3rd Duke of Exeter during his term of office as Constable from 1420 to 1447. It has never been determined whether it was the duke's own brainchild, built by Tower craftsmen to his specifications, or if he had brought it back from his travels overseas. Whatever may be the truth, it was often referred to as 'The Duke of Exeter's Daughter', a title form first encountered in a report of the torturing of one John Hawkins in 1467. In the absence of all references to its use over the intervening twenty years, there is a strong probability that it was not introduced until slightly later when Henry Holand, 4th Duke of Exeter, son of the previous duke, held office as Constable from 1450-61.

It consisted of an open iron framework with wooden rollers at each end. The victim was stripped off and laid on his back in the centre of the frame whilst his hands and feet were lashed with ropes to the rollers. The first model appears to have needed two operators at each end to turn the rollers in opposite directions but a later model, known as 'The One Man Rack', featured a central roller over which the prisoner was laid and to which the ropes from each end were attached thereby allowing one man to operate the winch.

In the few surviving warrants of the Diary period, two particular names – those of *Thomas Norton* and *Richard Young* (cf. *Langbein* pp. 106-109) – make regular appearances in view of the fact that they held office as rackmasters. This is not to say that they actually turned the winches themselves; they were more in a class of advisors to the commissioners to torture (those putting the questions) and the winch operators who were Yeoman Warders. In the State Papers of 1583 (*Tortures of the Tower*, p. 20), William Cecil, Baron Burghley sought to allay public concern by issuing the following disclaimer:

'The Queen's servants, the warders, whose office and act it is to handle the rack, were ever by those that attended the examinations, specially charged to use it in as charitable manner as such a thing might be.'

As soon as the ropes had been drawn to full tension, interrogation could begin. Refusal to answer or an unsatisfactory reply would induce another click of the ratchet mechanism gradually stretching the limbs until 'the bones started from their joints'. Reports by those who survived this ordeal could not be found; but the chances are that they were incapable of writing.

The Tower rack was lost to the flames of the Grand Storehouse Fire on 30th October, 1841 and, for many years after, a number of small scale models were displayed in the White Tower to satisfy public curiousity. These models were later withdrawn to storage on account of being too small (about eighteen inches long) to locate among so many larger exhibits. Having personally examined a number of these models in the Armouries stores, the author is of the opinion they should never have been displayed because the workmanship, especially on the childlike figurines tied to the machinery – who appear to be enjoying the experience – leaves much to be desired.

When a new torture display was opened in the Bowyer Tower in 1977, an enlarged drawing from Foxe's *Book of Martyrs*, showing Cuthbert Simpson's ordeal at the rack, was mounted on the wall; but problems with visitor movement caused the display to be moved to the lower Martin Tower where, with the extra space afforded, a full size replica could hold central pride of place. The 'one man rack' that was exhibited there is based on the only first-hand illustration and description which appeared in Isaac Reed's edition of Shakespeare's plays, published in 1799.

At the moment of writing, the lower Martin Tower has been converted into a Jewel House shop, most of the instruments having been moved to the Royal Armouries new premises at Leeds, Yorkshire. It is understood that the replica rack is still held in store at the Tower but that there are plans afoot to place it back on display once more.

———•———

THE SCAVENGER'S DAUGHTER

As the diarist intimated, this instrument is said to have taken its name from that of the inventor, a person named 'Skeffington'; but some confusion was encountered over which member of this family can claim the credit.

The most popular contender is Sir Leonard Skeffington, who held office

TORTURE AND PUNISHMENT

as Lieutenant of the Tower in 1534. But modern opinion comes down against this official who held no known qualifications in metalwork.

However, Sir William Skeffington, whose relationship to the above Lieutenant is not known, enjoyed the confidence of King Henry VIII and Thomas Cromwell. He was a royal lieutenant in Ireland from 1529 to 1532 and from 1534 to his death in the following year. Previous to this, Sir William had been a master of ordnance and in the interval 1532 to 1534, when he was not in Ireland, he returned to gunnery. Could this be the 'Lieutenant' who dreamed up the idea?

On the other hand, Sir William's son, Leonard, never rose any higher than that of being a Yeoman of the Ordnance at the Tower, an office he held from 1534 until his death ten years later. His skills were better suited to designing and producing such an invention. The mere fact that he flourished in the Tower at the same time as the aforementioned Sir Leonard could qualify a reason for the Lieutenant of the Tower having the laurels heaped upon him.

Originally known as 'Skeffington's Yrons or Gyves', the inventor's name was later corrupted to 'Scavenger' and, as we already had one 'daughter' – the rack – this new invention became her sister. In use, however, it had quite the reverse effect from the rack because, whilst the latter stretched the limbs, the Scavenger's Daughter crushed the body into a tight circumference.

There appear to have been several models of the Scavenger's Daughter. That which was named as such in the Tower Armouries collection and once displayed in the Martin Tower has one loop for the neck, two more for the wrists and two others for the ankles. This particular instrument of punishment has no facility to adjust the size to enforce further constriction of the victim's body. Sometimes called *The Spanish Cravat*, it weighs eleven pounds and twelve ounces and is forty four inches long. An early catalogue of the Tower Armouries related that it was 'among the spoils of the invincible Armada', thereby dating it to three years after the closure of the *Diarium*. Nonetheless, this does not explain why it was so clearly illustrated in Foxe's *Actes and Monuments*, the English translation of which was published in 1563!

Another model, probably the one to which Hart referred, is not on display but is believed to have been a broad hoop of iron hinged into two halves. The prisoner was forced to kneel on the hinged centre while the arms were brought together across the small of the back. With assistance from a warder, the victim would be forced to compress himself into as small a compass as possible until such time as the movable arms could be brought together and locked over the prisoner's back (*see* Illustration). There might well have been some form of adjustment, very much like a jubilee clip, in the area of the locking device to allow for the victim's size.

Entry 5 of the *Diarium* has often be cited as authority for saying that the allotted period of confinement was always an hour and a half. But, being a form of punishment which was never mentioned in torture warrants (despite Hart's suggestion in entry 55), the Lieutenant of the Tower could employ it at his own discretion without specifying any time limit.

———•———

THE GAUNTLETS

Although alluded to in Hart's preface, these gained no mention in any of his Diary entries; and the official torture warrants only begin to show usage of the gauntlets or manacles from 1590 onwards. Even so, the mere fact that Hart alluded to them suffices to show they were available in the torture chamber if needed, albeit just to act as a threat.

It would be impossible to provide any better description of their use than that written by Father John Gerard who, having endured a number of sessions in the manacles, managed his daring escape from the Cradle Tower with John Arden in 1597 and later wrote his autobiography. The official torture warrant naming Gerard was dated 13th April 1597 (*APC 27:38* cf. *SPD 28:544-456*). Having arrived in the cellar of the White Tower, Gerard recounted:

> Then they took me to a big upright pillar, one of the wooden posts which held the roof of this huge underground chamber. Driven into the top of it were iron staples for supporting heavy weights. Then they put my wrists into iron gauntlets and ordered me to climb two or three wicker steps. My arms were lifted up and an iron bar was passed through the rings of one gauntlet, then through the staple and rings of the second gauntlet. This done, they fastened the bar with a pin to prevent it slipping and then, removing the wicker steps one by one from under my feet, they left me hanging by my hands and arms fastened above my head. The tips of my toes, however, still reached the ground [due to his being so tall, Gerard was often nicknamed 'Long John'] and they had to dig away the earth from under them. They had hung me up from the highest staple in the pillar and could not raise me any higher, without driving in another staple... such a gripping pain came over me. It was worst in my chest and belly, my hands and arms. All the blood in my body had seemed to rush up into my arms and hands and I thought that the blood was oozing out from the ends of my fingers and the pores of my skin...

From 1590 onwards, the few surviving torture warrants on record reveal a sudden change in policy by which the manacles were put into use much more than the rack which, other than for a few isolated instances,

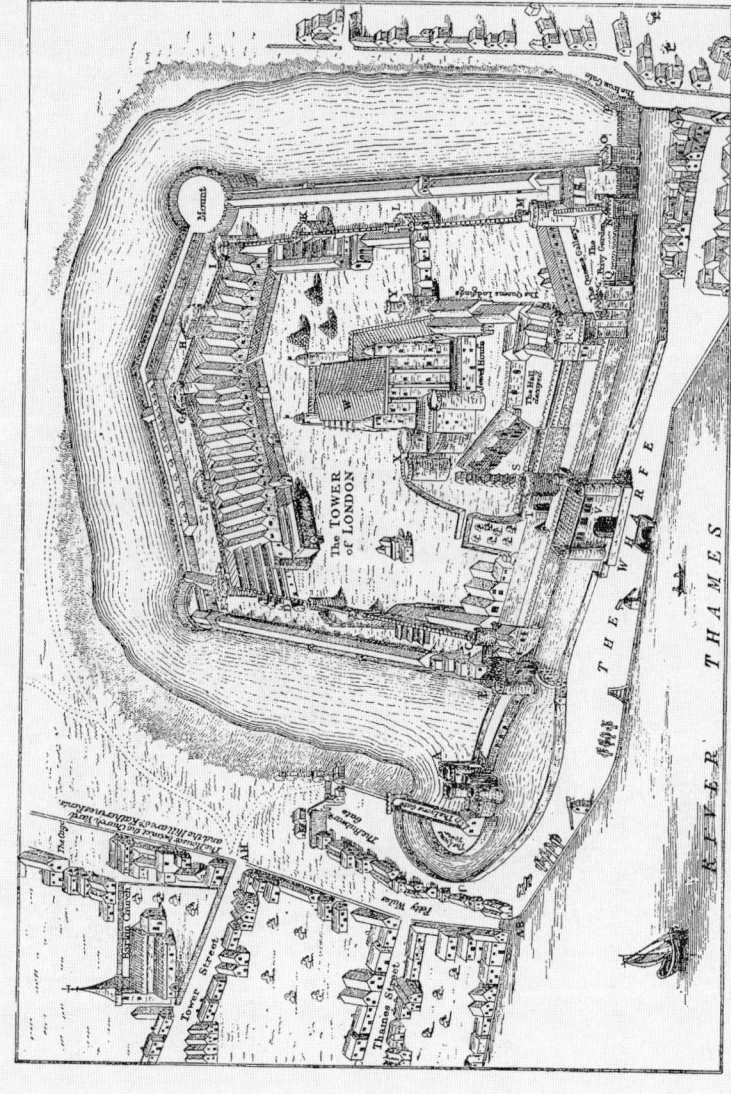

The Tower of London in 1597.
(with kind permission of
the Royal Armouries)

H M TOWER OF LONDON

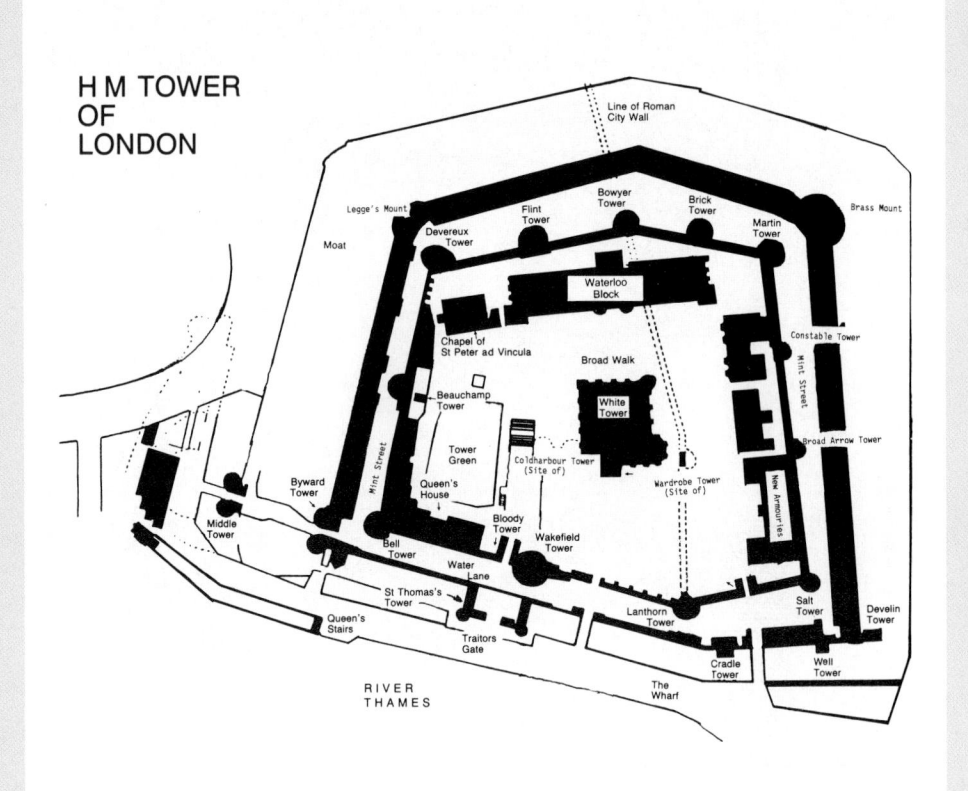

Prisons of London

1. The Gatehouse, Westminster
2. The Fleet
3. Newgate
4. The Bridewell
5. The Compter in Wood Street
6. The Compter in The Poultry
7. The King's Bench
8. The Marshalsea
9. The White Lion
10. The Clink
11. The Tower of London

1761 Plan of London
(with acknowledgement to the Guildhall Library, Corporation of London)

The Beauchamp Tower (between first and second tree from the left) where Thomas Miagh and John Colleton have left their inscriptions. *(Author's own photograph)*

The Lieutenant's Lodgings (Queen's House) where Sir Owen Hopton lived with his family from 1570 to 1590. *(Author's own photograph)*

Inscribed wall in The Beauchamp Tower showing Thomas Miagh's lament on being tortured. *(Author's own photograph)*

Inscription 84 in The Beauchamp Tower in which the priest John Colleton records his arrival on 22 July 1581. *(Author's own photograph)*

Inscription on the tomb of Sir Robert Tyrwhitt in All Saints Church, Bigby.
(By kind permission of Rev S.R. Kenyon)

Front view of Sir Robert's tomb - from the South.
(By kind permission of Rev S.R. Kenyon)

Tomb of Robert Tyrwhitt and his wife Bridget in the North Sanctuary of All Saints Church, Bigby (presumed damaged by Roundheads during the Civil War).
(By kind permission of Rev S.R. Kenyon)

Original Tudor frontage of Lyford Grange, Berkshire where Edmund Campion and his colleagues were captured (Entries 26 and 27 & Appx. 3 refer).
(Author's own photograph, by kind permission of the owner)

The Scavenger's Daughter.
(By kind permission of Geoffrey Abbott)

The Rack in use at the Tower.
(By kind permission of Geoffrey Abbott)

was almost phased out of use. At the same time, the Bridewell prison became the more regular venue for torture until 1597 when Gerard came to the Tower.

Although Sir Owen Hopton had retired in 1590, his status as Lieutenant of the Tower would have had no bearing on changing the method and venue of torture over the next seven years; it can only be conjectured that these changes were occasioned by the death of Sir Francis Walsingham and the appointment of Sir Richard Topcliffe, who held a personal preference for the manacles.

It would be wrong to refer to John Gerard's torture as *Strappado*, a similar form of torture employed on the continent by which the victim had his hands tied behind his back before being hoisted up to a point of suspension. The stress upon the shoulder joints in this method is much greater and could be worsened by adding weights to the prisoner's feet.

John Hart's description of the gauntlets, in which he writes of the hands being crushed, reveals he either had no notion of how the gauntlets affected the body or that he had confused them with the thumbscrews or a similar device. The ingenuity of the rackmaster and commissioners to torture knew no bounds.

———— • ————

THE FETTERS

The fetters once displayed in the Martin Tower have often been called 'manacles', leading to the belief that this is the instrument in which John Gerard suffered his ordeal.

Those held by the Royal Armouries weigh 11lb 12 oz and have a loop at each end for the wrists or ankles. Metal bars run from these loops to another central loop that could either have been attached to a wall or had a chain running through it for the warder to escort his prisoner under restraint.

———— • ————

THE LEG IRONS

Commonly known as 'bilboes', a set is held by the Royal Armouries. They weigh slightly more than fourteen pounds and are fitted with a type of escutcheon plate that might have been screwed to the floor. Two U-shaped brackets, about two feet apart, are attached to the central bar which runs from the escutcheon plate. A prisoner's ankles were fastened into these brackets; but mention has been found of certain classes of prisoners gaining exemption from this restraint by paying 'Fee of irons – £5', a regular source of income for the Lieutenant.

APPENDIX 6

THE ORDER FOR EXILE

The original, just one sheet, may be found in *State Papers Domestic, clxxvi, n. 9* of January 1585. An extract is also quoted in *Records of the Society of Jesus* by H. Foley but this has inadvertently transcribed the name of Richard Slack to be 'Richard Clark'. An unofficial yet accurate copy is incorporated into the *Ellesmere Papers*, E.L. 6153.

Shortly after the order was issued, a commission dated 20th January 1585 and signed by the queen entrusted one William Bolles, a Yeoman of the Queen's Chamber, and Anthony Hall, a skinner of London, with the task of conveying the twenty-one named exiles to the coast of France. Hall later testified as a prosecution witness at the trial of Sir Philip Howard, Earl of Arundel and Surrey.

The twenty-one named exiles embarked at Tower Wharf on 21st January and landed at Abbeville, Normandy on 2/12 February 1584-5. The Privy Council was later handed a full report of the journey by Bolles and Hall, to which was attached a certificate signed by all twenty-one undesirables, dated 3/13 February and testifying that they had not been ill-treated on the journey.

A Privy Council warrant of 28th February authorised payment to Bolles and Hall for the performance of their duties. Edward Rishton compiled an intimate report of this journey which was later published in all three editions of *De Schismate*. It is reproduced at Appendix 7.

The Order for Exile reads as follows:

COMMISSION FOR BANISHING JESUITS AND SEMINARY PRIESTS

Elizabeth by the grace of God, Quene of England, Fraunce and Ireland, Defender of the Faith, etc, to our right trustie and wellbeloved Counsellors, Sir Thomas Bromley, knight, our Chauncellor of England; and to our right trustie and right wellbeloved Cosens and Counsellors, George, Earle of Shrewsburye, Earle Marshall of England; Edward, Earle of Lincoln, High Admirall of England; Ambrose, Earle of Warwick, Master of our Ordinaunce; Fraunces, Earle of Bedford, Justice of all our forest chases, etc on this side Trente; Roberte, Earle of Leicester, Master of our horses, Charles

Lord Howard, our Lorde Chamberlen; Henry, Lord of Hunsdon, Governor of our towne of Barwick; and to our trustie and right welbeloved Counsellors, Sir Frauncis Knollis, knight, Treasurer of our Household; Sir Henrie Sydney, knight, President of our Counsell in our Principalitie of Wales; Sir Christofer Hatton, knight, our Vice-Chamberlayn; Sir Frauncis Walsingham, knight, our Principall Secretarie; Sir Ralfe Sadler, knight, Chauncellor of our Duchie of Lancaster; Sir Walter Mildmay, knight, Chauncellor of our Exchequer; and to our trustie and Welbeloved Sir Christofer Wraye, knight, our Cheif Justice of England; greeting.

Wheare James Bosgrave, late of London, clarke, John Harte, late of London aforesaid, clarke, Edward Rusheton, late of London afforesaid, clarke, and Henrie Orton, late of London afforesaid, gentleman, stand and be indited and attainted of high treasons againste us commmitted, as by the record therof more fullie and att lardge it doth and maye appere; and wheare also Jasper Haywood, late of London aforesaid, clarke, William Tedder, late of London aforesaid, clarke, Samuell Coniers, late of London aforesaid, clark, Arthure Pittes, late of London afforesaid, clarke, William Warmyngton, late of London aforesaid, clark, Richard Slack, late of London aforesaid, clarke, William Hartley, late of London aforesaid, clarke, Richard Norris, late of London afforesaide, clark, William Deane, late of London afforesaid, clark, and William Bushoppe, late of London afforesaid, clark, stand and be also indited of high treason for divers and sundrie hainous and horrible treasons againste us committed, as by the inditements thereof more and att large it doth appere; and wheare also Robert Nutter, Thomas Stephenson, John Collyton, Christofer Tompson, Thomas Worthington, John Barnes and William Smith, clarkes, have byn and are holden vehementlie suspected of and to be touched with the like haynous offences; we, by good and due meanes understanding them to drawen thereunto through a blind zeale and affeccion that they beare unto the Pope, being, for our profession of the true religion of Christe, a capitall enemy to us and our realme; and hoping neverthelesse that time and better instruccion may persuade them to a more loyall and conformable course, of our gracious clemencie not mynding to deale with them or execute them by justice as by our lawes we might, do (though without any their deserte) for us, our heires and successors give full power, warraunt and auctoritie by theis presentes to you, our said Lord Chauncellor, Lorde Treasorer, Earle of Shrewsburie, Earle of Lincoln, Earle of Warwick, Earle of Bedford, Lord Howard, our Lord Chamberlein, Lord of Hunsdon, Sir Frauncis Knollis, Sir

James Croftes, Sir Henrie Sidney, Sir Christofer Hatton, Sir Frauncis Walsingham, Sir Raffe Sadler, Sir Walter Mildmay and Sir Christofer Wray, or to any sixe or more of you, withowte farther corporall punishement, only to banishe out of and from all places under our obedience, the said James Bosgrave, John Harte, Edward Russheton, Henrie Orton, Jasper Haywood, William Tedder, Samuell Conyers, Arthure Pittes, William Warmyngton, Richard Slack, William Hartley, Richard Norris, William Deane, William Bushoppe, Robert Nutter, Thomas Stephenson, John Colliton, Christofer Tompson, Thomas Worthington, John Barnes and William Smyth and everye of them, with order and direccion to be given unto them and every of them under the hande writing of you or any sixe or more of you, that neither they nor any of them returne into this realme of England or any other dominions withowte our expresse licence and warrante in that behalfe firste had and obtayned uppon payne to have the justice and execucion of our lawes to be presentlie theruppon executed uppon them and every of them retorning, whiche we will and commaund to be don and executed uppon suche their severall returning withowte our licence with all due expedition.

And wheare divers other Jesuites, seminarie priestes and other wandring and Massing priestes of like affeccion have comen and dailie doe come from the partes beyond the seas into this our realme of England and other our dominions to thintente to withdrawe sundrie our good and loving subjectes from their due obedience unto us, and doe also seke what in them lyeth to sowe sediccion and stirre rebellion within the same our realme and dominions; whereof some stand and be indited and some also attainted, some of praemunire, some of high treason by them severallie committed, and the reste not yett in any wyse dealte with by way of inditemente or attainder. And wheare also their be divers others, aswell wandring and Massing priestes as other lay persons that are seductors of our said loving subjectes or otherwyse by meanes afforesaid seduced them selfes, wherof great daunger might ensue in tyme unto us and our said realme and dominions if the same be not by us the sooner foresene and prevented, we therefore, reposing great truste and confidence in you our said Lord Chauncellor, Lorde Treasurer, Earle of Shrewsburie, Earle of Lincoln, Earle of Warwick, Earle of Bedford, Earle of Leicester, Lord Howard, our Lord Chamberlayn, Lord of Hunsdon, Sir Frauncis Knollis, Sir James Croftes, Sir Henrie Sidney, Sir Christofer Hatton, Sir Frauncis Walsingham, Sir Raffe Sadler, Sir Walter Mildmay, and Sir Christofer Wraye, doe by vertue of theis presentes for us, our heires and successors, give full power, warraunte and auctoritie unto you or any sixe or more of you, wherof the Lord Chauncellor or the Lorde Cheif Justice to be one from tyme to tyme, to banishe owte of and from this realme of England and all other our dominions, and owte of and from all places under our obedience, all the said Jesuites, seminarie priestes and other priestes and lay persons, seductors or seduced as afforesaid, and every of them or as many of them as by you or any sixe or more of you shalbe thought convenient or fitt so to be dealt with; and that to be done in soche order, manner and forme, and under soche condicions, prescriptions and lymitacions as you or any sixe or more of you shall sett downe, signed with your or any sixe or more of your handes according to the severall qualities of their condicions and offences.

And our will and pleasure is, and we do by theis presentes graunt for us, our heires and successors unto you our said Lord Chauncellor, Lord Treasurer, Earle of Shrewsburie, Earle of Lincoln, Earle of Warwick, Earle of Bedford, Earle of Leicester, Lord Howard, our Lord Chamberlen, Lord of Hunsdon, Sir Frauncis Knollis, Sir James Croftes, Sir Henrie Sidney, Sir Christofer Hatton, Sir Frauncis Walsingham, Sir Raffe Sadler, Sir Walter Mildmay and Sir Christofer Wraye, and to everie of you that theis presentes or the inrollment, exemplificacion or duplicate therof shalbe aswell to you as to all other our justices, ministers and officers to whome by your or any sixe or more of your order or direccions in manner and forme as is afforesaid or otherwise yt shall or may appertaine a sufficiente warrante and dischardge for the doing, executing and performyng of every matter and thinge in anywyse abowte, touchinge or concerning the premisses or any of them in soche order and sorte as by you or any sixe or more of you under your or any sixe or more of your handes shalbe ordered, sett downe, appointed or prescribed. And we doe will and straightlie chardge and commaund by theis presentes all our judges, justices, sheriffes, lieutenauntes, bailiefes, constables of any of our castells, gaolers, ministers and officers, and all other our subjectes to whome it shall appertaine, that they and every of them be aiding and assisting to the due performaunce and execucion of the premissis, and that they and everie of them do allowe and performe the same in every respecte according to the purporte, effecte and true meaning of theis presentes. Ane theis presentes or the inrollment, exemplificacion or duplicate therof, shall likewise be unto them a sufficient warraunte and discharge withoute any other warrante or discharge from us, our heires or successors in that behalf in any wise to be had or obteigned.

And our will and pleasure is, and we doe by theis presentes straightlie charge and commaund that a true note and certificate be from tyme to tyme made and certified by our principall secretarie for the tyme being of and concerning all your doinges andproceedinges in this behalf into our court commonlie called the kinge's Benche, there to be entred and enrolled of record by the Clark of our Crowne in the office called the Crowne Office belonging to our said court.

And theis presentes or the inrollment, exemplificacion or duplicate thereof shalbe aswell to our said Secretarie and to the Lorde Cheif Justice anmd other the justices of our said courte, as also to the Clark of our Crowne for the tyme being, and to all other to whome it shall appertayne a sufficiente warrante and discharge for the entring and enrolling of record of the said certificate or note by our said Secretarie att any tyme or tymes hereafter to be sent as is afforesaid. In witness whereof we have caused thes our letters to be made patentes. Witnes our self at Westminster, the fifteenth day of Januarie in the seaven and twentith [year of our reign].

[The Royal Seal is pendant from a double tag.]

APPENDIX 7

THE JOURNEY INTO EXILE

Originally composed in Latin by Edward Rishton in *De Origine ac Progressu Schismatis Anglicani* (Translated by David Lewis 1877)

At that time both the old and the new prisons were filled with the confessors, and in one prison, the Marshalsea – that is the name of one of the prisons in London – there were about thirty priests beside laymen. Some also of those who with Father Campion, or soon after, had been condemned to death, were kept in the Tower and in other prisons of the City, waiting these three years for the headsman. Those, but not all of them, though under the same sentence, nor yet the only ones, were chosen for banishment, and with them certain others taken out of nearly every prison in London. Others then were shut up in the many prisons throughout the land, but of these not one was released.

When the authorities had determined the day on which these prisoners were to embark, they sent to the keeper of every prison the names of those who were to be sent out of the country, with orders to inform the prisoners of the day on which they must depart, in order that they might make provision for their journey and their sustenance afterwards, for they were to be maintained at the public expense – expected by many – only so long as they were on board the vessel that carried them. But as they in the meantime were kept in prison, and allowed to speak to no one except in the presence of their gaolers, they could not obtain much help for their journey, or for the endurement of the banishment to which they were driven. In this light alone, that banishment must have been regarded as most calamitous by men deprived of their all. When they were told of the Queen's resolution, they laboured, every one of them to the utmost of their power, to obtain from their friends some provision for their needs, in the way of clothes and money.

The day came at last, though often changed, but for what purpose I do not know; and those persons who had been charged to see us transported went from prison to prison, demanding of the keepers thereof those who had been singled out for transportation. We were all brought to the ship moored in the Thames, near the gate of the Tower [probably Queen's Stairs virtually opposite the south of the Byward Tower], and ordered to go on board. Thereupon some of us, especially the reverend Father Jasper Heywood, made a public complaint in the name of all, that we ought not to be driven out of our country without cause, having committed no crime, without a legal trial and clearly not convicted. He also said that we would go no further, and with our own consent would never forsake our country and the Catholic people who dwell therein; but would rather die there in their presence as a testimony to the faith which we and they shared in common. Our country and their salvation were to us infinitely more precious than our lives.

Then, when nothing was not to be gained in this way, we asked to be shown at least the letters and orders of the queen by which we are condemned to be banished for life. But nothing was shown; the vessel sailed, and we went to sea after many a farewell and with the pity of our friends.

When we had been two days at sea, and had gone far from land, the reverend Father Jasper Heywood and others once more pressed the queen's servants with great earnestness to allow them to see and read the sentence of our banishment. The men were persuaded and showed the warrant, in which we read as follows: 'The aforesaid persons, by the confession of themselves and others, found guilty of sedition and of plotting against her majesty and the state, all of them either legally convicted of those same offences, or for like offences kept in prison, though deserving the last penalty of the law, are, under this warrant, ordered by her majesty, who in her goodness wills to deal more gently with them for this once, to be transported beyond the limits of the realm'.

When we read this they all cried out in one mournful protestation that the most false accusation had been brought against them, and that they were most grievously wronged, seeing that not one of them, or of their fellow Catholics, had ever uttered one word that could be construed into a confession of rebellion or conspiracy against the queen or country; and that one [John Colleton – see entry 36 and footnotes] certainly of those whom they were taking away at the time had been publicly acquitted, after a trial, of that most false charge. Father Heywood then spoke much to the same purpose, again and again imploring those who were in charge to take them back to England that they might be put on trial publicly, or at least that they might be put to death for Christ and in defence of their innocence, rather than be sent to a strange land accused of offences which they had certainly never committed. To this the answer was that it was not within their power to do that which we asked of them; and that they must obey the orders of the queen.

We went on, consoling one another as well we could, and rejoicing that we could bear patiently this reproach for the name of Jesus. At last, by the help of God, we landed at Boulogne and, having said farewell to those who brought us thither, we departed for different towns in France, each one according to his means. At last we came to Rheims, finding our brethren and our superiors in great distress about us in every place to which we came. They had heard the lying stories which the heretics, or those who wished us ill, had spread abroad; namely, that frightened by the dangers that were around us in England, we had of our own accord taken measures to bring about our banishment; that we had abandoned our work; or – and this was still worse – had come to some agreement with the heretics in matters of religion. But they rejoiced in our Lord when they heard the story fully related; and when many of us, moreover, declared our readiness to return, whenever our superiors bade us, without counting the cost. But our enemies, everywhere without restraint, speak of us whom they did not put to death, but banished, as instances and evidences of the queen's kindness. They persist in this, and urge it with so much shamelessness, that they have it that the more they banish, the more must the great kindness of the queen be remarked; and the more it must commend itself to foreign nations. The same fraud and cruelty were lately practiced upon two-and-twenty prisoners taken out of the gaols of York and Hull, and carried over to France; all except one being priests, and even he was a deacon. These, for the most part, were worn out not only by bonds and imprisonment, but by old age. Some of them were sixty, others seventy years old, others were still older, and one of them was eighty years of age.

Some of these, though they were very old men, had spent a great part of their lives in prison; and there were those among them who, for six and twenty years, had most patiently and bravely borne all those miseries which the wickedness of so many years, and of such heretics, is wont to inflict upon prisoners.

Soon afterwards, on the 24th of September, thirty priests and two laymen, brought together out of different prisons, were with the same intention driven out of the country. This is the way they think they can obtain a reputation for humanity and mercy. But it is very foolish, and nothing else but the kindness of thieves, who are wont to boast that they have given their lives to those from whom they have not taken it. It is more probable that they act thus for the purpose of burdening the seminaries, which they know to be poor, for the maintenance of so many priests. But there is no counsel against God; 'The earth is the Lord's and the fullness thereof'.

APPENDIX 8

THE CANONISATION OF THE FORTY MARTYRS 1970
(cf. *CTS Pamphlet H469*)

There is no doubt that the Second World War and the many difficulties in giving impetus to the historical studies of the lives of the martyrs caused a hiatus in the normal progression from beatification to canonisation. Eventually the hierarchy petitioned the Holy See for permission to resume the cause of a small representative group of English martyrs according to certain and specific criteria. Firstly, the extent and quality of devotion to certain of the beati in the group; and secondly their representative nature.

The petition came at an awkward moment in 1960 as it was suggested in some quarters that canonisation was importune and could damage the improved relations between the Anglican and Catholic Churches in England and Wales. This apprehension was finally cleared by issuing a statement from the British Council of Churches on 17th December 1969 in which it was recognised that 'the martyr tradition is one in which all have shared and from which all may draw strength even across denominational boundaries'.

In advancing the cause for the forty martyrs in 1960, documentary proof had to be provided, from a historical point of view, that martyrdom had actually taken place. The newly formed Sacred Congregation for the Causes of Saints produced a volume of more than four hundred pages of evidence. After countless enquiries into alleged miracle cures, two very special and outstanding cases were selected on the advice of a professional medical panel. Exhaustive examinations of these cases by special tribunals was eventually able to show the strict truth of one of these miracles and, by the Pope's intervention, the second case was dispensed with. In May 1970, Pope Paul VI announced that the entire group would be canonised on Sunday 25th October 1970.

At the ceremony of canonisation, the Pope made the following historic statement:

> May the blood of these martyrs be able to heal the great wound inflicted upon God's Church by reason of the separation of the

Anglican church from the Catholic Church. Is it not one – these martyrs say to us – the Church founded by Christ? Is not this their witness? Their devotion to their nation gives us the assurance that on the day when – God willing – the unity of the faith and of Christian life is restored, no offence will be inflicted on the honour and sovereignty of a great country such as England. There will be no seeking to lessen the legitimate prestige and the worthy patrimony of piety and usage proper to the Anglican Church – this humble 'Servant of the Servants of God' – is able to embrace her ever beloved sister in the one authentic communion of origin and of faith, a communion of priesthood and of rule, a communion of Saints in the freedom and love in the Spirit of Jesus. Perhaps, we shall have to go on, waiting and watching in prayer, in order to deserve that blessed day. But already we are strengthened in this hope by the heavenly friendship of the Forty Martyrs of England and Wales who are canonised here today.

Further resumption of the causes for beatification and canonisation of other martyrs is still continuing. The martyrs who were canonised on that day in 1970 are:

Reign of Henry VIII

John Houghton	Richard Reynolds
Robert Lawrence	John Stone
Augustine Webster	

Reign of Elizabeth I

Cuthbert Mayne	Swithun Wells
Edmund Campion	Eustace White
Ralph Sherwin	Polydore Plasden
Alexander Briant	John Boste
John Paine	Robert Southwell
Luke Kirby	Henry Walpole
Richard Gwyn (alias White)	Philip Howard
Margaret Clitherow	John Jones (alias Buckley)
Margaret Ward	John Rigby
Edmund Gennings	Anne Line

Reign of James I

Nicholas Owen (Little John)
Thomas Garnet

John Roberts
John Almond

Reign of Charles I

Edmund Arrowsmith
Ambrose Barlow

Alban Roe
Henry Morse

The Commonwealth

John Southworth

Reign of Charles II

John Plessington
Philip Evans
John Lloyd

John Wall
John Kemble
David Lewis

APPENDIX 9

THE OATH OF SUPREMACY

(cf. *Tanner* under bibliography)

The Act of Supremacy of 8th May 1559 was aimed at 'restoring to the crown the ancient jurisdiction over the state ecclesiastical and spiritual and abolishing all foreign power repugnant to the same'. To this end, a special oath was introduced that had to be sworn by all who held state or church offices. Because this oath played such an important role in all subsequent events – more especially during the period of the Diary – the exact wording is reproduced below to help the reader understand why it was opposed in some circles.

> I, A_ B_, do utterly testify and declare in my conscience that the Queen's Highness is the only supreme governor of this realm and of all other Her Highness's dominions and countries, as well in all spiritual and ecclesiastical things or causes as temporal, and that no foreign prince, person, prelate, state or potentate hath or ought to have any jurisdiction, power, superiority, pre-eminence or authority, ecclesiastical or spiritual, within this realm; and therefore I do utterly renounce and forsake all foreign jurisdictions, powers, superiorities and authorities, and I do promise from henceforth I shall bear faith and true allegiance to the Queen's Highness, her heirs and lawful successors, and to my power shall assist and defend all jurisdictions, pre-eminences, privileges and authorities granted or belonging to the Queen's Highness, her heirs and successors, or united or annexed to the imperial crown of this realm; so help me God and by the contents of this Book.

APPENDIX 10

THE TIRWHIT MARTYR

In entry 2, John Hart reported the alleged ill-health and death of Robert Tirwhit (Tiruit, Tirwight, Tirwright, Tyrrwhit, etc). 'soon after' committal in June 1580. In this appendix, it is intended to examine all available evidence from other sources because, whilst Hart is not alone in reporting the death of one of the sons of Sir Robert Tirwhit, these other sources do not agree to it being Robert.

That William and Robert Tirwhit were placed into the Tower in the month cited is not disputed; proof was furnished by the committal warrant mentioned in footnote 3 to entry 2. The mere fact that Hart was at fault with dates is purely academic but, when that error is placed alongside the other glaring mistakes he wrote, they suffice to illustrate he must have written them out at some later date. Whilst submitting that Robert could not have died the way Hart implied, the case merits closer inspection.

The story begins somewhat earlier in 1580 when a small social gathering assembled at a splendid stately home in Kettleby, Lincolnshire. During a protracted stay in anticipation of the wedding of one of the daughters of the house, one of the assembly had secret reasons for suspecting that his hosts were holding religious beliefs that run counter to national policy. On discovering that his young master, the intended groom, was being gradually 'converted' to Catholic ways, the guest had a number of violent confrontations with the host family that almost ended in blows. After witnessing his master's wedding to the charming lady, he became more disgruntled and suspicious about the activities in the steward's chamber the next morning, vehemently suspecting that the bridal party, including his master, were attending an illegal Mass conducted by a mysterious stranger. Recalling other episodes over the previous weeks, the guest began to suspect that the regular visits to 'Twigmore House' might also be connected and that his hosts might even have been attending illegal worship whilst there. At the end of the visit, the faithful but disappointed servant decided that his only course of action was to write out a report of what had occurred and send it to the Privy Council.

In *The Articles Drawen out of the Declaration of Richard Smith, late Scholemaster unto the Lorde Sheffeilde, concerning the religion, contract and marriage of the Lorde Shefeilde in Sir Robert Tirwight's House and of the religion of his sonnes and familie* (*see* transcription at Annex 1 to this Appendix), we discover the revealing report which betrayed the Tirwhits. Because Smith's report was not dated, it was somewhat difficult to locate as it had been erroneously calendared into papers belonging to 1583. Nonetheless, when linked with the subsequent arrests, his allusions to 'Passion Week' and 'Whitsuntide' tend to place the visit to Thornton College into March, April and May 1580.

It would certainly have been as a direct result of Smith's letter that Sir Robert appeared before the Privy Council on 8th June 1580 *(APC)* and was commanded to send for the Steward of his house, his son Goddard and one Nicholas Tirwhit. Sir Robert was also instructed to arrange that 'every one of them may make their appearance before their Lordships as soon as convenient to answer their defaults at their extreme perils. And Sir Robert was enjoined to do his best to accomplish this order'.

As none of those named by the Council appeared in any later prisoner lists, we may only assume that William's arrest from Wigmore or 'Twigmore' House and the subsequent arrest of Robert from Thornton College were part and parcel of the purge against those whom Smith had reported.

It is of particular interest to notice the Council's reference to Nicholas Tirwhit being one of those whom they were anxious to interview. His relationship to the arrested brothers could not be determined; but it has been confirmed that Nicholas was a seminary priest who had been ordained from Douay on 23rd March 1577 and had been active in England since August 9th of the same year *(Anstruther)*. Is it possible that he had been the mysterious stranger lurking in the steward's chamber earlier in 1580? Little, if anything, is known of his work in England but he must have found somewhere safe in which to hide – where safer than with his own kith and kin?

Whereas the queen and council must have been incensed at the report of a covert act of treason by one of the leading landowners in Lincolnshire, the mere suggestion of a nuptial Mass after the wedding would have been the cause of great embarrassment to Robert Dudley, Earl of Leicester, a leading courtier who had befriended Elizabeth when she was imprisoned in the Tower in 1554. Dudley's clandestine liaison with Lady Sheffield, mother of the Kettleby groom, was still a matter of some delicacy involving a cuckolded husband who had died in circumstances which led to a suspicion that Dudley had arranged for him to be poisoned in order that his affair with the lady could blossom. And blossom it certainly had! Whether they had been secretly married or not, Lady Sheffield was delivered of a bouncing boy on 7th August 1574 – a half-brother to the young man who was married at Kettleby six years later (*Complete Peerage*).

This delicate but close relationship between the groom and one of Elizabeth's favourites could possibly qualify why no action was taken against the young Lord Sheffield. Consequently, on July 10th, 1580 *(APC)*, the

Privy Council wrote to the Bishop of Lincoln instructing him to drop all charges against the bride, Ursula Tirwhit, because, as a result of 'Lord Sheffield's earnest suit, his wife was now conformable in religion'. And, at their meeting six days later, the Privy Council agreed, 'Lord Sheffield is reformed in religion since leaving Sir Robert Tirwhit's house' and they thought good 'he should be forborned and also John Tirwhit in respect of his conformity'. The latter appears to have been Sir Robert's fifth son.

But let us turn our attention back to the first and second sons in the Tower. On 27 June, the day following that on which Robert had joined his elder brother in prison, the Council issued the order *(APC)* for them to be examined in matters of religion. This was a straightforward questioning and there was no recourse to torture.

Even though John Hart reported Robert's death 'soon after', both of the Tirwhit brothers were still very much in the world of the living on January 8th following when William Wykeham or Wickham (1539-1595), then Dean of Lincoln, was granted free access to speak with them on 'their obstinacy in religion'. And on 25th January 1580-1, we find the council calling for a search of William's home at Wigmore House in an effort to discover 'suspected persons and Popishe and supersticious stuff'. It was not possible to find a report on what was found in the house; but this was an age of cunningly constructed 'priest's holes' (*see* Eliot's account at Appx 3) and ingenious hiding places in most Catholic residences and the absence of a report would suggest the searchers returned empty-handed.

More importantly, on 13th June 1581, Sir Owen Hopton, the Lieutenant of the Tower, received the Privy Council order *(APC)* calling for him to take £300 from William and £200 from Robert as their bonds for release. Full clearance was issued the following day for both of them to be handed over to the Dean of Lincoln in order to receive instructions in the established church. Under these conditions, we can imagine the wayward brothers riding through the Bulwark Gate of the Tower with their guardian, inwardly congratulating themselves at the happy conclusion of an adventure that could just as easily have led to their being handed over to the sheriffs of London at that same gate prior to being drawn to Tyburn.

Just before we lose sight of the three horsemen riding gaily northwards, it is necessary to backtrack for a moment to examine a letter which William had sent to the Council during the year of his incarceration. The contents of his undated letter are considered so important to this case that they have been transcribed and reproduced in full at Annex 2 to this Appendix. It will be noted how, in the formal language of his day, William pleaded for leave to return to Lincoln for the recovery of his health but mainly to sort out the estate of his brother Marmaduke, lately deceased. A reply to his appeal was not found – there might only have been the one copy which William thrust into his saddle bags while packing for the journey north –

but such letters are known, in many cases, to have been the instruments by which certain prisoners secured their liberty on bond.

From the schoolmaster's declaration of the previous year, we know that Marmaduke, Sir Robert's sixth son, had been a witness to his sister's betrothal to Lord Sheffield, even though his appearance before the council had never been called for. Nonetheless, he was now dead and his elder brothers were dashing back home to sort out his belongings, recover their health and begin the usual three months of religious training under William Wykeham.

Whilst they might have succeeded with the first two objectives, it became patently obvious that their religious re-education under the dean was hitting troubled waters. Their names cropped up once more at the council meeting on 17th October 1581 during which the agenda included a discussion of the havoc being created in Lincolnshire 'by reason of the great resort that is had unto them'. The irate councillors therefore resolved to take further bonds from William and Robert to guarantee their appearance in London. When they did appear, they were cast into the Fleet prison but a precise date was not ascertained.

It was noticed that their father had already been cast into the same notorious gaol but, other than a brief mention of his being granted Liberty of the Fleet and his wife 'to resort and remain with him' on 4th September 1580, nothing more is known. As will be seen from the inscription on his impressive tomb at All Saints Church, Bigby, Sir Robert died on November 13th, 1581. Linking this date with the previous mention of his being in the Fleet shortly before, it might wrongly be assumed he had died in custody in the Fleet; but the family history (*Notices and Remains of the Family of Tirwhit* (anonymously and privately produced but never published, a copy is held at the British Library)) claimed, 'He died at his house at Thornton College'. This irregular publication, being more concerned with the lineage of a modern branch of the family descended from one of Sir Robert's brothers, is most suspect for its accuracy, more especially when it was seen that the author was not only unaware of most of the foregoing data but was totally ignorant of the very strong probability of the family having its own martyr.

Whatever might have been the circumstances of Sir Robert's death, his funeral now commands our attention as it has some bearing on the case. As the eldest son and heir, William was granted liberty from the Fleet prison on or before 20th November – a week after his father's death – this time to the more expensive tune of £1,000 thereby allowing him to plan the funeral and sort out Sir Robert's extensive estate. But then came an unexpected delay which prompted the Council to further extend William's bond by stipulating that he should rejoin Robert in the Fleet on 20th February following *(APC)*.

The delay over the funeral was qualified in the family history by 'the absence of roads and the consequenting difficulty of bringing together the persons who made up the attendance'; yet, when it is learned that the funeral at Bigby did not take place until 20th January 1581-2, this appears to be a rather weak excuse. Even with the absence of roads as we know them, a horseman could quite comfortably cover as many as twenty miles per day with little or no effort. Just how widespread were the Tirwhit family when they needed as long as two months to reach Bigby? It may only be surmised that the long delay was brought about over a controversy as to whether a Catholic could be buried in the church.

Having noticed how William was liberated on his bond and the council's generous grant of extension – it was further extended to May 1581 – it came as something of a surprise to learn from the family history, 'The chief mourner was not William, heir of the deceased, but his son-in-law, Philip Constable of Everingham'; but the credibility of this source was shattered by a comment on the same page which claimed, 'The standard was borne by Marmaduke, 4th son to Sir Robert (the deceased)'. This must certainly be a gross mistake as it has already been shown that young Marmaduke, Sir Robert's sixth son, had died while his elder brothers were in the Tower between June 1580 and June 1581. Therefore the standard bearer at the funeral, if named Marmaduke, can only have been the deceased's next brother, another Marmaduke.

It was not possible to determine why the author of the family history had suggested that William was not the chief mourner at the funeral. Short of slipping bail, there was no logical reason for supposing that William, the devoted Catholic son, had purposely absented himself from his father's funeral. If he had slipped bail, why did the council see good to extend it well beyond the original time limit? For these reasons, the remarks passed by the author of *Notices and Remains...* give rise to a great deal of doubt and suspicion.

Because *Acts of the Privy Council* from 1582 to 1586 are missing from the archives at the PRO, there was no method of discovering if William did return to the Fleet at the end of the time limit imposed by the council. We may, however, rest assured that he remained constant to his Catholic ideals as was evidenced by a letter (*State Papers, Domestic, vol 183, fol 60*) which was sent to the Privy Council by the sheriff of Lincoln on 27th October 1585 in which he reported, 'The recusant William Tirwhit has not provided a horse as demanded because he is not in the county'. From this isolated comment, it would seem that William had taken to hiding elsewhere outside his home county, probably succoured by another Catholic family.

Notices and Remains showed that William's will, dated 1st May 1591, was proved on 3rd December of that year. In his last will and testament,

William requested that he be buried near his father in Bigby, as has proved to be the case. The allusion to his daughter Elizabeth being married to Ambrose Rookwood (of Gunpowder Plot fame and whose name is inscribed in the Martin Tower) can only be an error for his younger sister as there is no evidence of William having a daughter of that name.

Having seen the mortal remains of William buried in Bigby church, let us return our attention back to his brother Robert whom we last saw in the Fleet prison. Of particular relevance is a report made by Richard Topcliffe (*SPD, vol 152, fol 154*) wherein, during February 1581-2, he accused Robert Tirwhit of being present at a Mass in prison in the company of two priests, William Deane (already a prisoner) and Edward Osborne (a visitor who was apprehended later that month). The report must therefore have been made some time in early February which would infer that Robert had enlisted the help of these priests to serve a requiem Mass to coincide with the funeral at Bigby on 22nd January. It suffices to say that Robert was eventually liberated from the Fleet by authority of the council's warrant dated 22nd November 1582 (*CRS, Miscellanea, vol II*, p. 223) after which he faded from the scene; but this is relatively unimportant. More significant, from all the facts thus far presented, it is patently obvious that Robert (or even William) had not died 'soon after' committal to the Tower in June 1580, as Father Hart claimed in his *Diarium*. Nevertheless, this does not mean the investigation of the Tirwhit martyr is concluded because we must now examine other corroborative statements written by independent authorities.

For this we will need to backtrack to June 1580 to recall a few isolated yet interrelated events. It was, although he failed to say so in as many words, the month in which Hart was captured. It was also the same month in which many others had slipped into the country from the continent, amongst whom were the Jesuits Robert Parsons and Edmund Campion. For the next thirteen months, the latter had eluded the security network as they toured the country visiting countless Catholic households.

With Campion's capture in July 1581, Parsons knew the next phase would be to hunt him down and therefore resolved to leave the country; but the queen and Walsingham had not heard the last of him. During his time in England, Parsons had kept copious notes of his observations on all aspects of the Catholic persecution. One of the overriding reasons for fleeing England was to establish a printing press on which he could produce the books so urgently requested by the people he had met. Such a facility would also prove useful for producing his own literary assaults against Elizabethan policies, more importantly after Campion's execution in December 1581.

Of the many writings that would flow from his pen thenceforward (we have already commented on his later contribution to *De Schismate*), a remarkable insight of the painstaking notes he had taken in England is provided by his *Epistle of the Persecution of Catholics in England* (Douai, 1582). His own controversial comments on the subject of a Tirwhit martyr are brief, to the point and well worth reciting in full. As expected, it was all composed in Latin and a translation could not be found. This might therefore be the first time it has been fully cited in English. Here, verbatim, is what Parsons had to say:

> TIRWHIT, son of the knight Robert Tirwhit.
>
> A young man of great and honourable family who was accused of the crime of hearing a Mass which was said to have been celebrated at his sister's wedding. He had flown from his father's house and hid in London in the previous year. From the exertion of his flight and from the heat of the summer, he fell into a grave fever. When this became known to his enemies, they immediately seized him and imprisoned him as he was so weak and afflicted with sickness. This seemed to the onlookers both inhuman and deadly; they pleaded and beseeched that the sick man should be cared for. They should not add affliction to affliction; nor kill such a generous, noble and fair youth. They even offered security that he would be brought before the judge as soon as he was better; but this was not acceptable. Doctors met who advised that it would impair his health if he were removed to the unhealthiness of a prison. They took no notice. They took him to the penitentiary and shut him away in a cell. He died two days later; and they buried him with no thought or scruples.

Bearing in mind all that has been shown of the arrest, release and recommittal to the Fleet of William and Robert, this heart-rending account could not have been written with them in mind; yet the annoying omission of a Christian name in Parsons' account seems to be of paramount importance and shall be looked at later. Our investigation is not helped in any way by Bishop Challoner's claim in *Memoirs of Priests... that have Suffered in England 1577 to 1684* in which the writer submitted that both William and Robert had died whilst imprisoned in the Tower; but this opinion may be seen to clash with all the other evidence thus far presented and has never been endorsed by any other writer of recusant history.

Moreover, when Parsons compiled his account of the Tirwhit martyr, his notes from England were hardly dry on the paper; he was safely ensconced in his seminary and was free to pick and choose the phrases he wanted to use in putting together his Latin notes of what had happened in England; and, from his choice of words, it must be obvious that he held more intimate knowledge of the case than Father Hart. Admittedly, Parsons did not cite a Christian name; nor did he name the 'penitentiary' into which the captive was cast, only to die two days later. If he had been certain of it being the Tower of London, he would have been sure to have said so in his account, purely to prove to the authorities in England exactly how much he knew.

Even so, there are certain points in Parsons' report that merit closer scrutiny. It must firstly be stressed that Parsons was still wandering around the English countryside when William and Robert were allowed to leave the Tower with the Dean of Lincoln. Such momentous tidings – two recusant prisoners actually gaining their freedom from the Tower – must have spread like wildfire and would certainly have been carried to Parsons and Campion within a matter of days. For this reason, Parsons knew there was no question of their having died in custody.

In similar Latin terms as those used in the *Diarium*, Parsons mentioned the alleged Mass 'at his sister's wedding'; yet then went on to mention the flight 'from his father's house' where, from the schoolmaster's deposition, we are assured the wedding took place. But notice the important reference to the fugitive's escape 'in the previous year' which must have been 1580, the year of the wedding, placing the sick man's death into the summer months of 1581, at about the same time as the former Tower inmates were riding forth out of the fortress. Although John Hart's wording regarding the ill health of the victim compares quite favourably against the words Parsons employed, the latter alluded to a 'penitentiary' in which the captive died as opposed to the former who named the Tower.

Having made this brief comparison of writing styles and leaving a few questions in the air for the moment, we now need to move our time frame forward by almost three hundred years to the year 1874 when a long listing of martyrs was submitted to Rome for consideration of the individual causes for possible beatification. Cutting completely across all that Parsons and Hart had recounted, Robert Tirwhit made no appearance in this impressive list; and yet, featured in position fifty-seven in the dossier of 353 names, it came as something of a shock to find the name of William Tirwhit being cited as a martyr who 'died in prison in London in 1581'.

Whereas the committee responsible for compiling this list had wisely negated the name (Robert) and the year (1580) which John Hart had advanced, sufficient evidence has now been presented to prove that William could not have died in prison in 1581, having been liberated from the Fleet towards the end of that year to organise his father's funeral and estate in the following year.

However, the various original sources which we have been fortunate to examine were not as readily available to the members of the 1874 committee – of which, more shall be said in a moment – and so the cause for the Tirwhit martyr was postponed in 1886 as being worthy of further investigation; since which time the cause seems to have made little or no progress. As such, in common with other names in the same list, William Tirwhit – still resting peacefully alongside his father's remains in Bigby church since 1591 – has been classed *Dilatus*, a title style which denotes that martyrdom will be recognised when and if more evidence comes to light.

Within the limited framework of this present study, it was impossible to determine the reasoning behind the decision by which William Tirwhit's name was inserted into the 1874 list of recommendations. Neither of his contemporaries, Hart and Parsons, had advanced his name; and the subsequent postponement of his cause in 1886 suffices to show that the Devil's Advocate had been able to raise sufficient doubts over his death to warrant the delay for further investigation. The reason for advancing William's name could possibly mean that a closer inspection of Hart's *Diarium* had penetrated a flaw in the description under entry 2 and that they assumed that, if Robert had not died, the only other likely contender who appeared to fit Parsons account must have been William.

Yet why did John Hart name Robert Tirwhit; Parsons suggest a Tirwhit with no Christian name; and the 1874-86 committee advance William's name? The only common denominator applicable to all three is that they all proposed a son of Sir Robert Tirwhit. From his fine monument in the church at Bigby, we discover that he was the proud father of as many as nine sons but, as only five of them were named in Smith's letter of deposition, we may discount the other four, either because they were too young or had not been present in the house at the time of the wedding.

William, the elder son and owner of Wigmore House, and Robert, the second son and a witness at the wedding, have now been eliminated beyond all reasonable doubt. We have also seen that John, the fifth son, avoided prison by conforming in religion. Nothing more was found of the fourth son Goddard who had witnessed the wedding; but we do know that the only other witness, Marmaduke, the sixth son, had died some time while William and Robert were in the Tower.

The reader might have noticed that the bulk of information presented thus far has been gleaned from *Acts of the Privy Council* with occasional references to *State Papers, Domestic* (Elizabeth). It should not pass without mention that the former documents were not calendared into published form until 1896, ten full years after William's dubious cause for beatification had been postponed. The latter documents, covering the period up to 1580, did not become public knowledge until 1856; and those beginning in 1581 became available for study in 1865. Whereas the committee tasked with compiling the list of martyrs might have availed themselves of the opportunity to study *State Papers, Domestic*, the few isolated entries therefrom would not have sufficed to prove or disprove the cause of William

Tirwhit. Nevertheless, it must be accepted that, with all the extra data provided in *Acts of the Privy Council*, much more is now known than was available to the Victorian committee.

Having sorted through the names of Sir Robert's sons and with this new found knowledge available, let us try to determine which one could be the probably martyr. We have previously deleted William, Robert and John from our suppositions and, with no further mention of Goddard, he also seems a non-starter. However, let us just remember that all-important mention of another death in the family, that of their brother Marmaduke.

Nothing definite was found of the circumstances surrounding this bereavement in the family. From the schoolmaster's report, we know for certain that Marmaduke had been at Lord Sheffield's wedding at Kettleby; but why had the Privy Council not called for his appearance when they interviewed Sir Robert on 8th June 1580? Why is there no mention of Marmaduke conforming in religion or being apprehended at a later date? One could frame a hundred and one questions along this theme; but the most salient must be 'Was this the son, reported by Robert Parsons with no Christian name, who had flown from his father's house and hid in London the previous year?'

Combining that question with the known departure of his brothers from the Tower in June 1581 in response to the undated letter that William had previously written (*see* annex 2), we then start to notice serious undertones. In William's letter we notice his request 'to settle provision for his brother's children...his own estate which was wholly committed to his brother...the question of inheritance...making of provision against Easter term, etc'. Of all the many arrangements demanding his attention, one important detail is never mentioned. On no occasion in his letter does the petitioner allude to planning the funeral, as was the later case when his father died. But, if the account composed by Parsons is any indication, there was no necessity for a funeral as the martyr had already been 'buried with no thought or scruples'.

In summary, sufficient evidence has now been brought to light from sources not previously consulted to show that William and Robert were imprisoned in the Tower in June 1580; during the period of their incarceration, their brother Marmaduke passed away; William, on learning news of this tragedy, petitioned for release in order to arrange certain legal matters; and, as a result, both brothers were liberated on bonds in June 1581. It could be said that they were allowed free to recover their health or to sort out Marmaduke's legal affairs; but, behind the wording of their release warrant, we can envisage the machinations of Sir Francis Walsingham. His sole reason for letting them go was to bring about their religious conformity. This was the only key that could guarantee release; the bonds they paid were but an added bonus for the queen's coffers. Faced with the choice between conformity or constant prison, the brothers had no other option but to bow to the demands of the Dean of Lincoln if they wished to recover their health and probably improve their own finances from Marmaduke's estate.

Having gained their liberty and reached home, it would appear that the brothers were treated as cult heroes in their own county and, within a space of only four months, they had become such a thorn in the side of the government that order was given for their committal to the Fleet, it being patently obvious that they did not intend to conform and that harsher methods were necessary. Nonetheless, the evidence is conclusive enough to prove they did not die in custody either in the Tower or the Fleet.

In view of all that has now been disclosed, the most likely contender for the honour of martyrdom appears to be Marmaduke Tirwhit. Until further evidence is uncovered from hitherto untapped sources, we must either take the above findings as acceptable and creditable or must place the cause for a Tirwhit martyr back into the files of the countless unsolved mysteries of Tower and recusant history.

ANNEX 1 TO APPENDIX 10

The Declaration of Richard Smith

As was shown earlier in the Appendix, this original *State Paper* was difficult to locate as it had been calendared into documents of 1583 but with a query. It will be found at the Public Record Office under *State Papers Domestic, Elizabeth, vol 165, fol 28.*

In common with most writings of the period, a virtual lack of punctuation caused difficulty in following the writer's flow. Punctuation marks have therefore been inserted where considered necessary.

Line spacings have been retained as they appeared in the original text but a few spellings have been altered where a definition could be confusing or even incomprehensible.

In this day and age, it is difficult to appreciate why a schoolmaster would attend all the arrangements leading up to the occasion of his student's wedding. The teacher makes extraordinary references to 'reading to my Lorde' and then almost comes to blows over a controversy of the books being loaned to his ward. To comprehend such a situation, it must be understood that marriages were contracted at a much earlier age than is today's practice.

Whilst Edmund, 3rd Baron Sheffield must have been a very young man when he married Ursula Tirwhit, the *Dictionary of National Biography* and various publications on the peerages cannot agree to his exact date of birth; but, taking a cross sectional average of all that was found on his birth, he could not have been much older than sixteen. The age of the bride was never alluded to; but no doubt she was somewhat younger than her new husband.

The document reads as follows:

> Articles drawen out of the declaration of Richard
> Smith, late Scholemaster unto the Lorde
> Shefeilde, concerning the religion, contract
> and marriage of the L. Shefeilde in Sir
> Robt Tirwight's House and of the religion
> of his Sonnes and familie.
>
> Imprimis, the L. Shefeilde, at his first coming to the house
> of Sir Robte Tirwight did professe the true Christian
> Religion published throughout Her Majesty's dominions as
> did appear by his open speache againste the Doctrine of
> the B. of Rome; and the exercise of prayer he used in his
> Chamber in the Booke of common prayers used by her
> Highness' autoritie. Wherein the said L. , after some tyme
> growinge verie slacke and negligent, his scholemaster
> complayned to Sir Robte Tirwight who answered that
> it was sufficient for my L. to use that prayer with
> him in his Great Chamber and that, evenings and mornings,
> he might use private prayers to himself for (saied he)
> it will weary him to use so much to pray; whereto Mr.
> Smith, offeringe to replye, was sharply rebuked by
> Sir Robte Tirwight.
>
> Item, Smith, at the motion of Mr. Deane of Lincoln
> intending to reade Mr. Nowell's Cathachisme unto my
> L. , did in the presence of Goddard Tirwight offer to give
> my L. a Lecture thereon which my L. , at the first, seemed
> somewhat to mislike; and, after a little private conference
> had between his L. and Goddard in the presence of Smith,
> the L. Shefeilde did utterlie refuse to read it. Whereupon
> Smith, complayning to Sir Robte, was verie earnestlie
> reprimanded of him for goinge about to bring my L. back,
> as he termed it, to his A. B. C. againe and willed Mr.
> Smith, if he doubted of my L.'s Religion or of his, he should

examine them there; and at that time, also after he
had been rebuked of Sir Robte and commanded to departe,
Robte Tirwight, his second sonne, came unto him to
move him to reade some other Booke to my L. and to
forbeare to overthwart him for feare it might be a breach
unto the marriage or else that his father wolde put the
saide Smith awaie; and so in th'end was constrained to
read unto my L. stories de Gloria at the instigation
of Goddard Tirwight.

The saide Smith in a shorte space after seeing the
manifest corruption of my L.'s religion daily increasing
and plainely declaring to Sir Robte that my L. was a
papiste and became perverted, the saide Sir Robte waxed
exceeding angerie and wisshed Smith to take heade
what he said for that (sayed he) my L. might utterlie
undoe him for raysing a slander uppon his L. And the
saide Sir Robte (then) demandinge of Smith how he
knew my L. to be a papist answered that because,
insteade of godlie prayers, he used a booke of erroniouse
Doctrine: as prayers to Saints, to his good Angell [and] for
sowles in Purgatorie. The which Booke Goddard hadd
then in keeping and within half an hower after delyvered
the same to the steward. Att these speaches, Sir Robte was
also verie angerie with Smith.

Also Smith uppon another Complaint unto Sir Robte
that my L. hadd refused to be taught anie longer by
him because, as he said, Smith was not of ye Catholic
Churche, Sir Robte mused thereat [and] said that the over-
thwarting of the saide Smith, the godlie conversion
of his sonnes and the desolute liefe of the other
Religion was the cause of my L.'s turning and was angry
with Smith for crossing my L., saying it wolde make him
more earnest; after which tyme Smith never reade unto
my L.

Concerning the contracte and marriage
of the L. Sheffeilde with the Daughter
of Sir Robte Tirwright

Uppon the thursdaie after the date of the L. Treasurer's
letters, Sir Robte Tirwight came to Thorneton College with

the same to my L. who, uppon the sondaie after, sent for
Smith immediatelie before Dinner unto Sir Robte Tirwright's
Dyning Chamber where, he attending to know his L.'s
pleasure, Mistress Ursula, daughter unto Sir Robte Tirw,
came upp; and there my L. tooke her by the hande
and said, "I, Edmonde Sheffield, take thee Ursula
tirwyght to my wief for ever". And she, for
her parte, after Goddard Tirwright (when my L. and
she had drawen hands), rehearsed the same; then said
Goddard, "I praie you, my Masters, beare witness for my L.
intends never to have other marriage but this".

This was don in the presence of

Robte }
Goddarde }
John } Tirwright
Marmaduke }
John Routhe
John Sheffield
Richard Smith
and others

The next day after, in the morning, he heard it whispered
in the house that there sholde be a stranger in the
Steward's Chamber, there kepte secretlie and not to be
seen; who he was, he could not learne; but the Daie following
he heard that my L. was married in the Stewarde's
Chamber at a masse whereof he could learne no manifest
profe but of one kept there close he did conceave by their
probable arrangements. The usuall carrying hither of
meate, drinks and fyer with the excluding of the
Boye that used to make the Steward's bedd up.

Touching Sir Robt's Childeren
in his house.

Since the first coming of Smithe to Sir Robt's house
his sonnes did at no tyme use prayer with their
father and the rest in the great Chamber; neither did they
go to anie Churche to his knowledge.
ffrances and Ursula, his Daughters, never since the
beginning of Lent would come unto prayers savinge

ffrances now of late since Whitsontide used againe
to come to prayers.
Smith hathe been earnestlie delte withall bothe by faire
and fowle meanes by Goddard and Robte Tirwright to
turne from his religion and [they] have greatlie repayned att
him for that he did withold some of the household whom
they had attempted to perverte.

Goddarde Tirwight offered to strike Smith in the
presence of dyvers [others] for that he said (when the Steward
[was]
whipping out the doggs) byd them awaye to the Churche
that there was no Churche in England fitt for them
except the Churche of Twigmore, a place suspected
where Willm Tirwright dwelleth.

Touching Sir Robt's ffamilie

Three parts of Sir Robt's household servants have not
since Smith's being in that house used at anie tyme
to come unto prayers in his Hall.

All the papists in Sir Robte Tirwright's house went
to Mr. William Tirwight's at Twigmore betwixt
thursdaie in passion weeke and mondaie in
Easter weeke last paste, where, it is thought, they
heard masses.

———•———

ANNEX 2 TO APPENDIX 10

The undated Petition of William Tirwhit from the Tower to Sir Francis Walsingham

The original letter, written on one large sheet of heavy paper, is found in *State Papers, Domestic, Elizabeth, volume 148, fol. 18*. On the outside of the folded sheet, the petitioner has written, 'The Peticion of William Tirwhitt' below which another hand (probably Sir Owen Hopton) has written:

For Liberty for 3 months to go into Lincolnshire to:

1. Provision for his brother's children and their stockes.
2. In light unto his own estate which was wholly committed to his brother, lately deceased.
3. Question of inheritance of 500m by year triable at the next assizes there or by compromise.
4. Help for his disease of the stone.

The body of the letter reads as follows:

> Humbly beseecheth your honour William Tirrwhitt that, whereas Marmaduke Tirrwhitt his brother is lately deceased, who hath committed unto your supplicant the custody of his children and the dividing of their several possession; which Marmaduke had the oversight and dealing altogether of your supplicant's causes; and whereas besides there is a rift now depending now betwixt him and Mr. Stanhope for some part of the inheritance to the value of 500 marks which is to be tried by nisi prins or compromised by friend in Lent assizes next; and for that your supplicant's great debt for the which he standeth bound with divers of his friends in several bonds unto be politely ordered besides his [illegible] unto her Majesty in Easter term next; and for that the disease of the stone daily groweth upon him to his great and excessive pain of body whereof, if remedy be not sought, it will be his utter undoing.

> May it please your good honours for these mighty causes to grant him liberty for three months to go into Lincolnshire as well for the better recovery of his health as to determine his causes as aforesaid; and so shall he daily pray for the continual prosperity of your good Lord with much increase of honour.

APPENDIX 11

JOHN HART'S LETTER OF SUBMISSION TO SIR FRANCIS WALSINGHAM

Written on three sheets of heavy paper, the original is in *State Papers Domestic, Elizabeth, 1581, vol 150, n.80.* Bearing in mind the writer's anguish at having just evaded his own execution and the fact that his friends Campion, Sherwin and Briant were even at that very moment being butchered at Tyburn, Hart's handwriting is remarkably clear. The few examples of deletions, corrections and errors in spelling and grammar were commonplace in most written documents of the era and cannot be mistaken as a sign of any inner turmoil in Hart's conscience. Nonetheless, the choice of wording and his scheme to act for Walsingham does reveal a weakness beneath his hard exterior.

To facilitate reading the transcription, the general tenor has been left unchanged. However, Hart's alterations have been ignored; spellings of certain words have been modernised; and punctuation, where needed, has been inserted.

Here is the full letter:

Most Honourable,

So soon as I understood by Mr. Lieutenant of Your Honour's special favour toward me in making earnest suit in my behalf and putting me in such undoubted hope of my life if my conformity shall be agreeable thereinto; forthwith, it came into my mind how I might declare unto Your Honour (to whom, with others of Her Majesty's most honourable Privy Council, this whole matter doth belong) that dutiful obedience towards Her Majesty and Your Honours by some untoward fact of mine which already, with most solemn attestations, I have word. The thing then wherewithal I was bound to trouble Your Honour especially is, in my simple discourse, of some weight and may perhaps (if Your Honour shall also like thereof) come to good effect and purpose; and it is this.

Whereas I do now, by divers and sundry examinations, very well perceive that some great matter is intended (whereof, I dare say, Your Honour is not ignorant; forasmuch as whilst conspiracies be but yet thought upon, Your Honour, for your singular wisdom, doth forecast how to prevent before they take place). Whereunto must needs be that Doctor [William] Allen, of all others whom I know beyond the seas, must needs be made privy. It were not remiss, in my simple judgement, speedily to think upon some means how to know the very secrets of his whole heart, if it were possible. Which thing may be done in this wise.

If I be not much deceived in him whom now of many years of pain thoroughly knows and being very much conversant withal than any in the whole seminary that was, of my state and condition; and, hereof I am utterly ashamed, that there is nothing can please him better than to understand of his scholar's stoutness in suffering at this time imprisonment, with such like troubles, for their Catholic faith; and it is a wonder to see how he will rejoice at the only hearing thereof.

Which thing maketh me verily to think that whereas I, who was before this so dear unto him that in every deed he made some account of me and, for that cause, was not willing that I should depart from him when I did, acquainting me always, or for the most part even then, with all matters in manner of study and setting forth of books; that whereas (I say) I have in this wise been very much made of him when, as yet, I did nothing in this excellent part as he supposeth – that is, in suffering for the cause which liketh him so well – when as he shall now understand of my stoutness that it hath been such as to abide a whole year and more, close imprisonment, and that in the Tower, the only name whereof is very terrible abroad. Yea. And yet much more – to have been at the rack (though I endured nothing thereon (but that is unknown to him)), to have been indicted, arraigned and condemned for the same as both he and his fellows (I know it) are fully persuaded and now presently do stand at Her Majesty's mercy for my life without any speeches as I suppose (otherwise than to Your Honours and a few others who are secret enough for that matter) that I am so minded, as I have professed to Your Honours, to reform myself according to Her Majesty's Godly and virtuous proceedings. If I were now with him in this case, I should be so made of as I cannot express it in any words, and I think verily he would now make me privy to very many things which hitherto, untrusting my constancy in this behalf, and by this that now I have said, having met certain tokens of the same, he hath kept secret from me and others of my calling – imparting them only to a few (all of which I know very well) of the chief seniors in the house; so that if he should perhaps herein be more circumspect that they (as it is very likely he will), yet I have very vehement conjectures of coming to some knowledge of matters by others about him with whom he often dealeth very secretly; and, for the cause which now I said, are no less fond of any that shall suffer in the cause than he, but much more talkative.

And this is the matter wherewithal I thought good to give Your Honours intelligence as a thing which perhaps may serve for some little point of policy whereunto I know Your Honour hath, for your high calling, very great regard. Which thing will better serve for the setting forth of that true cause indeed which Your Honour, under Her Majesty, doth so mightily defend; I mean the religion this day professed in this noble Realm of England. For as for my bare yielding and conforming of myself which I have promised to Your Honours unformedly, though it may do some good thereunto by giving others of my profession example to do the like. Yet that thing is not of such importance as this which hitherto I have spoken of and which is much more than may be done by many others with as great profit. This thing either by some other or, at best, not so conveniently, for reasons which I retain in mind, as by me alone.

All which I have said (I protest before Your Honour) not to the intent I would pull the wreck out of the cellar again as though I was sorry for what I have done or said in my submission to your honour; but because I am desirous to do some service to my Prince and Your Honour which may be gratefully accepted as I, for my part, am willing to perform it.

But this whole matter and mine own life also to be disposed of, I leave to Your Honour's further consideration – myself not able any way to move Your Honour either one way or another. But only after my rude and unskilful manner to lay down what conceit and meanings I have when I perceived such marvellous clemency toward me on Your Honour's behalf, for which I am bound to pray all the days of my life. And thus craving pardon at Your Honour's hand for my boldness, I make an end, beseeching God, of his infinite goodness, to endue Your Honour with all blessings in greatest abundance in this world and, afterwards, with life everlasting.

The 1 of December 1581

Your Honour's most humble and comely servant

John Hart

APPENDIX 12

YEOMAN WARDERS OF 1580

In 1326, due to civil unrest, the establishment of Yeoman Warders had been increased from 'ten armed footmen' to thirty, a figure that remained constant until 1605 when, with the large influx of Gunpowder Plotters, a further ten men were recruited to raise their number to forty, a figure around which the strength has hovered ever since (*Yeoman Warder Records*).

The original listing, a claim for the wages of Yeoman Warders, may be found in the *Tower Bills* file at Chancery Lane under *E407-56*. Each of the thirty Yeomen, who had been specially selected for employment as a reward for former services to the crown, received the princely sum of eight pence per day for performing their manifold duties in ensuring the security of the Tower and her prisoners. In a later age (1794), the duty of guarding state prisoners attracted a further three shillings (15p) per week over that paid for gate duties – seventeen shillings (85p) as opposed to fourteen shillings (70p) – suggesting that the added incentive was introduced to make prisoner duties more 'attractive'.

Other than a few isolated cases of claims for overdue fees in discharging these duties, the PRO file gives little or no mention to which Warder had the responsibility for which prisoner. As none of the Warders were mentioned in the Diary, there was no method of determining which of the thirty named below was detailed to care for John Hart. The Warders named were:

John Waynewrighte	Robert Shawe
Henry Hille	Thomas Searle
William Mercer	Simonde Malone
Ralfe Gascone (Gascoigne)	William Simenes
Richard Powell	Henry Higbye
Peter Wells	Robert Morris
William Hodges	Henry Campion
Anthoine (Anthony) Beare	William Johnsone
Robert Chadwicke	Robert Savage
Thomas Westmoreland	Thomas Meares

Thomas Dowsinge	Andrew Palmer
John Haywarde	Leonard Summesytte (Somerset)
Robert Butler	Henry Bellamie
Anthonye Davis	Mathew Twyford
John ffreeman	Thomas Butler

APPENDIX 13

BRIEF BIOGRAPHIES OF THE PERSONS NAMED IN THE DIARY

The fact that only eighty-five prisoners were named in the pages of Hart's Diary does not mean they were the only ones to pass through the Tower during the period covered. Just as many, if not more, were committed for other non-religious offences such as piracy, coining, murder, robbery, fraud, treason or political misdemeanours; but these were of little or no import to the diarist who simply wished to concentrate on the persecution of his fellow Catholics. In light of the brevity of the Diary entries, the reader might well appreciate inclusion of these brief biographies in order to learn just a little more about the characters encountered therein.

In a number of cases, the only knowledge we have of some personalities is that cited in the *Diarium*. In such cases, the relevant entry and associated footnotes are all that can be covered in the following pages in which names are arranged alphabetically.

Unless stated otherwise, the information on Seminary Priests was obtained from the brilliant work of scholarship composed by Anstruther. Nonetheless, this study has revealed certain errors in these valuable volumes and, where applicable, they are mentioned below to assist the reader in forming his own opinions.

ADDIE, ADDY or ADY (ABDY), Patrick
Named in entries 86 & 90.

Due to the Latin spelling form, *Bayley* translated the surname to read 'Abdy' when the above was intended.

At one time Addy had served as a servant to John Leslie, Bishop of Ross, an earlier prisoner who left an inscription in the Bloody Tower. According to *SPD* at the time of his arrest, Addie was a Scots priest who had been captured with William Creighton by the Admiral of Zeeland on board a ship bound for Scotland from Dieppe. When this ship had been boarded by the admiral's men, Creighton was seen to tear up a letter and throw it overboard. Unfortunately, the prevailing wind had blown the scraps of paper back on deck. When assembled by the admiral, the letter was found to contain certain plans against Elizabeth I.

Being captured on 3rd September 1584, both captives were conducted back to Ostend. News of their capture and information about the letter caused Elizabeth to call for their extradition which was readily granted. Both were committed to the Tower on 16th September (entry 86). This date is supported by claims for them in *Tower Bills*.

Shortly before the diarist and his twenty companions departed into exile, Addy was reported (entry 90) as being cast into the Pit for four days, probably for petty infringement of prison rules.

With the conclusion of the Diary, Addy was still retained at the Tower. It was proposed in the Prisoner List of 27 May 1585 (*CRS Miscellanea, Vol 2*) that he should be banished; yet he continued to feature in demands for his fees up to and including 30 September 1586. The absence of five *Tower Bills* covering the period from 1st October 1586 to 24th December 1587 means that the conclusion of claims in his name could not be ascertained; but it is known that he was sent back to Scotland at some later date with orders never to return.

ALFIELD or AUFIELD, Thomas, alias Badger
Named in entry 47 only.

Born in Gloucestershire in 1552; educated at Eton and Oxford; ordained at Chalons on 4th March and sent to England on 29th March 1581; witnessed the executions of Campion, Briant and Sherwin on 1st December 1581.

It is a sad reflection of his day that Alfield was betrayed to the government by his own father and was arrested on 7th April 1582. Brought to the Tower on 24th of that month, order was issued for him to be questioned about Jesuit practices. 'If not willing to talk, to be put to the rack...' (*APC 13:400-401; cf.SPD 2:57, 153, 243, 249*). He might also have suffered further interrogation under torture on 1st May but the original warrant was sufficient authority for this to proceed. It has been implied that he offered his recantation under these tortures. He was certainly at liberty before 13th September 1582.

His second term in the Tower is recorded in *Tower Bills* wherein claims for 'Thomas Alphilde' were entered for the full quarter from 25th March to 24th June 1585. On this ocasion, Alfield was charged with 'dispersing slanderous books against the execution of justice'. Without mentioning these three months at the Tower, *Anstruther* quoted a list from Newgate prison in which the keeper recorded Alfield's arrival there on 14th June 1585 (yet another example in which Sir Owen Hopton (Lieutenant of the Tower) had demanded fees for ten days longer than he was entitled).

Tried with William Wiggs and Thomas Webley on 5th July 1585, Alfield was condemned to death on an accusation of distributing Cardinal

Allen's *Modest Answer to the English Persecutors*. Refusing all offers of his life in return for acknowledging Elizabeth's supremacy, Alfield was hanged at Tyburn on Tuesday 6th July 1585 and beatified in 1886.

APRICE or PRICE, William
Named in entries 84 & 87.

On accusation of concealing priests and papists, this man's committal was recorded in the Diary for 27th August 1584 (entry 84). It was also intimated that he had either concealed or murdered a boy named Jackson to prevent his giving evidence against him. On arrival he was cast into the Pit for twenty-three days and suffered similar punishment on 24th September 1584 (entry 87).

Aprice remained languishing in his cell after the diarist and his twenty companions departed into exile on 21st January 1584-5 (entry 91). The Prisoner List dated 27th May 1585 (*CRS, Miscellanea, Vol 2*) recommended that he should be removed to another prison; yet claims for his fees in *Tower Bills* continued through to 30th September 1585. Subsequent bills are lost from the series. However, it was found (*CRS, Miscellanea, Vol 2*) that he was moved to the Clink prison whence, in December 1586, comment was passed, 'William Price is discharged'.

ARDEN, Edward
Named in entries 62, 63, 65, 67, 70 & 72.

A native of Park Hall, Warwicks; born either 1532 *(BDEC)* or 1542 *(DNB)*; his father had died during his infancy and he became the ward of Sir George Throckmorton, whose daughter he later married. It was this relatively innocent association that was destined to lead to his loss of life.

For some considerable time before, Walsingham's espionage agencies had been watching Francis Throckmorton and reporting back on his scheming with Catholic elements. Subsequent to the scare of a bye-plot led by John Somerville, certain answers given by Somerville after his committal led to Arden being named. Despite constant denials of any knowledge of Somerville's intentions, Arden was brought to the Tower where he was named 'Edmund Arden' in the *Tower Bills* starting on 6th November 1583. Hart reported his arrival the next day. Arden was sent to torture at the rack (entry 67) on the same day as Francis Throckmorton, 23rd November 1583, but the warrant that might have given authority is not on record.

Edward was tried at the Guildhall on 16th December and, as evidenced by *Tower Bills*, sent to the condemned cell at Newgate with Somerville three days later. Whilst there is no doubt over Arden's innocence of the charge, there is much confusion about his eventual execution. The 1586 edition of the *Diarium* showed it taking place on 22nd December 1583. When reproduced in *Bayley*, the date had been changed by the author or his printers to show 26th of the same month, which was possibly a simple compositor's mistake. However. when Robert Parsons rewrote his *Annals of the Schism* from Rome, he cited 20th December 1583 which, in view of the many errors committed by John Hart in his diary, seems to be the most reliable and has been accepted as accurate by most historians.

The *DNB* appears correct to say he suffered at Tyburn. No evidence or reason could be found to support the claim made by Parsons (and repeated in *BDEC*) that he was put to death at Smithfield.

ARDEN, Francis
Named at entry 79 only.

(Should not be confused with John Arden – who escaped with John Gerard in 1597 – as was the case when A.H. Cook DCM, MM, BEM linked them both together under the one name 'Francis John Arden' in his handwritten catalogue of *Prisoners of the Tower.*)

Francis, who might have been related to the others of the same surname, was brought to the Tower on 23rd February 1583-4 on which date claims for his fees started in *Tower Bills* (Appx 2). This date of committal also agrees with the Diary entry. Such claims continued to feature through to 24th June 1585, five months after Hart and the other exiles had departed. However, no further claims were entered either for John or Francis after that date.

On 4th April 1585, it was explained in a letter that a decision had been reached whereby Francis, due to his becoming dangerously ill from confinement, could be discharged if he could only provide £500 in sureties. Being unable to pay his prisoner fees or find friends who were prepared to back him to the tune of such a large sum, he was still held at the Tower on 27th May 1585 when another letter reported that he faced an indictment of treason 'but the matter against him is not full enough to be remanded to Her Majesty's Bench' i.e. face trial.

Although the Lieutenant of the Tower had entered demands for his fees up to 24th June 1585, it was reported from the Marshalsea that Francis had arrived in that prison ten days earlier on 14th June 1585, after which nothing more is known.

ARDEN, Mary
Named in entry 65 & 70.

The wife of Edward Arden who, having been named by Somerville, was brought to the Tower on 16th November 1583 (entry 65). Although her husband is named in the *Tower Bill* for Christmas 1583, she does not appear therein and, because the next bill is missing, we only begin to notice generous demands for her from 26th March to 25th June 1584. She faced trial at the Guildhall on 16th December 1583 (entry 70) and was condemned to death.

Whilst she later gained a pardon, it was not possible to say when she went free because the bill for Michaelmas 1584 is also missing from the series; but she is not named in the bill beginning on 1st October 1584.

ARMAGH, Archbishop of, *see* **CREAGH.**

BADGER, Thomas, *see* **ALFIELD**

BARNES, John (Thomas)
Named in entries 83 & 91.

John Barnes was born in Winchester and was ordained from Cambrai on 29th March 1578; he was sent to England on 3rd August 1579 and was able to continue his ministry undetected for some considerable time; but then, in common with most of the missionary priests, he was captured. Citing the *Tower Bill* starting on 30th September 1582, *Anstruther* suggested that the 'Thomas Burnes' named therein was the seminary priest. However, the diarist was explicit in describing the person who arrived with Stephen Rowsham on 19th May 1582 (entry 49) as 'laicus' (a layman).

Nonetheless, the wording of entry 83 clearly shows the committal of Thomas Barnes, 'presbyter' (priest) on 24th August 1584. There is no doubting that this was John Barnes the priest, who had evaded capture for eleven months longer than had originally been imagined. Yet again, the apparent collusion between the diarist and the Lieutenant's clerk is detected from the *Tower Bills* wherein John is named as 'Thomas'. The claims for this 'Thomas' continued through to 21st January 1584-5 when his name was marked 'dismyssed' to signify he was one of the twenty-one exiles.

The *Commission for Banishing Jesuits and Seminary Priests* (Appx 6) named the exile correctly as 'John Barnes, clerk'. He reached Rheims on 3rd March 1584-5, departed for Lorraine on 26th January 1588-9 and was still living there in 1596.

BISHOP or BUSHOPPE, William
Although not named as such in the *Diarium*, this man was one of the 'ten other priests' mentioned in the final entry for 21st January 1554-5. Bishop was brought to Tower Wharf from the Marshalsea. This seminary priest later became the first Catholic Bishop of Chalcedon to be officially permitted by James I to return to England in 1623. Bishop died in England the following year.

BOSGRAVE (BOSGROVE), James
Named in entries 8, 33, (35) & 91.

Born c. 1548 at Godmanstone, Dorset; left England to enter the novitiate of the Society of Jesus in 1564, when only seventeen years of age; entered the Society on 17th November 1564 at Rome. He was ordained at Krems on 30th November 1573 and spent the next eight years working in Moravia, Poland and Lithuania. Becoming ill, he was despatched to England in 1580 in the hope that his native air would speed up his recovery. In autumn, he landed on the coast of Suffolk and was arrested at Orford probably on account of his poor command of the English language after such a long time abroad.

He was forthwith sent up to London and cast into the Marshalsea prison. Due to his ignorance of the religious changes that had taken place in his absence, he freely consented to attend Anglican worship and was allowed free. When friends advised him of his error, he wrote to the Privy Council revoking his decision and declaring his Catholicism, for which he was returned to the Marshalsea.

The council ordained his transfer to the Tower with Hart on 24th December 1580 (entry 10) incorporating a clause that, with Paschall from the Compter in the Poultry, all three were to undergo torture because they had 'lately arrived in the realm from Rome and other places beyond the seas with the intent to pervert and seduce Her Majesty's subjects' (*APC 12:294-295*). Whereas the Diary failed to mention Bosgrave's torture ordeal, the mention in entry 11 of Orton being tortured can only be an error on the part of the diarist as Orton was never named in any extant warrants for torture.

It will be seen from the *Tower Bills* (Appx 2) that the claims for Bosgrave started on 24th December 1580. In later prisoner lists, he was occasionally named 'Jacob Bosgrave', 'Jacob' being the Latin for 'James'. Entry 33 described how he appeared in court with other priests; and entry 35 recounted how he was condemned to death.

On account of his initial error of appearing to offer conformity to the Church of England, he wrote an apology in 1583 which was published under the title *The Satisfaction of M. James Bosgrave, the Godly Confessor of Christ, Concerning his going to the Church of the Protestants at his first coming into England*.

As a prisoner, he was confined to the Well Tower wherein he carved out two inscriptions that still endure. Under number 9 he etched out:

JAM. BOSGRAVE. PRIEST

PRIESTE, JESUITE. 1582

His other inscription (number 10) is slightly eroded and has been misread in the past to the point that one authority (*RCHM*) claimed the dating was '1589' leading to a false impression that he was held for much longer than was actually the case. This is not an isolated example where the carving of a figure '4' in stone has been mistaken for a '9' and vice versa. For this reason, the inscription is meant to show:

JA. BOSGRAVE
VINCULIS PRO FIDE CATH.
1584

It is of particular interest to learn that, after his condemnation, the queen granted him a special reprieve from the death penalty at the express request of the King of Poland. As a result, Bosgrave was retained at the Tower until, as evidenced by *Tower Bills*, 21st January 1584-5 when he was one of the twenty-one exiles (entry 91 and appendices 6 and 7). Upon landing in Normandy, he made his way back to Poland to resume his Jesuit duties and died there at Kalisz on 27th October 1623.

BOURKE or de BURGH, Richard, 2nd Earl of Clanricarde
Named in entry 3 only

The son and heir of Ulick, the 1st Earl, was born some time after 16th September 1527; succeeded to the earldom after his father's death on 19th October 1544. Richard is often refered to as 'the Sassanagh' [sic] on account of the services he had rendered to England in 1548, 1552 and 1553.

The Diary claimed that he was being held 'at the same time' on 19th June 1580; but the diarist must have meant that the earl was held during the period covered by his diary because claims for the earl did not appear in *Tower Bills* until 4th December 1580. These claims continue through to 24th June 1581; but the bills for the rest of that year are missing from the series.

He was in custody for the part he had played in Desmond's Insurrection in Ireland. Once this uprising had been fully crushed, he was released in the latter half of 1581 and died on 24th July 1582 (*Complete Peerage*).

BRIANT (BRYANT), Alexander
Named in entries 23, 24, 34, (36), 38 & 39.

Born either in Somerset, Exeter or Dorset in 1556 (*Anstruther*) or 1553 (*DNB*); educated at Hart Hall, Oxford; returned to the Catholic faith whilst an undergraduate in 1574; arrived at Douay on 11th August

1577 and ordained at Cambrai 29th March 1578; sent to serve the Catholic community in England on 3rd August 1579; worked undetected in Somerset, during which period he reconciled many to the Catholic faith, including the father of Robert Parsons, the Jesuit superior.

Briant came to London – probably with the aim of meeting Parsons – and was arrested by pursuivants in March 1581 from a house next door to that in which Parsons was sheltering. Firstly sent to the Wood Street Compter prison where, in an endeavour to learn where Parsons might be hiding, he was deprived of food and drink for two days.

Briant was moved to the Tower on 25th March 1581 and was said to have suffered further tortures two days later but any warrants to that effect are no longer on record. He was consigned to the Pit in the cellar of the White Tower on 6th April 1581 and might then have been sent back to the prison in Wood Street because a letter from the council on 3rd May 1581 gave order for his return to the Tower and incorporated orders for him to undergo torture (*APC 13:37-38* cf. *SPD 2:22*). Whatever tortures were applied, Briant would not reveal the wanted information. At some later stage, one of his torturers described him as 'a miracle of pertinacity'.

It must be more than accidental that so few of the documents relating to the 1581 martyrs survive in the archives. Even the *Tower Bills* for the latter part of this year are missing. Historians consider that many of these papers were destroyed to conceal knowledge of what had transpired in those months.

Tried with others at Westminster on November 16th for plotting at Rome and Rheims, Briant was condemned to death on 21st of that month. From his prison, Briant applied for membership of the Society of Jesus but, although his entry could not be arranged in the brief time available, he is often cited as being a Jesuit.

With Campion and Sherwin, he was hanged, drawn and quartered at Tyburn on Friday December 1st, 1581, being the first of the group to suffer at the hands of the hangman. John Stow was wrong to say they suffered on 1st September 1582. Briant was beatified in 1886 and canonised by Pope Paul VI on 25th October 1970.

BRINKLEY, Stephen
Named at entries 28 & 61.

A highly skilled printer from a good family, Brinkley had earlier joined a secret society of gentlemen dedicated to assisting Catholic priests in England and the conversion of Protestants, an association that had received Pope Gregory XIII's blessing on 14th April 1580.

There seems no doubt that Brinkley was one of the leading lights in setting up a secret printing press for publishing a spate of Catholic pamphlets and tracts. Immediately after Parsons and Campion arrived on the English Mission, Brinkley's printing machinery was put to use in producing and circulating a number of controvertial works under the guise of originating from 'Doway'; but the government had grounds for suspecting that they were being produced somewhere in England.

For the purpose of producing Campion's *Ten Reasons*, the printing works was set up in Stonor House and, after the booklet had been distributed, Brinkley and his men should have moved with their equipment to another safe location. Yet, for unexplained motives, Brinkley, his assistants and all their equipment stayed in the house hidden away in the woods near Henley-on-Thames.

With the capture of Campion and his associates from Lyford Grange in July 1580 and their subsequent torture in the Tower, the secret location of the printing works was forced from Campion's lips; but, when naming Stonor, he was convinced that his assistants had conformed to their usual practice of moving elsewhere. Nonetheless, the disclosure resulted in the search of Stonor and the capture and committal of those named in entry 28. The *Biographical Dictionary of English Catholics* suggested that Brinkley underwent 'considerable torture' on arrival at the Tower. Whilst this might have been correct, it is unusual to find it gaining no mention in the Diary and no warrant in Brinkley's name has been found on record.

Brinkley was not named in *Tower Bills* as he was deemed capable of paying his own prisoner fees (*CRS Miscellanea vol II, p. 229*). The mention of his being released on 24th June 1582 (entry 61) is probably as accurate as we may ever discover with any degree of certainty because the official warrant that might have shown this transaction would possibly feature in the missing *Acts of the Privy Council* for that year.

In 1585, he finally managed to escape the persecution by fleeing to Rome where he joined forces with Robert Parsons, spending the rest of his life in running a printers' shop. It would therefore be safe to assume that Brinkley played some part – if not a major role – in production of the second and third editions of *De Schismate* and might even have inserted entry 61, recording his liberation, into the *Diarium Turris*. The date and place of his death are unknown.

BRISCOW, BRUSCOE, BRISTOW OR BRISCOE, Thomas
Named in entry 19 only.

A Yorkshireman born in 1553; educated at Oxford; fled the country to seek training at Douay whence he was transferred to the College at Rome in January 1557-8. Although he had not yet been ordained, he was one of the group of fifteen who left Rome with Edmund Campion, Robert Parsons and others, reaching Rheims on May 31st, 1580.

It is known that he left Rheims for Dieppe in the company of Edward Bromborough or Brombury but the circumstances of the journey across France and the apparent absence of his companion on the English Mission has never been explained. By describing Briscoe in the Diary as 'layman recently a pupil at the College of Rome', John Hart confirmed that the captive had not yet received holy orders. The reason for allowing Briscoe to return to England at this time was the recent death of his brother and the letters he had received from his mother pleading for him to return to care for her.

According to *Tower Bills*, claims for Briscoe started on 24th December 1580. It was therefore unusual to find the Diary reporting how he had been 'taken at the port and brought to the Tower' on 8th February following. If nothing else, it helps to show how stringently Hart was held.

Even though he had not been ordained, 'Thomas Bristowe' was named in an undated listing headed 'Priests in the Tower' (*CRS Miscellanea Vol 2, p. 221*) which would suggest that the authorities did not look on him as a layman due to the training he had already received at Douay and Rome.

Whereas he was not shown in the list headed 'Prisoners in the Tower, 27th May 1585' (*CRS, Miscellanea, vol 2, p. 238*), his name headed the next available list of 18th June 1586 (*ibid, p. 251*) in which mention was given to his 'conveying over a young gent'. The final appearance for his fees in *Tower Bills* was for the first nine weeks of the Michaelmas Quarter 1586, ie, from 24th June to 27th August which would infer that he might have been moved to another prison or even liberated to clear space for the Babington conspirators who were just beginning to arrive in custody.

It was noticed that Sir Francis Walsingham included 'Tho. Bristowe' in his pre-meeting notes for the Privy Council debate on 30th November 1586 (*CRS, Miscellanea, Vol 2, p.261*); and yet the final results of the meeting, summarised in 'The Lords' Resolution on Prisoners' of the same date (*ibid, p. 263-266*), failed to give Briscoe any mention at all, giving reason to believe he might have been liberated in August, even though *Anstruther* claimed he was retained in the Tower for eight years in all (1580-1588).

After release, he returned to Douay on 18th March 1593 and eventually gained holy orders from Valladolid later that year. He was sent back to England in 1594 and was next heard of at Lancaster in April 1605 when condemned to death but the execution stayed. He was later banished, reaching Douay in November 1605. He left for England once more in May 1606, was again arrested and banished from Newgate in July 1606. He stayed at Douay from then until February 1608 and then departed for England with a little more success. Although it is not known when he died, he was certainly still living in England in 1620.

BRUMLUM, William. *see* CROMLOME or CROMBLEHOLME

BURNS (BARNES), Thomas
Named in entry 49 only.

Much confusion surrounds this layman whose committal was dated 19th May 1582. Although the surname would correctly translate as 'Burns', *Tower Bills* starting on 30th September 1582 showed claims for the fees of 'Thomas Barnes'; but this can only allude to the layman who was brought in with Stephen Rowsham.

As these claims were continuous in all available bills up to and including 21st January 1584-5, it seems as if the layman was confused with the priest of similar name who, according to the Diary, was committed on 24th August 1584 (entry 83). It would appear that the layman was replaced by the priest of similar name during the period covered by the missing bill for Michaelmas for 25th June to 30th September 1584.

CAMPION (CAMPIAN), Edmund
Named in entries 26, 27, 30, 31, 33, 35 & 39.

The son of a London bookseller, born 25th January 1540; a junior fellow at St John's College, Oxford in 1557; won the patronage of Robert Dudley, Earl of Leicester; in 1560 Campion was a speaker at the queen's state visit to Oxford; was well patronised and became one of Elizabeth's favourites. It looked as if a successful and prosperous career was mapped out for him; but he then chose to abandon these preferments and went to Ireland to help found a new university in Dublin (later Trinity College) and consider his future.

During this period he wrote a *History of Ireland* which, after alterations, was incorporated into *Holinshed's Chronicles*. After long hours in meditation, Campion elected to flee to Douay to study for the priesthood. He was accepted into the Society of Jesus at Brno on 26th August 1573 and ordained in Prague in 1578. In preparation for joining Robert Parsons and other priests for service on the English Mission, he was summoned to Rome. Shortly before leaving Prague another of his companions painted the emblem of martyrdom, a garland of lilies and roses, on the wall above Campion's bed space.

The detachment under Parsons moved out from Rome on 18th April 1580. Reports of their move were sent back to Walsingham causing seaports to be placed on full alert. The party firstly reported to Rheims for a final briefing by Doctor William Allen. Having split into smaller groups of two or three, Campion left with Ralph Emerson and Robert Parsons. After Parsons had travelled ahead to investigate security arrangements at

Dover, Campion, disguised as a jewel merchant, followed with Ralph Emerson and landed at Dover on 24th June 1580.

Campion was mistaken for William Allen's brother Gabriel and taken before the mayor of Dover. Whether or not a bribe changed hands or the mayor was satisfied with his papers, Campion and his friend were allowed to continue to London. Often disguised as a flamboyant military gentleman, he was able to pass detection in his missionary work despite the hue and cry to watch out for him.

In the course of his travels, Campion worked in Lancashire, Yorkshire and the Midlands. At Stonor Park, Oxfordshire, he wrote and had printed his most famous work *Rationes Decem*, in which he advanced ten reasons challenging the Protestant faith. Four hundred copies of his booklet were secretly distributed onto the seats of St Mary's University Church, Oxford.

A few weeks later, he paid a visit to Lyford Grange, Berkshire. This isolated moated house in the middle of open country was ideally suited for illegal prayer meetings and celebrations of the Mass. The location was considered so secure that Campion needed little persuasion to remain a while longer to permit others to hear and see him. His eventual capture is adequately described at Appendix 3.

Under an escort comprising the sheriff and fifty or sixty horsemen, Campion, three other priests and eight laymen were carried off in grand procession towards London. Their journey was purposely delayed to ensure they arrived on market day, Saturday 22nd July 1581. At their head rode Campion with a crude banner above his head stating 'Campion the Seditious Jesuit'. Taken directly to the Tower, Campion underwent extreme sufferings from the time of his arrival. Mention has been given to starvation, use of the thumbscrews, needles being thrust under his finger nails, compression in the Scavenger's Daughter and another spell of eight days in the Pit; but it was not until 30th July 1581 that the use of the rack was authorised (*APC 13:144-155*). Further torture warrants in his name and others were issued on August 14th (*APC 13:171-172*) and October 29th (*APC 13:249*).

His chamber in Coldharbour Tower, adjoining the west side of the White Tower, was convenient for these sessions upon the rack by which the commissioners aspired to net Parsons and other Catholics. Accused of living under obedience of the Pope and plotting the destruction of the queen at Rome and Rheims, Campion was tried and condemned in November (entries 33 & 35).

Despite the strength of his defence and the way he discredited all witnesses, the jury found him guilty causing him to claim, 'In condemning us, you condemn all your ancestors, all the ancient bishops and kings, all that was once the glory of England.'

Being sent back to the Tower, he was brought out and tied upon a wicker hurdle for the journey to Tyburn on Friday 1st December 1581 to be hanged, drawn and quartered with Alexander Briant and Ralph Sherwin. All three were canonised by Pope Paul VI on 25th October 1970.

During June 1959 an electrician working on the restoration of Lyford Grange found a box hidden under an old floorboard, nearly under the eaves and close to the chimney breast, on the south side of the roof above the passage outside the oak room. Upon examination by Nan Morell and Margaret Whiting, the then owners of the Grange, the box was found to contain an *Agnus Dei* medallion wrapped inside a sheet of contemporary paper which still bore the marks of original wax upon it. There was no doubt in the minds of the finders – and those of later experts from the Victoria and Albert Museum – that this forbidden and compromising article must have been secreted in the hiding place by one of the captured priests at the time when Lyford was being searched by Elliott and his helpers in July 1581. The find was later presented to Campion Hall, Oxford where it is still retained.

CARTER, William
Named in entries 52 & 73.

Born in 1550; at age eleven he was apprenticed to serve a ten year course in printing under John Cawood, the queen's printer. Carter later became a personal secretary to Nicholas Harpsfield at £20 per annum. When his employer died in 1575, Carter possessed a collection of his manuscripts ready for printing. With his previous training, he set up his own printing and bookbinding business. When some of his illegal works had been traced back to his workshop, Carter was cast into the Compter in the Poultry and then the Gatehouse prison. On being liberated in June 1581 on a bond of a hundred marks, he was placed in house arrest with order to remain there till he agreed to attend Anglican church services.

A year later, having failed to comply, his house was subjected to a search causing the discovery of many incriminating documents including *The Treatise of Schism* that had been printed in his workshop (*DNB*). When sent to the Tower some time after June 1582, he was firstly able to pay his own diets and fees from his own pocket; but when his funds ran dry on 29th September 1583, his name began to feature in *Tower Bills* (Appx 2).

The final demand for his fees was dated 5th January 1583-4 and was endorsed 'executed'. Nevertheless, it was six days later, on Saturday 11th January, when he was hanged, drawn and quartered at Tyburn. He was beatified on 22nd November 1987 (*Foley* and *Usherwood*).

State Papers Domestic contain an undated letter addressed to Walsingham from Agnes Carter. With a query over its dating, it was placed among documents of 1587. In her letter Agnes pleaded for her son William to be taken out of the Tower and back to the Gatehouse prison. Detailed study by the Catholic Record Society confirmed this letter really belonged to the records of 1583 because it refers to the printer who was executed. It appears that the Record Office had confused the printer with another William Carter from Aylesbury who had been sent up to London in 1586 for making a false report of the queen's death. This latter offender was never in the Tower.

COLLETON (COLLINGTON) alias Peters, John
Named in entries 27, 34, 36 (37) and was one of the 'ten other priests' mentioned in entry 91.

Born 1548; educated at Lincoln College, Oxford in 1565. Travelled to Louvain and thence to Douay from where he was ordained on 16th June 1576. Three days later, he departed for service in England, firstly making his way to his home town of Milverton, Somerset where he reconciled his father, brothers and sisters back into the Catholic faith. In his own words, John the priest claimed his father had died for the faith in Gloucester gaol. Colleton continued his missionary work undetected until the surprise raid on Lyford Grange (Appx 3) when he was taken with Campion and the others, to arrive in the Tower on Saturday 22nd July 1581. Colleton was cast into the Beauchamp Tower wherein his inscription near the large east facing window still shows his name and the date of arrival. Whereas *Anstruther* submitted he was moved to the Marshalsea prison on 31st July 1581, he might not have been moved as he was named to undergo torture in the Tower two weeks later under terms of a warrant issued on 14th August 1581 (*APC 13:171-172*) and, although the Bills for Michaelmas and Christmas 1581, covering the period from 26th June to 24th December, are wanting from the series, his name features as 'Collington' in all available *Tower Bills* from 24th December 1581 (Appx 2).

Hart's description of Colleton's trial and acquittal (entries 34, 36 and (37)) is absolutely correct. The record of the trial showed that a Mr Lancaster gave testimony to the effect that Colleton could never have played a part in the alleged conspiracy in Rome and Rheims due to an inconsistency over time and place. As a result, he was the only man to be 'quit of the former high treason by the jewrie'. Notwithstanding this proof of his innocence, Colleton was returned to the Tower, probably segregated this time from the others by being placed into the Salt Tower where he again left a carving of his name under number 62-7. It is not possible to examine this latter inscription as the room in which it is carved is used as an armoury store.

The final claim for his fees was dated January 21st, 1584-5 and endorsed 'dysmissed' to mark him out as one of the first group of twenty-one exiles (Appx 6). During the Journey into Exile (Appx 7), strong protest was lodged against the injustice by which Colleton, although acquitted of the said treason, was being banished; but those in charge of the transportation had no alternative but to comply with the queen's order.

Facing likely execution for defying the banishment order, Colleton came back to work in England in 1587 and succeeded to evade capture until 10th December 1609 when, yet again, he was cast into prison for refusing the Oath of Allegiance. It has occasionally been suggested that this was another spell in the Tower; but *Anstruther* showed he went to the Clink prison and was soon at liberty in 1610. By 19th December 1613, he was back in the Clink once more and stayed there until 1618. He was cited as being in the New Prison [?] on 19th November 1621 when order was given for him to be exiled; yet he was still there on 5th April 1622 when order for release was issued.

In 1623, he was appointed vicar-general to the Bishop of Chalcedon, in which capacity he earned great admiration from Catholics and Protestants alike. He also held the trust of Charles I, having visited the Pope on his behalf in 1624 to urge sanction for the marriage of the then Prince of Wales to the Infanta Henrietta Maria.

John Colleton, the man who had failed to become a Carthusian due to ill-health, spent his final years at the home of the Ropers at Eltham, Kent where he died aged almost ninety years on 29th October, 1637. He was the author of several works including *A Supplication to His Majesty for Toleration* and *A Just Defence of the Slandered Priests*.

COMPTON, John
Named in entry 28 only.

Not to be confused with John Cotton, this man was one of Brinkley's printers who was taken from Stonor and came to the Tower on 13th August 1581. Compton's absence from all later documents was qualified by an entry in the Diary of that date in which it was shown,

> [Compton], being of a more timid nature, when the prison guards with drawn swords threatened him with death unless he promised to attend the heretic church, gave in and thus obtained his liberty.

CONIERS or CONYERS, Samuel

Although not named within the pages of the *Diarium*, Coniers was among those 'twenty one in number' in the final entry who were exiled to Normandy. Captured with John Nutter, Coniers had been a prisoner in the Marshalsea prison since 1st February 1583-4 and remained there until brought to Tower Wharf on 21st January 1584-5. He never returned to England and died in exile.

COPLEY, Robert
Named in entry 44 only.

This mention of his seven days in the Pit beginning on 22nd March 1581-2 was the only time his name was shown. He was unmentioned in *Tower Bills* as proof that he was a person of some property. His surname suggests an affinity with Sir Anthony Copley who, due to nonconformity, was living as a refugee in France at this time.

When Robert was arrested, negotiations had opened with Sir Francis Walsingham with a view to permitting Sir Anthony's return to England. Large sums of money were being offered in an attempt to persuade the queen to act leniently with Sir Anthony because all of his estates in England were still intact (*Conyers Read*).

CORYAT, George. see MUNDYN

COTTAM or COTHAM, Thomas
Named at entries 4, 5, 33 (35) & 51.

Born in Lancashire in 1549; ordained deacon in 1577 and entered as a novice of the Society of Jesus in Rome on 8th April 1579; after only six months of this austere life style, he was discharged from the Society and sent to France to recover his health. On learning news of the departure of Edmund Campion and others from Rome on 18th April 1580, Cottam hurried from Lyons to Rheims to meet them. For a part of that fateful trip, Cottam travelled in the company of Charles Sledd (or Slade), ignorant that his companion was one of Walsingham's most successful agents. Cottam's description was soon on the way back to England.

Hastily ordained at Soissons on 28th May 1580, Cottam then pleaded for permission to join his friends on the English Mission. Due to the large numbers that were already prepared to travel, it was agreed that he could join them but that they should all split into smaller groups to travel via different routes. Cottam was to travel with Humphrey Ely and John Hart by way of the Dunkirk to Dover ferry, leaving Rheims on 5th June.

At Dover, Cottam and Hart were immediately recognised and arrested. Ely was so free from suspicion that it was agreed that he could assist in escorting Cottam up to London. As already noticed, for his neglect in allowing his 'prisoner' to escape, Ely was placed into the Tower. On hearing of this, Cottam surrendered himself to Thomas Andrews at the sign of *The Star* in New Fish Street and was placed into the Marshalsea on 27th June, whence he was moved into the Tower on 4th December 1580.

Shortly after arrival, he was punished for his obstinate attitude by being placed into the Scavenger's Daughter. Catholic propaganda made a big issue of this, claiming he was tortured without recourse to official warrants, without the presence of commissioners and, worse of all, without being interrogated. Nonetheless, this was a mistaken opinion because the Lieutenant had no need to abide by such regulations when punishing his prisoners. In the strict sense of the word, the Scavenger's Daughter was never classed as torture and was never entered into any official warrants. Its use was at the Lieutenant's discretion.

Cottam faced trial with others at Westminster on 14th November 1581 and was condemned to death six days later on an accusation of plotting at Rome, Rheims and other places not specified with an aim of overthrowing the queen. Passing mention was found to his execution being deferred 'for reasons of state'.

On Wednesday 30th May 1582, he was drawn on a hurdle from Newgate to be hanged, drawn and quartered at Tyburn with Luke Kirby, William Filby and Lawrence Johnson. On the scaffold, Cottam made a futile attempt to convert Simon Bull the executioner to Catholicism.

It was ordained that their remains were to be buried under the gallows because the City gates were already filled with the relics of those who had suffered on 28th May.

The *DNB* and *Gillow* were at fault to place his execution on Sunday 13th May 1582 as executions were never carried out on the sabbath. All other sources, including *The Dictionary of Saints* and publications of the CRS and CTS, agree to his suffering on Wednesday 30th of that month. He was beatified in 1886.

COTTON, John
Named in entries 27 & 47.

Described as 'gentleman' in Eliot's report of his adventures at Lyford Grange (Appx 3) when this man was taken with the other Catholics and led to the Tower to arrive on 22nd July 1581. Not to be confused with John Compton (who arrived in the following month), Cotton had sufficient funds of his own to pay his fees thereby explaining his absence from *Tower Bills*.

He was not released on bond of 'good behaviour' (i.e. conformity) on 7th April 1582, as shown in entry 47, although news of his impending release might have been in the offing on this date. In fact, he was held until Wednesday 25th April 1582 when the council isued order (*CRS, Miscellanea, Vol 2*) for his delivery to his brother Richard who was to take him to their grandmother's house for three months instruction in the accepted religion. Because he made no later appearances in prisoner lists, it would seem that John Cotton heeded these lessons and conformed in religion thenceforward.

CREAGH, CREVAGH, CREWE and, in Irish, O'MULCHREIBE, Richard, Archbishop of Armagh
Named in entry 3 only.

Probably born about 1525; was translated to the archbishopric in 1564. Whilst celebrating Mass in a monastery near Drogheda, he was arrested and sent back to England bound in chains. The *DNB* suggested he arrived on January 18th but an entry in *APC* showed his committal on 22nd February 1564-5. It was not possible to learn how it was managed but, at Easter time of the same year, he escaped from prison. He fled firstly to Louvain and thence to Dublin.

Was apprehended once more in Connaught on 8th May 1567 and sent to trial for high treason in Dublin. Although acquitted, he was retained in detention from which he managed yet another escape. Before the end of 1567, he had been recaptured and was in the Tower.

Whereas he was not shown in the April 1570 prisoner listing, Creagh must be the person who was shown as 'The Irish Bishop – to be examined' in Sir Owen Hopton's prisoner list of 14th June 1572 (*CRS, Miscellanea, Vol 2*). Usually shown in first place as 'Richard Craigh(e)', *Tower Bills* contain claims for his fees beginning on 25th June 1572. He appears to have spent a while in the Gatehouse prison, Westminster but was back in the Tower from 4th March 1574-5.

A legal representative named William Birmingham was granted a pass to visit the archbishop on 22nd October 1575 to discuss financial arrangements needed to purchase 'apparel and necessaries' that were not paid for from the limited funds allowed to the Lieutenant for keeping him.

The *DNB* submitted that Creagh died, 'not without some suspicion of poisoning', on 14th October 1585; yet claims for his fees were still being demanded in *Tower Bills* up to 30th September 1586, eleven months later and probably beyond; but the next bill is missing from the series. The Jesuit Robert Southwell claimed that Robert Poley, one of Sir Francis Walsingham's most employed spies, 'poisoned the Bishop of Armacan [Armagh] with a bit of cheese that he sent him' and, many years later, a Catholic Nicholas Williamson alleged that Poley had 'poisoned the Bishop of Divelinge [Dublin?]', a somewhat garbled version of the same rumour.

There is no doubting that Poley was held in the Tower from 18th August 1586 to 29th September 1588 (*Tower Bills*), originally to watch other members of the Babington Conspiracy and later certain other persons. He was therefore in position to carry out the poisoning. More remarkably, Poley was also present with two other former Tower prisoners, James Typping and Michael Moody, at the mysterious death of Christopher Marlowe in 1593 (cf. *The Reckoning – The Murder of Christopher Marlowe* by Charles Nicholl (Jonathan Cape, 1992)).

Whereas Sir Owen Hopton might not always have been honest in submitting his claims for prisoner fees – often adding a day or so to round up a figure to subsidise his income – it was more than his job was worth to include claims for a prisoner for almost a year after his death. There had to be an answer to this riddle and it was finally unearthed from the burials register for the chapel of St Peter ad Vincula. Under the '1587[8]' heading is an entry reading:

Bishop Richard Crue, Irish, buried in the Chapel xxviijth January.

In finding this entry, Hopton was finally exonerated from any suggestion of dishonesty and proved he had every right to claim for the prisoner who had not died as much as fifteen months earlier.

CREIGHTON, CRICHTON or CREITON, William
Named in entry 86 only.

Born in Scotland c. 1534; entered the Society of Jesus on 5th December 1562; ordained at Rome in 1563. His capture is outlined below Patrick Addy with whom he was conducted back to Ostend. Due to the suspected part the Jesuits had played on 10th July 1584 in the death of William 'the Silent', Prince of Orange, Creighton was immediately condemned to death by hanging and a gallows for that purpose was set up in readiness. But, on hearing information about the torn letters, Queen Elizabeth I called for his extradition to England to face trial as a traitor.

On arrival in London, Creighton was questioned in the home of Sir Francis Walsingham, to whom he admitted being a priest and Jesuit but asked to be sent to Scotland to face trial there. Walsingham produced some intercepted letters that proved the prisoner had heard confessions of certain English Catholics at Lyons and had concealed their treasonable intents against the queen. Creighton denied all knowledge of the letters and considered that certain promises from the secretary of state would result in his release. Nonetheless, he was committed to the Tower on 16th September 1584 when claims for his fees started in *Tower Bills*.

He was firstly held in the Martin Tower and was later removed to the Coldharbour Tower. In both places of confinement, he was able to celebrate Mass daily and hear the confessions of other prisoners by the 'ingenious opening of doors and lifting of paving stones'.

Although claims for his fees came to an end on 30th September 1586, the absence of the next five *Tower Bills* in the series do not reflect exactly when he was liberated.

His liberation and return to Scotland were effected during May 1587. This was brought about by the evidence provided in February 1584-5 by Doctor William Parry who, before his execution on 2nd March, had declared Creighton was opposed to any attempts against the queen's life. Creighton died at Lyons on 9th June 1617 (*McCoog*).

CROMLOME or CRUMBLEHOLME, William
Named in entries 79, 88 & 90.

Entry 79 recorded the arrival of one 'Gulielmis Brumlumnus' on 22nd February 1583-4 and claims for 'William Brumlum' began to feature in *Tower Bills* next day. Unfortunately, the Bill for June to September 1584 is lost from the series; yet in the next Bill, starting in October 1584, the surname of this prisoner had been changed to 'Cromlome'. It was even more remarkable to find entry 88 for 16th October 1584 recounting how William Crumlum had been placed in the pit for two months and twenty-four days. The same surname, with a capital 'C' continued in all later bills up to 30th September 1585.

From these anomalies of spellings from 'Bromlome' to 'Cromlome', and their Latin equivalents, it is manifest that some form of collusion prevailed between the diarist and the person responsible for writing out Hopton's demands in *Tower Bills*. Because this character Bromlome/Cromlome did not appear in any other documents after 30th September 1585, it was not possible to say what became of him.

John Hungerford Pollen, in his valuable article on *Tower Bills* (*CRS Miscellanea, Volume 3)*, suggested, without giving reasons, that the prisoner's true name was *Crumbleholme*.

DEAN or DEANE, William
Although not named in the Diary, Dean was one of the 'ten other priests' to whom reference is made in the final entry.

Having been captured and imprisoned elsewhere since 1582, this missionary priest was brought from the King's Bench prison to Tower Wharf on 21st January 1584-5 to join up with the others who comprised the first group of exiles. He later made an illegal return and was hanged at Mile End Green on 28th August 1588. Beatified in 1886.

DELVIN, 14th Baron. see NUGENT, Sir Christopher

DUTTON, George
Named in entry 20 only.

Not to be confused with John Dutton who arrived shortly afterwards and is not named in the Diary. *Tower Bills* showed just one claim for George when demanding the sum of £5.19s.2d. for the full quarter from 24th December 1580 to 25th March 1581.

However, John Hart recorded on Friday 10th February 1580-1, that George Dutton, layman... for fear of torture, after 46 days, agreed in part to the demands of the heretics; that he would go to their churches; and, even though he openly said he would never accept communion, was allowed his freedom on those conditions.

Counting backwards from the date of this entry, forty-six days would bring us back to Christmas Day 1580 which virtually tallies with the start of claims for his fees. It therefore seems as if George did not remain for the full quarter for which Hopton submitted demands.

DUTTON, John

Although unmentioned in the Diary, this person could be quite easily confused with George Dutton due to the close proximity of their names in *Tower Bills* whence it will be seen that demands for John were for the comparatively larger sum of £15.12s.8d. being a back-dated claim from 20th February 1580-1 to 2nd June 1581.

Because this latter date came before the end of the accounting term, it looks as if John must have left on that date. Due to a lack of more data on him, it is not possible to learn if he was held for a religious offence and secured release by conformity or if he had been charged with some other offence and secured his liberty on proving his innocence.

FENN (FEN), James
Named in entry 76 only.

Was wrongly named 'John Fen' by *Strype*.

For refusing the Oath of Supremacy in 1559, he was put aside from further advancement in the following year even though he might have earned substantial rewards for conformity. He married and had two children, Francis and John. When his wife died, he left the country to seek dispensation for ordination as a Catholic priest. He reached Rheims on 5th June 1579 and was ordained on 2nd April 1580 at Chalons sur Marne. Set off for England on 10th May 1580 and took up work on the mission in Somerset.

Captured at Brimpton, Somerset, he was firstly placed into Ilchester gaol whence he was moved to the Marshalsea Prison before 20th September 1581. In preparation for his trial, Fenn was brought to the Tower on 4th February 1583-4.

He was arraigned at Westminster with others on 7th February on an accusation of living under obedience to the Pope. In the company of four others, Fenn was hanged, drawn and quartered at Tyburn on Wednesday 12th February 1583-4, having spent only eight days in the Tower. He was beatified in 1886.

FILBY or FILBIE (PHILBIE), William
Named in entries 27, 34, (36), 38, 48 & 51.

Born about 1555; ordained 25th March 1581 and sent to England later that year; captured by Eliot and the sheriff's men at Lyford Grange and was among the party that arrived with Campion to be placed in the Tower on 22nd July 1581.

Inscription 12 in the Well Tower, now heavily damaged and eroded, clearly shows:
WH...FI...PRISTE

This is accepted to be Filby's handiwork.

Tried and condemned with others in November 1581, Filby was sent back to the Tower. The final claim for his fees in *Tower Bills*, annotated *mort*, was dated Wednesday 30th May 1582 on which day he was dragged to Tyburn with Luke Kirby, Thomas Cottam and Lawrence Richardson for the usual form of execution. Being the youngest of the group was probably the reason for Filby being singled out as the hangman's first victim. He was beatified in 1886.

FITZGERALD, Gerald, 11th Earl of Kildare (and Baron Offaly)
Named in entry 3 only.

Born 2nd February 1525; son of the 9th Earl and half-brother of the 10th Earl; the title had been restored to him by Mary Tudor in 1554. Whereas entry 3 suggests he was a prisoner on 19th June 1580, the earl was actually brought to the Tower from Dublin Castle on 10th June 1582 with other Irish Catholics, all accused of playing a part in Desmond's Insurrection. Strict instructions were issued for the Lieutenant to place the earl in separate lodgings from all others. Being a person of property, he was not named in *Tower Bills*.

As the Irish situation abated, the rebels in custody were gradually allowed free. The earl was ultimately liberated in June 1583 on a bond of £2,000 and on condition of remaining within twenty miles of London but not to come within three miles of Her Majesty's court. He died in London on 16th November 1585 and was sent back to be buried at Kildare on 13th February 1585-6 (*DNB* & *Complete Peerage*).

FITZGERALD, Henry, 12th Earl of Kildare (and Baron Offaly)
Although not mentioned in the *Diarium*, he was the eldest son of Gerald, 11th Earl of Kildare and was committed with his father and other Irish rebels on 10th June 1582 charged with suspicion of high treason for engaging in Desmond's uprising.

Born in 1562, Henry was probably liberated either with or before his father but the authority was not found. He succeeded to the titles on his father's death in November 1585 and died without issue at Drogheda on 1st August 1597, being buried in Kildare Cathedral. The titles then passed to his younger brother William (*DNB* & *Complete Peerage*).

FOGAZA (FOGACA, FOCATIO or FUGATIUS), Anthony or Antonio
Named in entry 43 only.

From *Conyers Read*, it was learned that Antonio Fogaza was 'a rather amateurish Portuguese conspirator of no particular importance'. He was closely examined by the council throughout March 1579-80 and might have been sent to the Tower soon afterwards.

The Diary entry records, 'Fogaza ... after two years in prison and great suffering on the rack, when he was near to death ... was carried out on a litter and a few days later gave up his soul to Christ'.

Whereas a warrant for his torture on the rack might have been found in the missing *Acts of the Privy Council*, proof of his two years in prison was provided by *Tower Bills* wherein demands for Anthony Fogaca or Focatio covered the period from 30th September 1580 to 25th March 1582; but the final demand was not annotated *mort* as was Hopton's usual practice when a prisoner died in custody.

The implication of his dying a few days after leaving the Tower could not be confirmed or denied by this study. John Hart was in no position to check the rumour and could only write of what he was told without substantiation. It has been confirmed that there is no cause for recognising Fogaza as a martyr. If, as a foreign plotter devoted to the Catholic cause, he had conspired against the queen on behalf of his country, there would be no reason to advance his name for beatification.

FORD, Thomas, alias SATWELL or SALTWELL
Named in entries 27, 34, (36), 37, 48 & 50.

Born in Devon; ordained in 1573; worked on the English mission from 1576 onwards but then apprehended at Lyford Grange with Edmund Campion. Arrived at the Tower in the grand procession commanded by the sheriff of Berkshire on Saturday 22nd July 1581.

Ford was named to undergo torture at the rack under authority of the warrants issued on 14th August and 29th October (*APC 13:171-172* and *id. 13:249* respectively). He faced trial with others at Westminster on 16th November and was condemned to death on 21st of the same month.

It has been intimated that he was held in the Broad Arrow Tower where he set out an undated inscription of his name but this no longer survives. The final claim for him in *Tower Bills* was dated 27th May 1582 and had the traditional prefix *mort* alongside his name. He was hanged, drawn and quartered at Tyburn next day, Monday 28th May 1582, and was beatified in 1886.

GETTER, John. see JETTER

GODSALF (GODSHALL, GODSAFE or GOODSALF), George
Named in entries 25 & 78.

Born in Wells; educated at Oxford; arrived at Douay on 15th July 1576, having already been ordained as a deacon in Mary's reign; ordained a priest at Cambrai in December 1576; sent to England on 19th June 1577.

Although he confined his missionary work to Oxfordshire, it appears he was arrested in Warwickshire with John Payne and sent down to the Tower. In the absence of the *Tower Bills* from June to December 1581 (Michaelmas and Christmas quarters), the date of his arrival in custody was not confirmed; but most writers accept John Hart's dating as 14th July 1581.

Godsalf was removed to the Marshalsea prison with Stephen Rowsham on 12th February 1583-4, the dating given by Hart in the absence of the Lady Day 1584 *Tower Bill*. Godsalf remained so held until September 1585 when he was among the second group of Catholics exiled with order never to return. He died in Paris some time before 1592.

HALL, Hugh
Named in entries 63, 68 & 70.

The Arden's family priest was, according to John Hart, committed on 4th November 1583. The diarist also alluded to Hall being tortured on the rack on 24th November but no warrant survives for this. Although accused of similar offences to the Ardens and Somervilles, this priest is known to have given condemnatory evidence against the rest. By virtue of this service, he was condemned but later liberated.

Hall languished in prison at the Tower for a further nine months after the diarist and other exiles had departed. The final claim for him was dated 12th October 1585 which, coming before the end of the accounting quarter, was probably the date on which he left. *Bayley* explained, 'He was sent abroad through [Robert Dudley, Earl of] Leicester's influence'.

HARRIS or HARRYS, John
Named in entries 28 & 56.

One of Brinkley's skilled printers who was captured at Stonor House with him and arrived in the Tower on 13th August 1581. Whereas John Hart alluded to his being moved to 'another prison' on 16th September 1581, the keeper of the Marshalsea repeatedly mentioned in his reports that he had received the prisoner on 23rd August 1581, thereby placing Hart more than five weeks late in reporting the occurence. He was still listed in the Marshalsea on 8th April 1584 (*CRS, Miscellanea, Vol 2*) after which he gained no further mention, to imply he had conformed in religion.

HART, John
Named in entries 8, 11, 34, (36), 40, 58, 60 & 91.

Probably born in Oxfordshire; studied at Oxford but his college is not known; converted to Catholicism whilst at university and left England in 1569; received minor orders in 1575 and ordained at Cambrai on March 29th, 1578; offered to serve in England when Campion and his contingent from Rome reached Rheims and some of their number were found unfit to travel any further. Hart was allowed to depart with Ely and Cottam on 5th June 1580 but was arrested with the latter as they stepped ashore from the Dunkirk to Dover ferry. Thomas Andrews took him up to London and handed him over to the council at Nonsuch.

After an interview with Sir Francis Walsingham, Hart was sent to Oxford for three months re-education under John Reynolds, a minister of religion at Corpus Christi. When Hart returned at the end of this time and was found as resolute in his Catholic ideals as before, he was cast into the Marshalsea. The council ordered his transfer to the Tower on 24th December 1580. James Bosgrave was moved from the same prison and John Paschall from the Compter in the Poultry the same day.

In their warrant for transfer, all three were named (*APC 12:294-295*) to undergo torture in an endeavour to learn the whereabouts of Campion and Parsons. *Anstruther* placed their move into 29th December 1580, which was either the wrong date purposely entered by Hart into his Latin Diary or that the printers in Rome had mistaken Hart's figure '4' for a '9', a common error already commented upon.

Tried and condemned with others at Westminster in October 1581, Hart was actually taken out to be tied upon the same wicker hurdle as Edmund Campion on Friday 1st December 1581 and would have suffered with Campion, Briant and Sherwin if he had not pleaded for his life at the last moment and offered his conformity. This was sufficient for order to be given for the sheriffs to untie his bonds and send him back into the

Tower where he was made to write his letter of apostacy which still survives in the PRO (*see* Appx 11).

In his letter addressed to Sir Francis Walsingham, Hart pleaded for the chance to return to the seminary at Rheims whence he could spy and report on William Allen. Hart also explained that, although he had been led to torture on the rack, he had endured nothing thereon, but that would not be known to Allen.

There is a remote possibility that this letter secured his release, as suggested in the *DNB*; but when he withdrew his recantation, he was then sent back inside. We are most fortunate that the relevant Lady Day Bill 1581 for December to March 1581-2 is still among the series wherein a claim for the full term has been entered in his name. In fact, no intimation of a release was reflected in the many available *Tower Bills* which recorded uninterrupted claims for him from his date of arrival on 24th December 1580 all the way through to 21st January 1584-5.

Hart was also condemned to suffer execution at Tyburn with Thomas Ford, John Shert and Robert Johnson on 22nd May 1582; yet, for unexplained reasons, he once more evaded his date with the executioner.

The particular dates covered by the *Diarium Turris* are very important because, whilst it has often been said it was compiled by Edward Rishton, sufficient evidence is presented in the earlier pages of this book to prove Hart must have been the diarist. Viewed in this way, the Diary makes much more sense when it is noticed that Hart gains more mentions than anyone else. By misdating some of the entries (especially those that showed his name), Hart could disclaim ownership if ever it was found.

It was seen that the final claim for him was dated 21st January 1584-5. This claim was marked 'dismyssed' to denote that he was one of the first batch of twenty-one Catholics exiled to the coast of Normandy with order never to return. When entering up the event in his Diary for that day, Hart made a point of adding 'of the Society of Jesus' after his own name; yet he did not enter the Society until 14th November 1585 (although *DNB* suggests 1583). From Rome on 10th April 1586, he was granted permission to travel to Poland, having probably handed over his diary notes just before departure. He died in Jaroslow, Poland on 19th July 1586.

HARTLEY, William
Named in entries 28 & 56.

Ordained from Rheims in February 1580, he had then left for service on the English Mission on 16th June 1580 and had taken up residence at the home of Dame Cecilia Stonor, almost certainly serving Mass in the house chapel that still survives at that stately home which has been a centre for Catholicism for centuries.

Hartley had covertly distributed Campion's *Rationes Decem* after it had been printed at Stonor. Being captured in the raid that netted the printers and their machinery, Hartley arrived at the Tower on 13th August 1581.

The Diary recorded his move to 'another prison' on 16th September 1581; but the keeper of the Marshalsea Prison claimed he had received Hartley on 23rd August 1581 (*CRS, Miscellanea, Vol 2*).

Report was made on 24th August of the following year of his having celebrated Mass for twelve of his fellow prisoners. Charged with plotting the deposition of the queen, he was tried on 5th February 1583-4 and sentenced to death. For reasons that have never been qualified, he was then spared and remained at the Marshalsea till 21st January 1584-5 when he was brought back to the Tower once more to be loaded onto the ship waiting at Tower Wharf to carry him with twenty companions into exile. For unexplained reasons, Hart did not enter Hartley's name into entry 91.

Under an alias of Garton, he came back to England in defiance of the banishment order and was arrested in London on 18th December 1587. His very presence in England was cast as treason, causing his condemnation at Newgate on 18th September 1588. He was conducted to the theatre at Mile End to be hanged (only) on Saturday 5th October 1588. This unusual change of venue and method of execution cannot be explained. *BDEC* was at fault to cite his execution as taking place on 15th of the month when all other sources quote the former date. Hartley was beatified in 1886.

HARVEY, John
Named in entries 28 & 56.

Another of Brinkley's printers who was captured at Stonor House with him and arrived in the Tower on 13th August 1581. Whereas John Hart alluded to his being moved to 'another prison' on 16th September 1581, the keeper of the Marshalsea repeatedly mentioned in his reports that he had received the prisoner on 23rd August 1581 (*CRS, Miscellanea, Vol 2*). He was still listed there on 8th April 1584 after which he gained no further mention, to imply he had conformed in religion.

HAYDOCK (HADCOCK or HADDOCK), George
Named in entries 42 & 76.

Born Preston, Lancs; made a deacon in Rome on 3rd September 1581; due to ill health, he was sent to Rheims and was ordained therefrom on 23rd December 1581; left for England on 16th January 1581-2 and made a point of visiting his old friends from Lancashire who were held in the Fleet and Gatehouse prisons. From them he learned of his father's death.

Whereas visiting friends in prison could prove dangerous for seminary priests, the keepers and gaolers were not averse to bribes, considering this a major source of income. But another danger could not be avoided so easily. This was the constant threat of betrayal by one of Walsingham's agents. It was on 2nd February 1581-2 when one of these spies arrested Haydock and had him placed into the Gatehouse, Westminster.

Three days later, he was moved to the Tower when *Tower Bills* began to show claims for his fees. He was indicted at the King's Bench with thirteen other priests on 7th February 1583-4 when all were sentenced to death. As it happened, only five of their number were selected to suffer, Haydock being one of them. On Wednesday 12th February 1583-4, Haydock was the first of the select band of five to be hanged, drawn and quartered at Tyburn. He was beatified on 22nd November 1987 (*Foley* and *Usherwood*).

HEYWOOD (HAYWOOD), Jasper
Named in entry 91 only.

Born in London in 1535; had served Princess Elizabeth as a page of honour; he was a grand nephew of St Thomas More; Heywood joined the Society of Jesus in Rome on 21st May 1562. On coming back to England, he was appointed the Jesuit superior for the English Mission after Robert Parsons had been compelled to flee the country in August 1581. During a few months in Staffordshire, Heywood had received as many as two hundred and eighty persons back into the Catholic fold; but his high-handed dealings with laymen and priests alike gave cause for concern within the ranks of his superiors on the continent.

In an effort to soothe this bad feeling, he was recalled to Rome for consultation. While making his way towards this rendezvous, he was apprehended and placed into the Clink prison. On 8th February 1583-4 he was transferred to the Tower where claims for his fees began to appear in *Tower Bills*. His arrival in custody was unmentioned by Hart. These demands concluded on 21st January 1584-5 when his name was marked 'dismyssed' to show he was another of the group of exiles loaded for the journey to Normandy.

Before climbing the gangplank, Heywood acted as spokesman for the party of twenty-one Catholics, protesting at the way they were being treated and pleading with the onlookers at the unfair way they had been dealt with by the queen and her government. His appeals fell on deaf ears and the galleon set sail with its full complement (*see* Appx 7).

Heywood made his way from Rheims to Rome from where, on 10th April 1586, he was granted permission to travel to Naples. He never came back to England but served as a prefect of cases of conscience from 1593 until his death in Naples on 9th January 1598.

HILDESLEY (Ilsley), William
Named in entries 27 & 47.

Another Catholic 'gentleman' captured at Lyford by George Eliot and brought to the Tower on 22nd July 1581.

Hildesley was not shown in *Tower Bills* so must have being paying his own fees.

According to an entry in the Diary, Hildesley was liberated on Saturday 7th April 1582, 'after finding guarantors for his good behaviour'. Besides putting up the money for his release on bail, such guarantors would also have borne the onus of ensuring his conformity in religion. The entry could not be confirmed from any official papers.

HEMERFORD (HUMERFORD or HUMBERFORD), Thomas
Named in entry 76 only.

(His name is found under various spellings but Hemerford is the most used.)

Born in Dorset in 1554; educated at Oxford; after overseas ordination, he left for service in England on 25th June 1583. Captured in Hampshire, he was in the Marshalsea Prison before 28th December 1583, on which date a report was made in a letter.

Brought to the Tower with Fenn and others on 4th February 1583-4, Hemerford was indicted at the King's Bench with twelve others on the following day. On the 7th of the month, he was selected to be one of the five who would be executed. No one has ever been able to determine how this selection was made – it might just have been decided by the drawing of lots – but it meant that other condemned priests were spared. Hemerford was the fourth victim to be hanged, drawn and quartered at Tyburn on Wednesday 12th February 1583-4 and was beatified in 1886.

ILSLEY, William. see HILDESLEY

JACOB, John (or James)
Named in entries 27 & 56.

An Oxford musician who was captured at Lyford Grange and came to the Tower on 22nd July 1581. Whilst he was named in the listing of committals for that day (entry 27), the diarist was very much at fault to suggest he was moved to another prison on 16th September 1582 (entry 56). To be correct, Jacob had been moved alone to the Marshalsea prison on 16th August 1581 and had been caught in the act of celebrating Mass there on 24th August 1582 (*CRS, Miscellanea, Vol 2, pp. 221, 231 & 233*).

He was named in later Marshalsea Prison lists and was still there in

1583 when John Gerard the Jesuit was cast into the same prison. John Gerard commented in his autobiography, '...he was wasted to a skeleton and in a state of exhaustion from grinding at the treadmill, a most pitiful sight. There was nothing left of him except skin and bones and I cannot remember having seen anything like it – lice swarmed on him like ants on a mole-hill – but he was patient.'

Because Jacob was not named in the Marshalsea list of July 1585, it has been presumed that he had by then been moved to the Bridewell prison where he is reported to have died from ill treatment from his gaolers; but the circumstances are too vague to advance the cause for his beatification and there appear to be no moves to do so.

JETTER (or GETTER), John
Named in entries 54 & 55.

An entry in the Clink prisoner list of recusants showed:

> John Jetter, late servant to one Mr. Higgins of London, scrivener, committed on 7th August 1582 and sent from hence to the Tower.

In another listing entitled 'Prisoners Committed to the Tower Since the Beginning of the Monethe of June 1582' (*CRS, Miscellanea, 2, p. 228*), he is named as 'John Getter of Layscoffe in the County of Sussex'. He is also named in all *Tower Bills* up to and including 23rd July 1583.

It is stressed that Father Hart elected to call the captive 'a lay youth' which tends to be contradicted by the *Catholic Truth Society Pamphlet H 469* in which John Jetter was shown as a seminary priest, a distinction held by his brother George who, although active on the English Mission, was never apprehended. However, the mention of John's capture 'as he was returning from France' would infer that he had paid a visit to one of the seminaries with a view to taking holy orders.

The Diary dated his arrival to 14th August and then, on 1st September 1582, described his suffering in the Scavenger's Daughter, his confinement to the Pit for eight days and how he was tormented on the rack, for which no warrant survives.

In the absence of the Michaelmas 1582 *Tower Bill* (that might well have included claims from his date of arrival), we only begin to notice his name from 30th September 1582. Such demands conclude on 23rd July 1583. Two days later, he was moved to Newgate where he was confined to the dungeon known as 'Limbo'. It was reported, 'He was bound in fetters so heavily that his flesh was eaten away by the chafing of the irons. An infection then set in, his body began to swell and he fell into the consumption that caused his death.'

A priest who visited him remarked, 'Though but a youth, he showed more than a man's courage'. Shortly before his death, John was visited by his brother George who, having been ordained from Rheims, was able to console and fortify John during his sufferings.

It is therefore patently obvious that it must have been John 'the lay youth' and not George the seminary priest who died in Newgate. All in all, the circumstances are too vague to advance his cause for martyrdom but he is numbered as one of the *Dilati* to signify that a cause for his beatification is still being pursued.

JOHNSON, Laurence. see RICHARDSON

JOHNSON, Robert
Named in entries 4, 6, 7, 33, (35) & 50.

A former manservant of whom little is known of his early life; he was ordained at Brussels in 1576; arrived on the Mission and sent to the Compter in the Poultry with Henry Orton on 12th July 1580 after Walsingham's spy, Charles Sledd, had recognised them.

Tower Bills recorded Johnson's arrival in the Tower on 4th December 1580 and continued to show demands for his fees up to 27th May 1582, the last two entries being annotated *mort*.

Diary entry 6 for 15th December 1580 gave mention to Johnson being tortured on the rack with others; there is another brief allusion to Johnson's torture in *State Papers Domestic* of June 1581; but the warrants of authority cannot be located. Johnson was hanged, drawn and quartered at Tyburn on Monday 28th May 1582. He was beatified in 1886.

KAINES OR KEYNES, Edward and Humphrey
Named in entry 27 only.

Being defined as 'gentlemen' in Eliot's report of his success at Lyford (see Appx 3), these brothers came to the Tower on 22nd July 1581 and were still in custody on 12th September 1581 when their father, a Justice of the Peace in Somerset, wrote to the council pleading assistance for his sons who had been taken with Edmund Campion.

This failed to secure their immediate release; but they were named in the List of Prisoners Discharged Since June 1582 Uppon Bonds. It is conjectured that they were freed in July 1582 having served the mandatory year in prison for recusancy (*CRS, Miscellanea, Vol 2, p. 228*).

KILDARE, Earl of. see FITZGERALD, Gerald, etc

FITZGERALD, Henry, etc

KIRBY or KIRKBY, Luke
Named in entries 4, 5, 33, (35) & 51.

Born Bedale, Yorkshire in 1548; ordained at Cambrai in 1577; came to serve on the English mission in May 1578 but returned to the continent in July of the same year. Continued his studies at Rome until 18th April 1580 when he left with Campion and others destined for service in England. Reported firstly to Rheims and thence to the mission.

It is accepted that he was arrested on arrival at Dover but details are uncertain. Upon arrest, he was sent to London to be confined in the Gatehouse, Westminster. He was moved to the Tower on 4th December 1580 when *Tower Bills* began to show demands for his fees. The diarist was a day late in reporting his arrival.

The Diary recorded on 10th December how Kirby was punished in the Scavenger's Daughter. Many writers described this wrongly as torture (but see the comments above under Cottam).

During his time in prison, Kirby was visited by John Nichols and asked for his forgiveness in telling lies against him. Kirby pointed out that it was too late as he had already been condemned. Next day, Nichols went to Sir Francis Walsingham and 'began to rage and swear' but was sent away without satisfaction.

The final claim for Kirby was dated Wednesday 30th May 1582 in which document his name was annotated *mort*. He was hanged, drawn and quartered with three of his fellow priests at Tyburn that same day. Some of his relics are now held at Stonyhurst College, Lancs. He was beatified in 1886 and canonised on 25th October 1970.

LANCASTER, Thomas. see WORTHINGTON

LAYTON or LEIGHTON, Thomas
Named in entry 81 only.

Seven separate entries in *Tower Bills* suffice to show this man being held from 1st October 1584 to 27th August 1586. He was charged with conveying intelligence between the Queen of Scots and Francis Throckmorton.

Whereas the 18th June 1586 prisoner list (*CRS, Miscellanea, Vol 2, p. 251*) suggested he was 'lerned' [*sic*], it was later decided to banish him. His removal from the Tower was deemed necessary to create space for the impending arrests of Babington's conspirators.

Layton was sent to the Clink on 28th August 1586 and was still there at the end of September when the council was deliberating over what action to take for the many captives who were filling London's prisons.

Because Layton was not found in the December 1586 lists, it can only be assumed he had either been sent into exile or had offered conformity.

LEIGHTON, Thomas. see LAYTON.

LETHERBOR or LETHERBOROUGH, Ralph or Rudolph
Named in entry 57 only.

The above entry for 20th September 1582 alluded to the committal of this merchant from Rouen on account of his religion. This foreigner could not have stayed very long as he was named in the list of those who had been 'Liberated on Bonds Since June 1582' (*CRS, Miscellanea, Vol 2, p. 228*). His actual date of release can not be determined because it was not mentioned in the Diary or elsewhere. The diarist was more concerned with the propaganda effect of a foreigner being placed in the Tower. That he might have been liberated soon after was of no particular import to the diarist when his readers had been informed of someone, owing no allegiance to Elizabeth, being imprisoned for religion.

LOES or LOUS, Philip
Named in entry 27 only.

Whilst this name was incorporated into the list of committals on 22nd July 1581, no evidence was found to link Loes to the Lyford Grange captives. Eliot's description (Appx 3) only showed twelve captives; and the sheriff of Berkshire was paid for bringing twelve Catholics to the Tower. By showing Loes in the list, the diarist left an impression that he was a thirteenth captive.

Although Loes might have arrived the same day, his committal was an isolated incident even though he might have had some connections with Campion and his associates. It is quite likely that he was one of Brinkley's printers arrested in London while on an errand to purchase more paper for the press at Stonor.

As the relevant *Tower Bill* is wanting from the series, we only begin to notice demands for Philip Loes commencing on 24th December 1581. Because they came to an abrupt conclusion on 4th November 1582, before the accounting quarter ended, it appears he left the Tower on this date. It was not possible to say what happened to him but, as he was not named in the lists from other prisons in London, he might have gone free.

It was, however, noticed that 'Jone Lowys, wife of Phillip Lowys' was one of the recusant prisoners in the Marshalsea in June 1582. She must be one-and-the-same with 'Joane Lowe, condemned for receavinge and releavinge of priests [who] died in prison in ye White Lion... April 7th, 1589' (*CRS, Miscellanea, Vol 2*).

MANFIELD or MANSFIELD, John
Named in entry 27 only.

A 'husbandman' who, having arrived with the others on 22nd July 1581, agreed to offer his conformity when threatened with torture. Order was given for him to receive instruction from a minister and, if he truly recanted, he could be freed from all restraints.

MUNDYN (MUNDEN or MUNDIN), John, alias George Coryat
Named in entries 59 & 76.

Born at South Maperton, Dorset in about 1543; educated at Winchester College and New College, Oxford; suspended from Oxford in 1566 after he refused the oath of canonical obedience to the Protestant Bishop of Winchester. He was deprived of all preferments when it was learned that he had not been to communion since Elizabeth's accession. Over the next fourteen years little is known of him other than the fact that he was employed as a schoolteacher in Dorchester and other places.

He left the country in 1580 to seek ordination at Rheims, arriving there on 9th October, having been robbed of all his money and most of his clothing at Dover. Details of his ordination are not known but he was a priest by 13th June 1582 when returning to Rheims. He departed for service in England on the following 6th August, working under the assumed name of a former student two years his junior at Oxford, George Coryat.

A contemporary report recounted that Mundyn was apprehended 'towards the end of the month of February' 1583. Mondyn was riding towards London from Winchester or Windsor (reports vary) and was recognised at Hounslow Heath by another former school chum from Winchester, William Hammon. When told he was to be placed under arrest, Mundyn claimed that Hammon had no powers of arrest in that district, being a magistrate of Dorset; but there were many other henchmen with Hammon and, in this case, might was right.

The horsemen conducted their captive to Staines where the necessary warrant was formally made out, thence he was taken before Walsingham to be interrogated on 12th February 1582-3. When the secretary asked him to give his opinion of Nicholas Sander's landing in Ireland, the captured priest declared he knew nothing of the event and that Sander should be made to answer, not he. When asked if he recognised Elizabeth as *de facto* and *de jure* queen, he calmly replied he did not know the meaning of such terms, causing Walsingham to lose his temper and send him to the Tower under care of a pursuivant who was allowed to keep Mundyn's horse and trappings as a reward for his pains.

Another contemporary account showed, '...the holy man was thrown into that small prison-house called Broad Arrow Tower. There he was at once laden with iron fetters and for some time spent his nights on the bare stone floor.' Claims for his fees began on 12th February (*Tower Bills*) but the Diary dated his arrival four days later to 16th of the month and went on to show he spent twenty days in irons as a punishment for his insolence to Walsingham.

Claims for his fees came to an end on 29th December 1583 with the added comment 'executed' against his name; but this must have been appended at a later date because he did not face trial until February 5th following and was condemned on February 7th, 1583-4 on a charge of plotting the queen's deposition. He was specially selected for harsh treatment by the executioner, being the last of a group of five victims who were hanged, drawn and quartered at Tyburn on Wednesday 12th February 1583-4. Munden was beatified in 1886.

MYAGH or MIAGH, Thomas
Named in entry 3 only.

The spellings employed in Inscription 21 in the Beauchamp Tower are so unusual that their full meaning has never before been deciphered with any degree of accuracy. However, if the word divisions are sorted out and the lost letters added to the right (which were erased when number 25 was carved) it was probably meant to read:

O[H], LORD WHIC[H] ART OF HEAV[E]N KING
GRAWNT GRAS[E] AND LYFE EVERLASTI[N]G,
TO MIAH THY SE[R]VANT IN PRISON ALON[E],
WITH SPE[E]DY INLARGDMENT, HENC[E] TO BE[GONE]
TOMAS MIAGH

The prisoner who carved these words is encountered once more under number 29 in the same chamber. In this case, all first letters in each line have been lost or damaged by number 25. Even so, his wording is easier to read as:

THOMAS MIAGH WHICH LIETH HERE ALONE,
THAT FAYNE WOULD FROM HENCE BE GONE,
BY TORTURE STRAYNGE MY TRUTH WAS TRIED
YET OF MY LIBERTIE DENIED
1581.THOMAS MYAGH

Although not on view to the public without prior arrangement, the neighbouring Bell Tower contains another like inscription reading:

> BY TORTURE STRANGE MY TRUTH WAS TRIED,
> YET OF MY LIBERTY DENIED ,
> THEREFORE REASON HATH ME PERSUADED,
> THAT PATIENCE MUST BE EMBRASED,
> THOUGH HARD FORTUNE CHASETH ME WITH SMART,
> YET PATIENCE SHALL P[OSSESS MY HART].

It has often been suggested that Miagh also carved this work because some of the words are so similar to his Beauchamp Tower lament; but modern opinion now comes down against this due to his habit of adding his name at the end of his works. It can only be conjectured that the Bell Tower unsigned inscription was carved by another inmate before Miagh passed through that chamber for questioning in the Lieutenant's lodgings. Remembering a few lines of the work, he then adapted the wording to suit his own conditions when he returned to his room.

Despite Hart's claim that Miagh was a prisoner 'at the same time' on 19th June 1580, he probably meant 'during the same time as the Diary' because this Irishman did not arrive in custody until the early months of 1580-1. Charged with holding a traitorous correspondence with certain rebellious elements in Ireland, reports were submitted on 10th March 1580-1 about two sessions of torture he had undergone. The report explained how an earlier order had insisted on his being questioned in secrecy without the presence of Warders. Such torture would have been quite mild. A week later his obstinacy led to his being confined in the Scavenger's Daughter but even the excruciating pain of being bound into a tight ball failed to secure the answers sought by the Council. It was therefore ordained on 30th July 1581 that he should be assailed upon the rack (cf. *Langbein,* p 198).

We may never know exactly what transpired in the dark confines of the racking room; he was not heard of any more till November when granted the liberty of the Tower as an indication of poor health. He was released shortly after, having never faced trial. In summer 1583, he was appointed keeper of Naas Gaol in Ireland, having qualified for such employment in the country's finest 'finishing school'.

NICHOLS, John
Named in entries 16, 17 & 21.

(Was indexed wrongly in Bayley as 'John Nicholas'.)

Born 1555; went to Rome in 1578 when he gave himself up to the inquisition and publicly abjured the Protestant faith. Pleading ill health, he then left Rome in 1580 and returned to London. Details of his arrest are not known but he arrived in the Tower on 24th December 1580 when claims for his fees began to appear in *Tower Bills.*

Whilst these claims came to an end on 25th March following, he remained in the Tower to preach to the other inmates in the 'public chapel' of St Peter ad Vincula against the evils of Catholicism. On recanting and embracing Anglican worship once more, he was liberated on 6th May 1581 and rewarded for his conformity. He later travelled to Germany where he again converted to the Roman church. Reports of this were published in 1583. He is believed to have died abroad in 1584.

NORRIS, Richard

Although not named within the pages of the *Diarium*, Norris was among those 'twenty-one in number' in the final Diary entry who were exiled to Normandy. Norris was brought to Tower Wharf from the Marshalsea Prison on 21st January 1584-5. He never returned to England and died in exile.

NUGENT, Sir Christopher, 14th Baron Delvin (Devlin)
Named in entry 3 only.

Born 1544; succeeded to the barony in 1559; was a fellow-commoner at Clare College, Cambridge and went back to Ireland in 1565; distinguished himself against Shane O'Neill in 1565, for which he was knighted the following year; commanded the forces of the Pale in Ireland in 1579.

The Diary showed he was held 'at the same time' on 9th June 1580 but this proved to be a general remark to show he was held during the same period of the Diary years. To be exact, the baron was a prisoner in Ireland in June 1580 on suspicion of high treason. His name was shown in the council's order for committal on 10th June 1582 in which the Lieutenant was told to keep him in 'several [separate] lodgings' in readiness for his trial.

Details of his trial are not known; but he was allowed to return to Ireland some time in 1585 with a view to transacting business regarding his personal estate. He was informed in 1588 that he should remain there and never return to England. He served as leader of the forces of Westmeath in 1593 and was a commissioner to enquire into abuses four years later. Subsequent to another outbreak of rebellion by Hugh O'Neill, 2nd Earl of Tyrone, the baron was imprisoned in Dublin Castle wherein he died in 1602 (*DNB*).

NUGENT (NEWGENT), James
Named in entry 3 only.

The Diary gave passing mention to 'Nugetus' being one of the notable Irish prisoners held 'at the same time' as the period of the Diary. His name, with variations of spellings, began to feature in *Tower Bills* on 5th February 1581-2 which, coming near the middle of the accounting quarter, must be his date of committal. They continued through to 25th March 1583 but the next bill is wanting from the series.

When the series reopened on 24th June 1583, Nugent was no longer shown in any form of spelling. His surname suggests he was an Irishman related to Sir Christopher Nugent, 14th Baron Delvin, but his committal four months before the baron does not help in forming a link.

NUTTER, John
Named in entry 76 only.

Elder brother of Robert Nutter; born in Barnley, Lancs; educated Cambridge; arrived at Rheims with his brother on 23rd August 1579 but John was then sent to Verdun to teach juniors, thereby delaying his ordination which finally took place at Laon on 12th September 1582; departed for work in England on 24th November 1583. When falling ill with a fever, he was put ashore at Dunwich, Suffolk. On 15th January 1583-4, he was reported by the local parish minister after papal literature had been found in his possession.

Accompanied by Samuel Coniers, John was brought down to London and placed into the Marshalsea on 1st February 1583-4. John was another of those who were brought to the Tower on 4th February and faced trial at the King's Bench the next day. Of all those who were condemned, John was one of the five chosen to suffer death.

Pending his appointment with the hangman, John was brought to the Tower and lowered into the Pit in the cellar of the White Tower where he met up with his brother Robert for a last farewell before being dragged off to Tyburn for hanging, drawing and quartering on Wednesday 12th February 1583-4, having spent only eight days in the Tower. He was beatified in 1886.

NUTTER, Robert, alias Askew or Rowley
Named in entries 75 & 91.

The younger brother of John Nutter; educated at Blackburn Grammar School, Lancashire; arrived at Rheims on 23rd August 1579; ordained at Soissons on 23rd December 1581 and sent to England on 16th January 1581-2. For the next two years, under his alias of Askew, he worked undetected in the Home Counties.

He was captured at Oxford and sent down to the Tower where the Diary reported his arrival on 2nd February 1583-4. Two days later, he was punished by being placed into the Pit. He was still there when his brother was lowered down to join him for a brief reunion before being taken off for execution.

Having seen John dragged away from him, Robert must have made quite a scene because Sir Owen Hopton was compelled to confine him in fetters for forty-three days and then confine him in the Scavenger's Daughter on two occasions.

The final claim for Robert in *Tower Bills* was for 21st January 1584-5 when he joined the first group of exiles destined for the coast of Normandy. Even though ordered not to return on pain of death, Robert assumed his new alias of Rowley and set off once more for service on the English mission.

He was captured at sea with three others who were brought ashore at Gravesend on 11th November 1585. Whilst there was no doubt that he intended to resume his missionary work, Robert denied the charge of entering the country illegally because he had been brought ashore 'against his will'. This argument saved him from condemnation.

He was firstly sent to the Marshalsea Prison whence, after his alias had been broken, he was moved to Wisbech some time in 1588. On 10th March 1600, he managed his escape and remained at liberty till May. On recapture, he had nothing to say in defence and was hanged, drawn and quartered at Lancaster on Saturday 26th July 1600. He was beatified on 22nd November 1987 (*Foley* and *Usherwood*).

ORTON, Henry
Named in entries 4, 11, 33 & (35).

Whereas this little known character was at Rome and left with the party on 18th April 1580, he was not studying for ordination but was 'a student of jurisprudence'.

Being recognised by Walsingham's agent Charles Sledd, Orton was placed into the Compter in the Poultry with Johnson on 12th July 1580 and moved to the Tower on 4th December 1580 when demands for his fees began to appear in *Tower Bills*. Being only a layman but a dedicated Catholic, he was tried and condemned for living under obedience to the Pope.

It should be noticed in the Bills for Lady Day and Midsummer 1582 that his name was clearly marked *mort* in anticipation of his execution; but he continued to feature in all subsequent demands without this comment. The final claim for his fees was dated 21st January 1584-5 and was marked 'dismyssed' to signify that he was the solitary layman banished with twenty Catholic priests to the coast of Normandy with order never to return on pain of death. Nothing more is known after his arrival in Normandy. It can only be assumed that he returned to the seminary to continue his studies of jurisprudence. There is no evidence of his ordination.

PASCHALL, John
Named in entries 8 and 14.

This manservant to Ralph Sherwin accompanied his master on the journey across Europe to serve on the English mission. At one stage of their travels, Paschall posed as the priest while Sherwin played the part of servant.

Both arrived in England in July 1580. Paschall was apprehended at some later date and placed into the Compter in the Poultry. The Lieutenant of the Tower received instructions on 24th December to accept him into custody with Hart and Bosgrave. The committal warrant gave authority for the use of 'the tortures' as the Lieutenant thought necessary (*APC 12:294*).

It has already been noticed that the arrival of these three men was wrongly dated as 29th December in the Diary. Having shown up this error, there was no method of confirming the statement shown for 15th January 1580-1 in which the diarist recorded,

> [Paschall] was led by fear of torture to make an open declaration against the faith' and was allowed free next day to the seduction of others.

PAYNE (PAINE), John
Named in entries 25, 32, 45 & 46.

The brother of Jerome Paine with whom he has often been confused; John was born in Peterborough, Northants and brought up as a member of the Church of England; details of his conversion to the Catholic faith are not known; entered the seminary at Douay in 1574 and served for a time as a bursar; he was ordained in 1576 and returned to England with Cuthbert Mayne in 1577.

John based himself at Ingatestone Hall, the home of the Petre family in Essex, whence he could minister to local recusants whilst posing as an estate worker. He was imprisoned briefly elsewhere in 1577, returned to Douay on gaining his liberty but came back to Ingatestone in 1578. It would appear that Paine was betrayed somehow by Walsingham's agent, George Eliot, which resulted in imprisonment at Greenwich on Walsingham's order.

Payne was brought to the Tower on 14th July 1581 and was named in a torture warrant on 14th August 1581, under terms of which he underwent severe racking in an endeavour to gain information about Robert Parsons (*APC 13:171-172*). After he had refused an offer of pardon if he would accept Anglican worship, order was given on 12th March 1581-2 for his delivery to the sheriff of Essex to face trial for living under obedience to the Pope.

At his trial he claimed 'his feet never did tread, his hands never did write, nor his wit ever invent any treason against Her Majesty'. The final demand for his fees in *Tower Bills* was dated 31st March 1582 and was annotated '*mort*'; but this somewhat premature because it was not until Monday 2nd April 1582 that he was hanged, drawn and quartered at Chelmsford, Essex. On account of his ministry to the region, he was so popular that the crowd pleaded with the hangman to allow him to hang until he was fully dead before the other mutilations. 'They very courteously caused men to hang on his feet' to speed up his death. John was one of the forty English martyrs canonised on 25th October 1970. The Bosworth Burse, a private collection, owns a representation of Christ rising from the Sacrament during the elevation of the Host at Mass. It is based upon a vision Paine had while he was at Douay.

PECKHAM, Sir George
Named in entry 9 only.

According to the diarist, Sir George was already in custody – probably in the Fleet prison – for failure to conform in religion. The diarist recorded his transfer to the Tower from another prison on 21st December 1580.

Whereas this date could not be confirmed from any official sources, it does tend to tie in very closely with the council's letter of 28th December 1580 (*APC*) when a John Babham was given permission to visit the prisoner with a view to discussing his living and payment of debts during restraint. Probably as a sign of failing health, the council granted Sir George the Liberty of the Tower on 7th February following and allowed his wife to join him from her place of imprisonment in the Fleet. His release, on a bond of £1,000 and a promise to conform, was approved on Wednesday 1st March, 1580-1; but this event passed without comment in the Diary.

PECKHAM, Lady

Although not named in the Diary, this lady was sent to the Fleet prison for her religious beliefs on some previous date. Instructions were issued by the council on 7th February 1580-1 for her to be 'enlarged therefrom and permitted to abide in the Tower with her husband', Sir George Peckham. She would have been liberated with him on 1 March 1580-1.

PIERPOINT (PARPOYNT or PERPOINT), Gervase
Named in entries 74 & 85.

It has already been noticed that the celebration of Mass during the Elizabethan era was illegal and therefore had to be conducted with as much secrecy as possible. At this distance in time, we can only imagine the looks of amazement on the faces of those caught out in such covert acts and on the faces of those making the discovery; it is difficult to determine who would have been the most shocked. But it is obvious that, when not one but *three* Masses are interrupted in adjoining rooms, all under the same roof of the leading prison of London second only to the Tower of London, reports and repercussions would ensue.

Such a report was made by the keeper of the Marshalsea prison on 24th August 1582 *(CRS, Miscellanea, Vol. 2, p. 221)*, one Mass in Richard Shelley's chamber conducted by Thomas Hartley; another in 'Denton's' chamber; and a third being celebrated in Gervase Pierpoint's chamber by Richard Norris.

Pierpoint was still named in the same prison in March 1582-3 *(ibid, p. 231)* but not in the next list so neatly compiled on 22nd March 1583-4 because, as the diarist noted, he had been removed to the Tower two months earlier, on 18th January. On the same day, William Shelley had been committed but no link, other than religion, could be found between the two prisoners, other than the suggestion of their undergoing torture by the rack on 12th February 1583-4 (unmentioned by *Langbein*). This session of torture is further discussed under Shelley.

Although the keeper of the Marshalsea had alluded to Pierpoint as 'gentleman', it will be seen from the *Tower Bills* (Appx 2) that claims for Pierpoint began on 19th January 1583-4 and continued through to 24th December 1584.

Because no claims for him were entered into the next available Bill beginning on 25th March 1585, it would seem he was removed from the Tower during the first three months of the year. He was listed as a prisoner in the Wood Street Compter in a report dated 30th November 1586 with recommendation for him 'to be continued in' (*CRS, Miscellanea, Vol 2, p. 262*). A later list from the same prison remarked that he had arrived there on 15th June 1586; but the few lists that now survive could give no clue as to where he was held from the time he left the Tower until reaching the Compter prison. By 1588, he was one of the many Catholics held at Wisbech Castle (*ibid. p. 279*).

He appears to have been one-and-the-same as the Jervys (Gervase) Pierpoint or Perpoint for whom orders were issued to the Lieutenant of the Tower on 6th July 1600 to accept him into custody along with Richard Thimbleby and Edward Fawcett and hold them until further examined.

Whilst Thimbleby and Fawcett must have arrived soon after this order was issued, it seems that Pierpoint was unfit to travel because, on 5th October 1600, the Warden of the Fleet was informed to deliver Pierpoint alone 'now that he is fit to travel'. The warden also explained that all earlier warrants to move him to the Tower had not been acted upon as the prisoner was 'too sicke to be removed'.

All three were granted liberty of the Tower on 14th November 1600 by reason of 'the indisposition of their health'. On 7th January following, the Lieutenant was told to deliver them to the sheriff of London who was advised to accept them and then place them into one of the prisons in the City until further instructions were issued. Nothing more was heard of them after this order.

PITT or PITTS, Arthur
Named in entries 42 & 91.

Born in 1557; left Douay for Rome in August 1577 and was one of the original students of the new English college that had been established there. Was ordained in June 1580; left Rome and made his way back for service in England by way of Rheims.

He was arrested with Haydock by Walsingham's agent on 2nd February and came to the Tower on 5th February 1581-2. Although indicted on 5th February 1583-4, it appears he was not condemned to death. Details are too vague to even try to comprehend the logic or reason behind the decision.

He remained at the Tower until 21st January 1584-5 when the last claim for his fees in *Tower Bills* was marked 'dismyssed' to show he was one of the group of twenty one banished from Tower Wharf that day.

In 1602, Pits spent a brief time in a French prison on a charge of disaffection to the King of France. After release, he crossed the Channel once more in the certain knowledge that, if caught this time, he would certainly meet his end. He took up residence with the Stonor family at Blount court, serving as family chaplain, and died some time after 1635, being buried in the church of Rotherfield Peppard, Oxfordshire.

POUND or POUNDS, Thomas
Named in entry 29 only.

Born on 29th May 1539 at Belmont, Hants; a nephew of the Earl of Southampton; became a great favourite at court after Elizabeth's accession in 1558 but then renounced this lifestyle in 1570 to embrace Catholicism. In 1574, whilst endeavouring to flee the country with an aim of enlisting into the Society of Jesus, he was arrested and, but for a few brief intervals, spent the next thirty years in as many as sixteen prisons on his own admission.

Although never ordained, he was admitted into the Society of Jesus as a lay brother on 1st December 1578, probably while in one of his places of confinement (*McCoog*). He was a prisoner at the Marshalsea in June 1580 when visited by Robert Parsons. His imprisonment there was not too severe as he was able to take Parsons to his room, serve a meal and discuss plans for the Jesuit mission in England.

Just before Parsons and Campion left London, Pound was able to absent himself from prison (probably by bribing the turnkey) and paid them a visit, urging them to publicise the fact that their mission was of a religious and not political nature.

Pound was brought in for his first spell in the Tower by order of the council on 14th August 1581. In a prisoner list from the latter part of 1582, he was named as one of four Tower prisoners who were paying their own diets, thus explaining his absence from *Tower Bills*. He was still in the Tower on 27th May 1585 when a certificate described him with Roscarrock as 'dangerous men fit to be banished' (*CRS, Miscellanea, Vol 2, p. 238*).

Whilst this was a time when many Romanists were being sent away with order never to return, Pound was not as fortunate but was removed to the White Lion prison on 1st September 1586. Two years later he was transferred to the Catholic concentration camp at Wisbech Castle.

Having been brought back from Wisbech on the strength of Bagshaw's testimony, Pound was firstly held in the Wood Street Counter. Evidence of his being removed therefrom were shown in the *Tower Bills* beginning on 25th March 1599. He might have been brought in before this date but the previous Bill is missing from the series.

In the summer months of 1601, Pound was moved with others to the castle at Framlingham. By July 1602, he had been moved yet again, this time to Newgate. *Caraman* was of the opinion that Pound was finally liberated in 1603 (see his *Translation of Weston's Autobiography*, p. 174); but the *Tower Bills* for Christmas 1604 and Lady Day 1605 provide evidence of his being brought back to the Tower on 3rd December 1604 and was held 'vntill the Three and twentieth of February, next following on which day he was delivered to the Warden of the ffleete by warrant of the Starrechamber'(*E 407-56*).

Pound later claimed to have spent as much as £4,000 in fines for his religious ideals. After final release from the Fleet prison, he lived out the rest of his life in London but died in his home town in Hampshire on 5th March 1615-6.

RICHARDSON, vere JOHNSON, Laurence
Named in entries 34, (36) & 51.

As an inherent part of their work on the English Mission, many seminary priests often assumed another name to protect their families either before ordination or on setting out for England. In most cases these aliases are known; but, in the case of this priest, his adopted name was used more often than his true name Johnson.

He was born in Great Crosby, Lancashire and was ordained from Douay in 1577; served on the Mission from 1577 to 1579 and then went back to Rheims; set out for England once more on 27th January 1580 and was arrested in his home county in the following year.

When brought down to London, he was placed into Newgate prison whence, on 16th November 1581, he was moved to the Queen's Bench to face trial at Westminster (entries 34 & 36). After trial and condemnation on 21st November 1581, he was brought to the Tower. Claims for him in *Tower Bills* only began to appear on 24th December 1581 but he might have been named in the previous Bill that is missing.

The final claim, prefixed *mort*, was dated 30th May 1582 on which date, with Filby, Cottam and Kirby, he was hanged, drawn and quartered at Tyburn, being the third to suffer at the hands of the state executioner. Richardson was beatified in 1886.

RISHTON, Edward
Named in entries 33 & (35).

Born in Lancashire in 1550; educated at Oxford; began studying theology at Douay on 1st October 1573; ordained 6th April 1577. Was one of the large group that left Rome with Robert Parsons, Edmund Campion and others on 18th April 1580. Rishton left for England on 5th June and was captured with his brother and other men from Lancashire at the sign of *The Red Rose* (or *Lion*) in Holborn towards the end of 1580. News of his capture reached Rheims in late December.

Rishton was placed in the Gatehouse prison whence his name was cited in the prisoner list of 23rd June 1581. He faced trial with other priests at Westminster on 14th November (entry 33) and was condemned to death on 20th November 1581 (entry 35). As such, his name was cited by John Hart when reporting the event in the Diary. For reasons that have never been understood, Rishton was not selected for execution but was removed to the King's Bench prison wherein he stayed for the next three years.

It must be stressed, for reasons already explained, that Rishton was never imprisoned in the Tower. The only time he saw the Tower as a prisoner was on the morning of 21st January 1584-5 when brought to the Wharf to join the other twenty exiles bound for Normandy.

Landed at Boulogne-sur-Mer and conducted to Abbeville, Rishton went to the college at Douay and then settled at Rheims on 8th March 1584-5. After a brief sojourn there, he proceeded to the university at Pont-a-Mousson in Lorraine with the intention of taking a degree in divinity. Rishton was singled out for his expertise in Latin to write a new continuator to a manuscript that had been started by Nicholas Sander. The confusion over *Rishton's Diary* is adequately discussed under 'Who Wrote the Diary'.

Rishton died of the plague but the date is uncertain. An entry in the records at his seminary showed his death on 29th June 1585; but this was then deleted as if the archivist had been mistaken. However, Dodd's *Church History* cites the same date of death 'of the plague' and goes on to say that Rishton was buried at Sainte-Menehould by the care of John Barnes, a Benedictine.

ROSCARROCK, Nicholas
Named in entries 4 & 13.

Probably born in 1549. For his poetical writings in support of the Catholic cause, he was brought to the Tower in the early part of 1580-1 and was sent to torture on the rack under authority of a warrant issued on 14th January (not mentioned in *Langbein*). *BDEC* was emphatic in saying he was confined to the Martin Tower, despite the presence of his undated inscription in the Well Tower (7) which reads,

NICOLAS ... CARROCKE

The authors of *RCHM* suggested he was a priest but there is no evidence of his ordination. The undated list of prisoners in 1582 quoted his name as 'Rose Carrick' when saying he was paying his own diet. Had he been a priest, he could not have done so. The 27th May 1585 list linked his name to Pound when describing them both as 'dangerous men fit to be banished' (*CRS, Miscellanea, Vol 2, p. 238*).

After five and a quarter years in the Tower, Roscarrock had allowed his debts to the LT to reach the astronomical figure of £140. It was no wonder that Hopton wrote to the council on 6th March 1585-6 pleading for Roscarrock's discharge. This was agreed soon afterwards.

Whereas Roscarrock later spent a time in the Fleet prison for his religion, he lived quietly at Haworth Castle from 1607 and probably died in 1634.

ROWSHAM (RUSHAM), Stephen
Named in entries 49, 54 & 78.

In the original Latin *Diarium*, this priest was shown as 'Rausamus' which was wrongly interpreted by *Bayley* as 'Ransom'. Much research time was wasted in trying to learn something of this character who, in the end, was found to be so well known by Catholic historians.

Stephen Rowsham was an Oxfordshire man who was educated at Oriel College in 1572; he then became the Anglican minister of St Mary's church at Oxford University in 1578. Shortly afterwards, he embraced Catholicism and fled to Rheims, arriving there on 23rd April 1581; ordained at Soissons on 29th September 1581; set out for service in England on 30th April 1582 and was arrested almost immediately on landing with Thomas Burns.

According to the Diary, both arrived on 19th May 1582; yet they were not shown in the *Tower Bill* for the quarter ending 24th June 1582. As the next bill is missing from the series, claims for Rowsham's fees, preceding those of 'Thomas Barnes', only began to emerge in the next bill starting on 30th September 1582 and continued through to 29th December 1583.

On 13th February following, the Diary recorded his move to 'another prison'. This is another of Hart's entries that is one day later than the official warrant issued the previous day wherein the council ordered Rowsham's transfer to the Marshalsea. The keeper of that prison repeatedly mentioned in his reports how he had received Rowsham on 12th February 1583-4 (*CRS, Miscellanea, Vol 2, pp. 233, 236 & 240*). He was kept there until September 1585 when he joined the second group of Catholics who were exiled to Normandy with order never to return on pain of death.

Nothing daunted, Stephen left Rheims once more for service in England on 7th February 1585-6 and was arrested almost a year later at the house of a widow Strange in Gloucestershire. Placed in confinement in the local tolbooth, he was instrumental in converting at least six of his fellow prisoners whilst awaiting the statutory death sentence for returning from exile.

It is some measure of the respect he commanded when many local inhabitants flocked to his prison to hear him celebrate his final Mass. A precise date of capture and execution has never been determined but it appears as if he was hanged, drawn and quartered some time in March 1586-7. It was certainly before 10th May 1587, on which date Humphrey Ely gave brief mention to his death in one of his letters. Rowsham was beatified on 22nd November 1987 (*Foley* and *Usherwood*).

SHELLEY or SHELLY, William
Named in entry 74 only.

(Not to be confused with 'Richard Shelly of ffindowe [*sic*] in Com. Sussex, gent' who was a prisoner in the Marshalsea at the same time and might have been related to the above).

The first intimation found of this esquire from Sutton in the County of Hereford being in some form of trouble with the authorities was located in a prison certificate from the Fleet prison *(CRS, Miscellanea Vol 2, p. 222)* in which the keeper reported that William Shelly had been discharged from custody by an order from the Council at Oatlands dated 16th September 1582. The certificate also explained that Shelly had provided a bond of £1,000 on condition of appearing before the council on 20th October.

The outcome of that interview could not be determined but, as William was not found in any later prison lists, it must be assumed that he continued at liberty on the agreed bail of £1,000. Whilst the diarist reported Shelley's arrival in the Tower with Gervase Pierpoint on 18th January 1583-4, there was no evidence to suggest that Shelley had been held in the Marshalsea with Pierpoint. More importantly, the *Diarium* gave no mention of the committal of Sir Henry Percy, 8th Earl of Northumberland nine days earlier.

For his involvement in the Ridolfi Plot in 1571, Sir Henry had previously spent almost two years in the Tower, during which period he had succeeded to the earldom. Once he had settled a fine of 5,000 marks (£3333.33), he gained his liberty in May 1573.

Under suspicion of further intrigues against Elizabeth I, the earl had been arrested on 15th December 1583 and committed to the Bloody Tower on 9th January following. It was later claimed that, as a result of Shelley and Pierpoint suffering torture on the rack under authority of a warrant dated 12th February 1583-4, 'they proved Henry Percy's guilt.'

Because the above warrant was unmentioned by *Langbein,* the only suggestion of interrogating Shelley was found in a Tower prison list dated 27th May 1585 *(CRS, Miscellanea, Vol. 2, p. 238)* in which recommendation was made that 'The Earl of Northumberland [is] to remaine as he doth untill William Shelley and Wicklife be examined.' The said list made no reference to Pierpoint and there was no way of learning who 'Wicklife' might have been. Slightly more than three weeks after the issue of this instruction, the earl was found dead in his cell on the night of 20th-21st June 1585; but his murder/suicide falls outside the range of this study.

It suffices to relate that, although Shelley had been named in the said list, it will be found from Appendix 2 that his name did not feature in *Tower Bills* as further evidence that he must have been a person of substance capable of paying his own fees. The list of 2nd July 1588 *(ibid, p. 281)* proved Shelley was still in custody but wrongly cited his date of committal as 11th January 1583-4. The same list explained he had been condemned for treason.

Shelley is known to have been one of the small group of Catholics who assembled with Philip Howard, Earl of Arundel (and Surrey) to celebrate a Mass at the height of the Armada scare later in July 1588. Whereas this small congregation later claimed they had offered prayers for the safety of all Catholics in England in fear of repercussions, it was later construed by the government as an appeal for a Spanish victory, causing further penalties for Howard. By the end of the month, the remnants of the Armada had scattered; yet after the incident, nothing more was found of Shelley.

SHERT (SHIRT or SKERT), John
Named in entries 34, (36) & 50.

Born near Macclesfield, Cheshire; educated Oxford; arrived at Douay on 9th January 1576 and sent to Rome as subdeacon; ordained at Rome; reached Rheims on 23rd July 1578 and departed for work in England on 27th August of that year; was able to work undetected till 18th August 1580 when a spy's report gave mention to one 'Short, alias Stalie in Holborn'. A hunt was instigated yet it took some considerable time until he fell into the net.

He was finally brought to the Tower on 14th July 1581. With others, he faced trial in November (entries 34 & 36) and was condemned for the ficticious plot at Rome and Rheims.

In view of the above date of committal, claims for his fees must have featured in the missing Christmas 1581 *Tower Bill*; but he is named 'John Shorte' in the next two Bills (25th March 1582 to 27th May 1582) in which his name has the usual suffix *mort* to mark him out as a dead man. However, there are sound reasons for believing he was removed from the Tower – probably to the Marshalsea – because Sir Owen Hopton then received instructions to accept him back into his custody on 27th May 1582 in company with Thomas Ford and Robert Johnson. All three were hanged, drawn and quartered at Tyburn the next day, being Monday 28th May 1582. Shert was the second to suffer and was beatified in 1886.

SHERWIN, Ralph
Named in entries 4, 6, 7, 33, (35) & 39.

Born Rodesley, Derbyshire in 1549; fellow of Exeter College, Oxford; embraced the Catholic faith in 1574; joined the English College at Douay whence he was ordained on 23rd March 1577; sent to Rome to assist in founding the new English college there; left Rome with a small contingent of English priests on 18th April 1580 and reached Rheims for final briefing on 31st May. Was at Rouen on 3rd July and must have crossed to England for service on the Mission shortly after. Sherwin was arrested at Nicholas Roscarrock's house in London and placed into the Marshalsea some time before December 1580.

On 4th December 1580 he was moved to the Tower where, according to *Anstruther*, he 'was tortured several times' but any warrants that might have authorised this are no longer on record. Nonetheless, it is usually claimed he was racked on two occasions and deprived of food for several days in an attempt to learn who had reconciled him into the Catholic church. In the hope of bringing about his conformity, he was offered a bishopric in the Church of England.

Due to some missing documents from *Tower Bills*, the final claim for him was dated 24th June 1581. However, it is known that he faced trial with six others (entry 33) and was condemned to death on 20th November 1581 (entry 35) for the fictitious plot at Rome and Rheims.

Returned to the Tower, he only emerged therefrom on Friday 1st December 1581 when he was dragged off on a wicker hurdle accompanied by Edmund Campion and Alexander Briant to be hanged, drawn and quartered at Tyburn, being the second to suffer. Having seen Alexander Briant's sufferings, Sherwin took the executioner's blood-stained hand and kissed it before kneeling down in silent prayer. Once the noose had been fastened about his neck, the sheriffs called upon him to confess his treason to which he retorted, 'If to be a perfect Catholic is to be a traitor, then I am a traitor'. His last words before the cart was drawn away from under his feet were, 'Jesus, Jesus, be to me a Jesus'. He was allowed to hang until all signs of life had gone before being cut down for the other barbarities. *John Stow* was at fault to say they suffered on 1st September 1582. Sherwin was beatified in 1886 and canonised on 25th October 1970.

SLACK, SLACKE or SLAKE, Richard
Named in entries 53 & 91.

Occasionally but quite wrongly shown as 'William'. Richard was ordained at Laon on 19th December 1579 and was sent to service in England on 21st April 1581. He was captured at 'Sophley', Leicestershire and sent down to the Tower arriving, on evidence of the Diary, on 23rd July 1582.

In the absence of the relevant *Tower Bill*, claims for the fees for one 'Richard Clarke' from 30th September to Christmas Day 1582 can only allude to this priest who then began to feature in all subsequent Bills under his correct name.

These demands continued through to 21st January 1584-5 when he was one of the group of twenty-one Catholics loaded onto a galleon at Tower Wharf for exile to Normandy. After travelling around Europe, he arrived at Rheims on 23rd April 1588 and was still on the teaching staff there on 3rd December 1594, after which nothing more is known.

SMITH, William

Unmentioned in the Diary, this missionary priest was brought from the Marshalsea Prison to be loaded onto the waiting ship at Tower Wharf on 21st January 1584-5 (entry 91). He made a successful return to England and continued his missionary work without detection. He was still living in England in 1612 when described as 'a grave ancient priest and a very good linguist'.

PERSONS NAMED IN THE DIARY

SOMERVILLE or SOMERVYLE, Elizabeth
Named in entry 65 only.

Committed the same day as Mary Arden, this lady was described in the Diary as the sister-by-blood of John Somerville. She was likewise spared after her condemnation at the Guildhall. The claims for her fees in *Tower Bills* were precisely the same as those of Mary Arden.

SOMERVILLE or SOMERVYLE, John
Named in entries 62, 65, 69 & 71.

Born 1560; married Margaret Arden, the daughter of Edward Arden. Even whilst Sir Francis Walsingham's agents were busy tracking the movements of Francis Throckmorton, their attention was distracted by the irregular behaviour of John Somerville. Reports were coming in of his having boasted a number of times in the north of England that he intended to go down to London to shoot the queen with a dagg or small pistol.

That the culprit was not entirely of sound mind was of no consequence for Walsingham. By linking Somerville to the Ardens and Throckmortons, it was felt that the planned assassination was an integral part of Throckmorton's design or even a bye-plot. To protect the queen, Somerville had to be stopped and interrogated; and so he was brought to the Tower.

The Diary recorded his arrival on 30th October 1583; yet claims for him in *Tower Bills* were seen to start the previous day. This was just one of many instances on which the diarist reported an event the day after it happened. On being questioned, probably by use of torture for which a warrant no longer exists, Somerville uttered sentiments that tended to implicate his wife, mother and father-in-law, and the family priest, Hugh Hall. Order was given for their committal.

All five faced arraignment at the Guildhall on 16th December 1583 and were condemned for compassing and imagining the queen's final destruction. On Thursday 19th December 1583, Edward Arden and Somerville were transferred to Newgate in readiness for execution the next day. Within a space of two hours or so of arriving at Newgate, Somerville was found strangled in his cell. (*A.H. Cook* was at fault to show he died in the Tower.)

Rumours were put about that Somerville had been secretly hanged in Newgate to 'avoid a mischief' when addressing the crowds at Tyburn next day. Due to his known insanity, it seems more likely that he had simply taken his own life whilst the balance of his mind was disturbed. His head was later hacked off and set up over London Bridge alongside that of his father-in-law.

SOMERVILLE or SOMERVYLE, Margaret
Named in entry 65 only.

The daughter of Edward and Mary Arden who married John Somerville. When questioned, John had given the council reason to suppose that his wife was implicated in his plan to murder the queen, in consequence of which Margaret was another of those committed on 16th November 1583. In the absence of the relevant *Tower Bill*, claims for her fees only began to emerge on 26th March 1584. Whereas the evidence of Hugh Hall had been taken as proof of her guilt and resulted in her condemnation at the Guildhall, Margaret was certainly allowed free but not, as *Bayley* suggested, 'after the death of her husband in the same year'.

Claims for her fees did not conclude until 22nd February 1585-6 which, coming before the end of the quarter, must have been the true date on which she departed, proving she was held much longer than other writers suggest.

STEVENS or STEPHENS, Jerome
Named in entries 9 & 14.

His name was firstly located as 'Jerome Stephins, gent' in a list headed *Prisoners for Religion* which probably dates from April 1580 and which stated he was detained in Newgate (*CRS, Miscellanea, Vol 1, p. 60*). His transfer to the Tower 'from another prison' was recorded in the Diary for 23rd December 1580 (entry 9) but confirmation could not be found in official documents.
John Hart observed on 15th January 1580-1 (entry 14):

> ...Jerome Stevens, layman, [was] led by fear of torture to make an open declaration against the [Catholic] faith...the following day [he was] sent away to the seduction of others.

As he had not been named in the *Tower Bill* for Lady Day 1581, he must still have been capable of paying his own fees, despite the earlier expenses of Newgate.

STEVENSON or STEPHENSON, Thomas
Named in entries 77 & 91.

Born at Windleston, County Durham in 1552; went to Rheims on 22nd June 1581 and was ordained at Soissons on 23rd December 1581. Sent to the English Mission on 13th April 1583. After only ten months at liberty he was captured and placed into the Tower on 13th February 1583-4 when claims for his fees began in *Tower Bills*.

He faced trial on 4th May 1584 and was condemned for entering the realm on papal affairs. Spared the death sentence, he was one of the twenty one exiles loaded onto ship at Tower Wharf on 21st January 1584-5 for the journey to the coast of Normandy.

He enrolled into the Society of Jesus at Brno on 11th December 1585 (*McCoog*) and served as a professor of rhetoric, Greek and Hebrew. Despite the Order for Exile, he was on service in England from 1609 to 1613 and probably much longer. In 1621, he was ministering in Suffolk but moved to Watten to serve as confessor that year. Remained there until 1623 when he returned briefly to Liege. He died at Watten on the night of 22nd/23rd March 1624.

STONOR (STONER), John
Named in entries 28 & 47.

The second son of Sir Francis and Lady Cecilia Stonor. Sir Francis died in August 1550, leaving his widow to care for her children at Stonor House, Oxfordshire. It was John's idea to offer the use of the house for the printing of Edmund Campion's *Rationes Decem*.

Subsequent to Campion's capture and questioning in the Tower, the Privy Council wrote to Sir Henry Billingbeare on 2nd August 1581 ordering him to 'repair to Lady Stonor's house and to search for certain Latin books dispersed already in Oxford at the last commencement, which... have been printed in a wood... And further for the press and other instruments of printing, thought to be there remaining.'

The raid on the house took place on the night of 12/13th August, resulting in the apprehension of those named in entry 28. As the son of the house, John Stonor was committed to the Tower on 13th August and held for nearly nine months. During this time Sir Owen Hopton's daughter, Cicely, fell in love with him, was converted to the Catholic faith and was employed in carrying letters between prisoners in the Tower and those in the Marshalsea. When news of her treachery was disclosed, Sir Owen was almost dismissed. It was submitted in a letter dated 27th May 1585 (*CRS Miscellanea, Vol 1, p. 238* quoting *CSPD Elizabeth Vol CLXXVIII, no. 74*):

> 'That her Matie may bee pleased to remove the Lieutenant of the Tower: and to give him some recompence in respect of his povertie and that he bought the office. Sr Drew Drurie a fyt man to bee put in his place.'

However, Sir Owen weathered the storm and remained in office until 6th July 1590 when he handed over to Michael Blount, esq. who was eventually knighted but replaced by Sir Dru Drury in December 1595.

On 25th April 1582, bonds were accepted from John's elder brother, Francis, to convey him out of the Tower for three months religious instruction. The council ordained, 'If he does not yield to conformity, he is to be returned to any prison nominated by the Council'. The fact that he is not named in any later prisoner lists does not mean that he continued to conform in religion after release. In fact, he held true to his Catholicism, went abroad and entered the army of Alessandro Farnese, Duke of Parma, Governor of the Spanish Netherlands.

However, following the execution of Mary, Queen of Scots in February 1586-7, John considered that armed intervention against Elizabeth I was no longer justified because the young King James VI of Scotland would succeed as a Catholic King James I of England (and not, as it later emerged, as a Protestant one).

Despite this fact, the Spaniards distrusted the regiment of British exiles in their army and ploughed ahead with their plans for armed invasion. The lack of success by the Armada in 1588 led many of the British officers to resign their commissions, including John Stonor. He settled in Louvain where he married a Belgian lady, Catherine de Lyere.

Towards the end of Elizabeth's reign, John petitioned Robert Cecil asking him to intercede with the queen and allow him to return home. Nonetheless, John remained in the Netherlands until the demise of Elizabeth in March 1603 and then immediately returned to England. His elder brother, Francis, who had been knighted by the queen on 18th September 1601, wrote to Lord Cecil on 18th July 1603, explaining that his younger brother had recently returned and was seeking permission from James I/VI to remain. Enclosed with Sir Francis' letter was an appeal from John to Lord Cecil in like vein.

John's hopes were dashed to failure and he was compelled to return to Louvain where his years of exile came to an end with his death on 30th July 1626, aged nearly seventy. He was buried alongside his wife in the church of St Pierre (*Stonor*).

TEDDER, William

Although unmentioned in the Diary, this seminary priest was brought to Tower Wharf from the Marshalsea prison on 21st January 1584-5 to join the other exiles (entry 91) bound for the coast of Normandy. He later returned to England and recanted his Catholic principles.

THOMSON or TOMSON, Christopher
Named in entries 12 & 91.

(*Bayley* was at fault to translate his name as 'Tonson'.)

A Londoner who was ordained at Cambrai on 6th April 1677; he left Louvain on 24th April 1577 for service in England and was captured before 3rd November 1578. He was placed into the Marshalsea on 11th November charged with 'Papistry'.

Moved to the Tower on 24th December 1580 when claims for his fees began to appear in *Tower Bills*. The Diary wrongly dated his arrival to 3rd January 1580-1. It also claimed he was sent to the rack the same day but no warrant of authority was found on record.

Claims for his fees came to an end on 21st January 1584-5 when he was one of the first group of twenty-one exiles. Nothing more is known of him after he landed in Normandy.

THROCKMORTON, Francis
Named in entries 64, 67, 69 & 80.

Sir John's eldest son and a nephew of Sir Nicholas Throckmorton; born in 1554. Francis had previously been implicated in a number of Catholic plots abroad but, when he came to England and began setting up lines of communication between Mendoza, the Queen of Scots and the French embassy, Sir Francis Walsingham's agents began to take a keen interest in his activities.

It was considered that he was seeking out ways of organising a Spanish invasion to rid the throne of Elizabeth once and for all. The affair passed into history as 'The Throckmorton Plot'. The unrelated and scatterbrain scheme by which John Somerville planned to murder the queen forced Walsingham to bring forward his plans for Francis Throckmorton. When his house was searched, a number of incriminating documents came to light causing the owner's arrest.

He arrived in the Tower on 13th November 1583. Five days later, Walsingham sent a note to Thomas Wilkes asking him to bring Thomas Norton with him next day 'to witness the racking of Francis Throckmorton'. If they had abided by this letter – and there is no reason for doubting they did so – this first session on the rack would have taken place on 19th of the month; yet the Diary, often at fault with dates, dated this torture to 23rd November (not mentioned by *Langbein*).

It was on 21st May 1584 when Francis finally faced arraignment at the Guildhall but he was not put to death that same day as was shown in the *DNB*. In this case the Diary was correct to show he died on Friday 10th July 1584. This was also reported on the same date by *John Stow* who wrote in his *Annales*,

> [He was] conveyed by water to Black Friars Stairs; thence by land to the Old Bailey without Newgate where he was delivered to the Sheriffs of London, laid on a hurdle, drawn to Tyburn and there hanged, drawn and quartered.

When the Diary was reproduced by *Bayley*, the author or his printers wrongly inserted a 'June' heading where the original Latin edition had shown 'July' leading to a misunderstanding that the execution had taken place on 10th June 1584.

THROCKMORTON (THROGMORTON), George or Thomas
Named in entry 66 only.

In the Diary for 17th November 1583, it was shown that 'George Throckmorton, the brother of Francis [was] apprehended' which leads to a belief that he must have been placed with the other plotters in the Tower. However, Cassel's *History of England* alluded to a brother named Thomas who 'was arrested at about the same time as his brother Francis after Walsingham's agents had intercepted some letters addressed to him'. Nothing more was found on this enigmatic character.

TIRWHIT, TIRUIT, TIRWIGHT or TIRWRIGHT, Robert
Named in entry 2 only.

A younger son of Sir Robert Tirwhit, the order for Robert to be brought in to join his elder brother was issued on 26th June 1580 and not 19th of the month as suggested by the Diarist. Like his elder brother, Robert was not mentioned in *Tower Bills* as he had sufficient funds to pay his fees. Robert could not have died 'soon after' as submitted by John Hart; but, due to the complexity surrounding the assumed death of one of the family, the case is more closely examined at Appendix 10 and adjoining Annexes.

TIRWHIT, TIRUIT, TIRWIGHT or TIRWRIGHT, William
Named in entry 1 only.

As the Diarist stated, he was the eldest son of Sir Robert Tirwhit, a rich property owner from Kettleby, Lincolnshire. William was certainly placed into the Tower before his brother but an exact date could not be confirmed. We can only assume that John Hart's dating was fairly close to the date of committal. William was not named in the *Tower Bills* because he had sufficient funds to pay his own prisoner fees. The charge of hearing Mass at the wedding of his sister Ursula to Lord Edmund Sheffield is borne out by the *Declaration of Richard Smith* (annex 1 to Appx 10). Subsequent to his brother, Robert, joining him in prison on 26th June 1580, order was issued by the Privy Council next day for their separate examination.

On 11th January 1580-1, the Dean of Lincoln was granted access to speak with both brothers on 'their obstinacy in religion'. Sir Owen Hopton,

Lieutenant of the Tower, was authorised on Tuesday 13th June 1581 to release them both on bonds – William for £300 and Robert £200. Next day, the council gave order for them to be handed over to the Dean of Lincoln to receive religious instruction in the established church.

Whereas both brothers returned to Lincoln, they failed to heed the dean's lessons and, due to the 'great resort that is had unto them', they were therewith brought back to London and placed in the Fleet prison before the end of the year.

As we have noticed, there is a cause for the beatification of one of the Tirwhit brothers but, as the circumstances are so confused, he has been classed as one of the *Dilati*. From the evidence presented above it can be seen that neither William nor Robert died in the Tower in 1580 as was suggested in the *Diarium* and in the original cause for martyrdom. By the same token, there is no evidence of their dying in the Fleet in the following year. William was buried near his father in Bigby church in 1591. For more details of the Martyrdom, *see* Appendix 10 and Annex 1 & 2.

TUCKER, John
Named in entries 28 & 56.

Yet another of Brinkley's printers who was captured at Stonor House and arrived in the Tower on 13th August 1581. Whereas John Hart alluded to his being moved to 'another prison' on 16th September 1581, the keeper of the Marshalsea repeatedly mentioned in his reports (*CRS, Miscellanea, Vol 2, pp. 233, 236 & 242*) that he had received him on 23rd August 1581. In an earlier list (*ibid. p. 231*) John Tucker is named 'priest' by the keeper of the Marshalsea, probably due to his pious behaviour.

Whereas his companions Harris and Harvey were removed from the Marshalsea prison some time after 8th April 1584, John Tucker was still named in the Marshalsea list of July 1586 and might have stayed there even longer. He was patently a more obstinate Romanist who would not so readily conform. For this reason, it can only be surmised that he carved his initials 'I.T.' at the end of a Latin lament in inscription 64 in the Beauchamp Tower. It is dated 1581 and reads:

SPIRITUS CERTO LOQVITVR
NAM IN HOC LABORAMVS ET
PROBIS AFFICIMVR QVOD SPEM
FIXAM HABEAMVS IN DEO
VIVENTEO EST SALVATOR
OMNIVM MA 'E FIDELIVM
LTIMO...

(This is a faithful saying and worthy of all acceptance. For therefore we both labour and suffer reproach, because we trust in the living God, who is Saviour of all men, especially of those that believe...)

There is evidence of a man named Tucker being held at the Tower in 1588 but details about him are too vague to say if it might have been the printer shown here or if he might have been executed in the wake of the Armada.

WARMINGTON, William

Although unmentioned in the Diary, this seminary priest was brought to Tower Wharf from the Marshalsea prison on 21st January 1584-5 to join the other exiles (entry 91) bound for the coast of Normandy. He later returned to England and recanted his Catholic principles.

WEBLIN or WEBLEY, William
Named in entry 27 only.

Another husbandman who, having been captured with Manfield from their hiding place in a pigeon house at Lyford, came to the Tower on 22nd July 1581.

When recording his committal in the Diary, the author named him as 'Valbinus' that leads to a translation of 'Weblin'; but most accounts show him as Webley which was the name used by George Eliot.

With Manfield, Webley then agreed to conform under fear of torture and, with order to undergo instruction from a minister, was granted his freedom if he truly repented.

WORTHINGTON, Thomas, alias Lancaster
Named in entries 82 & 91.

Born either in 1548 or 1554; son of Peter and Isabel of Standish, Lancs; educated Oxford; travelled to Douay in 1573 and ordained at Cambrai 6th April 1577; sent to England on 9th September 1578 but went back to Rome in 1579. Left Rheims on 27th January 1580 and captured by Topcliffe in London.

According to the Diary, he arrived as a prisoner on 19th June 1584 but, in the absence of the relevant *Tower Bill* that would have shown this, claims for him only began to emerge in the next Bill starting on 1st October 1584.

These demands came to an end on 21st January 1584-5 when he was another of the exiles loaded onto the waiting ship at Tower Wharf. After performing a number of clerical duties at Brussels, Douay and Rome, he came back to England in 1615 and continued working for the Catholic cause till his death in 1622 (*DNB*) or 1626 or 1627 (*Anstruther*).

YATE or YATES, Edward
Named in entries 27 & 41.

The younger brother of Francis Yate, owner of Lyford Grange, was taken from his hiding place by George Eliot and his helpers (Appx 3) and arrived in the procession on 22nd July 1581. Edward was later described as 'a very earnest Papist and one that gave great entertainment to any of that sect'.

Entry 41 for 23rd January 1581-2 gave reference to Yate being sent to another prison and this was confirmed by written records of prisoners by the keeper of the Gatehouse prison, Westminster who recorded (*CRS, Miscellanea, Vol 2, p. 255*):

> Edward Yatte, a barkeshyere man borne, and sent in by Mr. Leefetenante of the Towewer [sic] by your honors a yere since.

Yate made another appearance in the Gatehouse certificate of 8th April 1584 but was not named in any subsequent lists, suggesting he must have finally conformed in religion.

BRIEF BIBLIOGRAPHY

Cook, DCM, MM, BEM, Arthur Henry. *Prisoners of the Tower*

A handwritten manuscript locally produced within the Tower in the 1950s but never published, although copies were presented to the Guildhall Library and British Library.

Seniority and Succession Rolls of the Corps of Yeoman Warders

Compiled in longhand into a blue bound volume by an anonymous Yeoman Warder [?] towards the end of the 19th Century and thenceforward constantly but irregularly maintained within the Tower of London until the 1980s, this historic record had then fallen into disrepair and disarray. Considering the earlier entries to be historically accurate and complete, Brian Harrison personally undertook to rewrite the Record from 1900 to date into a purpose-bound volume in his own Regimental colours (green and red for King's Royal Rifle Corps). As new Warders arrived, their personal details were – and are still – entered into this unique volume.

There had never been an intention of revising the pre-1900 era but, as further data was brought to light from his studies, Yeoman Warder Harrison could no longer find sufficient space in the blue book to insert such new discoveries. As a result, a second matching volume was purchased by the Yeoman Body into which Mr Harrison could transfer or correct all of the blue book information alongside the extra information, yet still leaving space for any more details that might be revealed in the future. Both volumes were presented to his replacement Honorary Archivist when Mr Harrison retired with a promise that, if ever these volumes were allowed to fall into neglect, future archivists would never be forgiven.

Tower Bills

An incomplete series held at the Public Record Office under E407-56. Although outside the range of this particular study, the academic reader might wish to know that certain other bills have been located under:

BL Harleian 284 Fo 96-99 (31st October 1551 to 30th April 1552)
BL Egerton MS 2723 Fo 89 (25th June to 10th October 1568)
CSPD, Elizabeth Vol lxxvii n.46 (1st February to 7th April 1571)
ibid. Vol lxxviii, n33,34 (5th April to 26th June 1571)

BL Egerton MS 806, Fo 26-27 (25th December 1591- 25th March 1591-2)
BL Add MS 38,843, Fo 1 (24th June to 29th September 1599)
BL Add MS 34,195, Fo 82 (25th June to 29th September 1680) also reproduced in *Bayley*, Part 2, p xc but excluding 'Sum Total – £194. 18s. 6.1/4d'.
Bayley, Part 2, p xc – xci (26th March to 24th June 1681) – not located elsewhere and excluding 'Sum Total – £165. 16s. 2.3/4d'.
Bayley, Part 2, p xci-ii (25th June to 29th September 1681) – not located elsewhere and excluding 'Sum Total – £308. 19s. 1d'.
BL Add MS 34,195, Fo 86 (26th December 1681 to 25th March 1682)
Bayley, Part 2, p xcii (25th June to 29th September 1682) not located elsewhere and excluding 'Sum Total – £155. 2s. 1.1/4d'.
Bayley, Part 2, p xciii-xciv (25th June to 29th September 1683) not located elsewhere and excluding 'Sum Total – £246. 2s. 3.1/4d'.

It is also relevant to note that the Bill covering the period from 29th September to 25th December (Michaelmas quarter) 1598 turned up at auction, to be purchased for the Royal Armouries. Another, covering prisoners of the Second Jacobite Rising and endorsed with the signature of King George II, was kindly presented to the Tower by a collector of Jacobean memorabilia.

Registers of the Chapel Royal of St Peter ad Vincula

These are held at the Tower and maintained on a regular basis by the Clerk of the Chapels Royal. During his time as a Yeoman Warder, Mr Harrison was able to transcribe the entries for burials and, with a description of all of the Chapel Monuments and Memorials, has aspirations for publishing his findings. Work is also in progress in transcribing the entries for Baptisms and Weddings. At the time of writing, plans are being mooted for placing everything on the Internet but a decision still has to be reached.

PRINTED WORKS
General – Tower of London

Abbott, Geoffrey. *Tortures of the Tower of London.* (London, 1986)
Bayley, John Whitcomb. *History and Antiquities of the Tower of London.* (T. Cadell, 2-volume set, 1825 & 1830)
Brand, Rev. John. *An Account of the Inscriptions on the Walls, Chiefly in Beauchamp Tower.* (Royal Society of Antiquaries, 1796)
Britton, J & E.W. Brayley. *Memoirs of the Tower of London.* (London, 1830)
Chandlery, P.J. *The Tower to Tyburn.* (Sands & Co. London, 1924)
Dick, Wm Robertson. *Inscriptions and Devices in the Beauchamp Tower...* (Peter Ramage, 1853)

RCHM *Royal Commission on Historical Monuments (England) Volume 5 – London East.* (HMSO, 1930)

General History and Reference

Anstruther, Godfrey. *The Seminary Priests.* (4 Vols) (Durham, 1968)
  A Hundred Homeless Years. (Blackfriars, 1958)
Bellamy, John. *The Tudor Law of Treason – An Introduction.* (Routledge and Kegan Paul, 1979)
Bellenger, Dominic. *English & Welsh Priests 1588-1800.* (Bath, 1984)
Buckley, Theodore. *Foxe's Book of Martyrs.* (Routledge & Sons, undated but possibly a WW2 economy edition)
Burford, E.J. *In The Clink.* (New English Library, 1977)
Burnett, Gilbert. *History of the Reformation.* (2 Volumes) (Richard Chiswell, London 1681)
Byrne, Richard. *Prisons and Punishments of London* (Harrap, 1989)
Camm, Dom Bede. *Forgotten Shrines.* (MacDonald & Evans, London 1910)
Catholic Record Society. *Miscellanea Series, Vols 1-5 and Vol 60*
Catholic Truth Society. *The Martyrs of England and Wales 1535-1680.* (Pamphlet H.469, London 1985)
Cheney, C.R. ed. *Handbook of Dates for Students of English History.* (Royal Historical Society, 1978)
Dasent, J.R. *Acts of the Privy Council of England.* (London 1921- 1938)
Deacon, Richard. *A History of the British Secret Service.* (Muller, 1969)
Farmer, David Hugh. *The Oxford Dictionary of Saints.* (OUP, 1987)
Foley, Rt Rev. B.C. *The Eighty-Five Blessed Martyrs Beatified 22 November 1987.* (Catholic Truth Society, 1987)
Fryde, E.B., Greenway, D.E., Porter, S. & Roy, I, editors *Handbook of British Chronology, Third Edition.* (Royal Historical Society, 1986)
Gasquet, Francis A. *Henry VIII and the English Monasteries.* (Hodges, 1888)
Gillow, Joseph. *Bibliographical Dictionary of English Catholics.* (Franklin, NY, 1968 reprint)
Gordon, Charles. *The Old Bailey & Newgate.* (T. Fisher Unwin, 1902)
Jenkins, Elizabeth. *Elizabeth and Leicester.* (Gollancz, 1961)
Johnson, Paul. *Elizabeth I – A Biography.* (Holt, Rinehart and Winston, 1974)
Langbein, Prof. John H. *Torture and the Law of Proof.* (University of Chicago Press, 1976)
Leader, John Daniel. *Mary Queen of Scots in Captivity.* (Leader and Sons, 1880)
Lemon, R. et al. *Calendars of State Papers Domestic Series.* (90 volumes) (London 1856-1872)
Lewis, David. ed. *The Rise and Growth of the Anglican Schism.* by Nicolas Sander. (Burns & Oates, 1877)

Marks, Alfred. *Tyburn Tree – Its History and Annals.* (Brown, Langham & Co., 1908)
McCoog, Thomas M. SJ. *English and Welsh Jesuits Vol 1* (CRS, 1994)
English and Welsh Jesuits Vol 2 (CRS, 1995)
Newton, Douglas. *Catholic London.* (Robert Hale, 1950)
Oxford University Press. *Dictionary of National Biography.* (63 Vols).
 It must be appreciated that the most recent and currently available impression at the time of writing was published in 1969. The author is fully aware of the plans and preparations for the *New DNB* that is envisaged to appear in 2003 and has kept the compilers regularly informed of the many errors he has encountered during his consultaions from the *Old DNB*, trusting these shall find their correct place in the new volumes.
Plowden, Alison. *Danger to Elizabeth.* (Macmillan, 1973)
Pollard, A.F. *Tudor Tracts 1532-1588.* (Archibald Constable)
Read, Conyers. *Mr Secretary Walsingham and Queen Elizabeth.* (Clarendon Press, 1925)
Rumbelow, Donald. *The Triple Tree.* (Harrap, 1982)
Sheppard, Edgar. *The Old Royal Palace of Whitehall.* (Longmans, Green & Co., 1902)
Stow, John. *The Survey of London.* (J.M. Dent & Sons, 1929 ed)
 Annales or a General Chronicle of England. Continued and augmented by Edmund Howes (Richard Meighen, London, 1631)
Tanner, J.R. *Tudor Constitutional Documents.* (Cambridge Univ. Press, 1951)
Usherwood, Stephen and Elizabeth. *We Die for the Old Religion.* (Sheed & Ward, London, 1987)
Various Editors. *Calendars of Patent Rolls.* (72 Volumes).
 Calendars of Close Rolls. (47 Volumes) (Published 1892-1963)
Weinreb, Ben & Hibbert, Christopher. *The London Encyclopaedia.* (London, 1983)

Biographies and Autobiographies

Burton, Edwin & J.H. Pollen. *Lives of the English Martyrs.* (Longmans, Green & Co., 1914)
Caraman, Philip. *John Gerard – The Autobiography of an Elizabethan.* (Longmans, Green & Co. 1951)
 William Weston – The Autobiography of an Elizabethan. (Whitefriars Press, 1955)
Kendall, Alan. *Robert Dudley, Earl of Leicester.* (Cassell, 1980)
Reynolds, E.E. *Campion and Parsons.* (Catholic Book Club, 1982)
Rupp, Gordon. *Thomas More – The King's Good Servant.* (Collins, 1978)
Stonor, R.J. *Stonor.* (Johns, 1951)
Waugh, Evelyn. *Edmund Campion, Jesuit and Martyr.* (Longmans, Green & Co., 1935)

INDEX

A

Abbeville, Normandy 131, 213
Abdy, Patrick. *see* Addie, etc
Addie, Addy or Ady (Abdy), Patrick 65, 66, 86, 99, 169, 170, 187
Alençon and Anjou, Duke of. *see* François
Alfield or Aufield, Thomas, alias Badger 53, 82, 171
All Saints Church, Bigby 150, 152, 155
Allen, Gabriel 180
Allen, William 24, 29, 30, 49, 57, 164, 171, 179, 194
Almond, John 143
Alphilde, Thomas. *see* Alfield or Aufield
Andrews, Thomas 30, 31, 184, 193
Anstruther, Godfrey 169, 170, 173, 178, 182, 183, 193, 217, 226
Aprice or Price, William 64, 65, 85, 86, 99, 171
Arden, Edward 58-60, 63, 84, 97, 171, 172, 219, 220
Arden, Francis 62, 63, 85, 98, 99, 172
Arden, John 63, 128, 172
Arden, Margaret 58, 84
Arden, Mary 58, 60, 84, 98, 172, 173, 219, 220
Ardent or Arden, John 63
Armagh, Archbishop of. *see* Creagh, etc.
Arrowsmith, Edmund 143
Arundel, Earl of. *see* Howard, Philip, 17th Earl
Askew, Robert. *see* Nutter, Robert, etc.

B

Babham, John 209
Babington Conspiracy 178, 186, 200
Badger, Thomas. *see* Alfield or Aufield
Bagshaw, Christopher 212
Bankside 120
Barlow, Ambrose 143
Barnes, John 173, 214
Barnes, Thomas (John) 53, 54, 64, 66, 85, 86, 95-97, 100, 132, 133
Barnley, Lancashire 206
Bayley, John Whitcomb 14-16, 40-42, 45, 49, 52-54, 58, 60-62, 64, 66, 72, 87, 169, 172, 192, 220, 224
Beare, Anthony (Yeoman Warder) 167
Beauchamp Tower 124, 182, 203, 204, 225
Bedale, Yorkshire 200
Bedford, Earl of. *see* Russell, Francis, 6th Earl
Bell Tower 203, 204
Bellamie, Henry (Yeoman Warder) 168
Belmont, Hampshire 211
Berkshire, Sheriff of 44
Bigby Church 225
Bigby, Lincolnshire 151, 152
Bilboes. *see* Leg Irons 129
Billingbeare, Sir Henry 221

Birmingham, William 186
Bishop or Bushoppe, William 66, 132, 133, 173
Black Friars Stairs 223
Blackburn Grammar School, Lancashire 206
Bloody Tower 67, 169, 216
Blount Court 211
Blount, (Sir) Michael 121, 221
Blount, Henry, 9th Earl of Nottingham, 1st Duke of Richmond 115
Blunte or Blount, William 116
Boleyn, Queen Anne 13
Bolles, William 131
Bonner's Cole Hole 118
Book of Common Prayer 71
Borough High Street 118
Borough Road 118
Bosgrave (Bosgrove), James 38, 39, 48, 66, 78, 81, 86, 90-98, 100, 132, 133, 174, 175, 193, 208
Boste, John 142
Bosworth Burse Collection 209
Boulogne 30, 139, 213
Bourke or de Burgh, Richard, 2nd Earl of Clanricarde 37, 77, 89, 90, 175
Bowyer Tower 126
Briant (Bryant), Alexander 42, 43, 48-50, 57, 79, 81, 91, 142, 163, 170, 175, 181, 218
Bride Lane 115
Bridewell Palace 115
Bridewell Prison 35, 76, 115, 116, 129, 198
Brimpton, Somerset 189
Brinkley, Stephen 45, 57, 80, 84, 176, 177, 183, 193, 195, 201, 225
Briscow, Bruscoe, Bristow or Briscoe, Thomas 41, 79, 90-97, 99, 177, 178
British Council of Churches 141
British Library 72
Brno 179, 221
Broad Arrow Tower 191, 202
Bromborough or Brombury, Edward 178
Bromley, Sir Thomas 131, 133, 134
Brown, Walter 116
Browninge or Brewninge, Francis 88-90
Brumlum, William. *see* Crumlum or Brumlum
Brussels 199, 226
Bryant, Alexander. *see* Briant (Bryant)
Buckley, John. *see* Jones, John
Bull, Simon 185
Bulwark Gate 149
Burgh, Richard de. *see* Bourke or de Burgh
Burghley, Baron. *see* Cecil, William
Burns or Burnes (Barnes), Thomas 53, 82, 179, 215
Bushoppe, William. *see* Bishop or Bushoppe
Butler, Robert (Yeoman Warder) 168
Butler, Thomas (Yeoman Warder) 168
Byward Tower 138

C

Cade's Rebellion 118
Calais 28
Calton, John 112
Cambrai 50, 173, 176, 192, 193, 200, 222, 226
Campion Hall, Oxford 181
Campion, Edmund 18, 19, 43-45, 47, 48, 50, 57, 72, 80, 81, 101-110, 137, 142, 152, 154, 163, 170, 176, 177, 179-182, 184, 190, 191, 193, 195, 199, 200, 213, 218, 221
Campion, Henry (Yeoman Warder) 167
Caraman, Philip 121
Carter, Agnes 181
Carter, William 55, 61, 83, 85, 97, 181, 182
Cassel's *History of England* 224
Catisbye or Catesby, John 118
Cawood, John 181
Cecil, Robert 222
Cecil, William, Baron Burghley 111, 125
Central Criminal Court 115
Central Hall 112
Chadwicke, Robert (Yeoman Warder) 167
Chalcedon, Bishop of 183
Chalcedon, Bishop of. *see* Bishop or Bushoppe 173
Challoner, Bishop Richard 153
Chalons sur Marne 170, 189
Chancery Lane 27
Charles I 143, 183
Charles II 143
Charles V, Holy Roman Emperor 115
Cheapside 117
Chelmsford, Essex 52, 53, 209
Christmas Quarter 88
Church History by Charles Dodd 214
Clanricarde, Earl of. *see* Bourke or de Burgh, Richard, 2nd Earl
Clare College, Cambridge University 205
Clarke, Richard. *see* Slake
Clerkenwell 112
Clink Prison 35, 55, 76, 119, 120, 171, 183, 196, 198, 200
Clink Street 119, 120
Clinton (or Fiennes), Edward, 16th Earl of Lincoln 131, 133, 134
Clitherow, Margaret 142
Coldharbour Tower 180, 187
Colebrook 109
Colleton, John, alias Peters 44, 48, 66, 80, 81, 92-97, 100, 106, 109, 110, 132, 133, 138, 182, 183
Commission for Banishing Jesuits and Seminary Priests 173
Commonwealth, The 143
Compter in Bread Street 116
Compter in the Poultry 116, 117, 174, 181, 193, 199, 207, 208
Compter or Counter Prisons 35, 76, 116
Compton, John 45, 80, 183, 185
Coniers or Conyers, Samuel 66, 132, 133, 183, 206

Connaught 186
Constable, Philip 151
Cook, A.H. DCM, MM, BEM, Chief Yeoman Warder 63, 172, 219
Cooper, Thomas 105, 106
Cooper, Thomas, Bishop of Lincoln 149
Copley, Robert 52, 82, 184
Copley, Sir Anthony 184
Corpus Christi College, Oxford 193
Coryat, George. *see* Mundyn, etc.
Cottam or Cotham, Robert 200, 213
Cottam or Cotham, Thomas 30, 31, 38, 42, 48, 53, 78, 79, 81, 89-93, 184, 185, 190, 193
Cotton, John 44, 53, 80, 82, 110, 183, 185, 186
Cotton, Richard 185
Cradle Tower 124, 128
Creagh, Richard, Archbishop of Armagh 37, 52, 77, 88-90, 92-97, 99, 186, 187
Creighton, Crichton or Creiton, William 65, 86, 169, 187, 188
Crofts, Sir James 133, 134
Crombleholme, William. *see* Crumlum or Brumlum, William
Cromwell, Thomas 127
Crumbleholme, William. *see* Crumlum or Brumlum
Crumlum or Brumlum, William 62, 63, 65, 66, 85, 86, 98, 99, 188

D

Dancer, George 114
Davis, Anthony (Yeoman Warder) 168
Dawson, Thomas, Printer 101
De Comburendo Heretico 27
Dean or Deane, William 66, 132, 133, 152, 188
Delvin, Baron. *see* Nugent, Sir Christopher
Denton, – 210
Desmond, Earl of. *see* Fitzgerald, Gerald
Desmond's Insurrection 175, 190
Devlin or Delvin, Baron. *see* Nugent, Sir Christopher, 14th Baron
Dickens, Charles 113, 118, 119
Dieppe 30, 169, 178
Dorchester 202
Douai 24
Douay 24, 27, 48, 50, 148, 175, 177-179, 182, 192, 208, 209, 211-213, 217, 226
Douglas or Duglas, Peter 88
Dover 30, 31, 113, 180, 184, 193, 200, 202
Dowsinge, Thomas (Yeoman Warder) 168
Drogheda 186, 191
Drury (Drewrie), Sir Dru 221
Dublin 179, 186, 190, 205
Dublin Castle 190, 205
Dudley, Ambrose, 21st Earl of Warwick 131, 133, 134
Dudley, Robert, 14th Earl of Leicester 131, 133, 134, 148, 179, 192
Duke of Exeter's Daughter. *see* Rack, The
Dungeon among the Ratts 27, 124
Dunkirk 30, 31, 184, 193

INDEX

Dunwich, Suffolk 206
Dutton, George 41, 79, 90, 188, 189
Dutton, John 91, 188, 189
Dyos or Deyos, William 114

E

Edward III 111, 112, 118
Edward VI 13, 21, 22, 115
Eliot, George 44, 80, 101, 102, 149, 181, 185, 190, 197, 199, 201, 208, 226, 227
Elizabeth I 21-25, 28, 35, 68, 72, 73, 76, 102-104, 117, 120, 131, 133-135, 138, 139, 142, 148, 152, 163, 169, 170, 175, 179, 184, 188, 211, 216, 219, 222
Elizabeth Tudor, Princess 196
Eltham, Kent 183
Ely, Humphrey 30, 31, 184, 193, 215
Emerson, Ralph 179, 180
English Civil War 120
Epistle of the Persecution of Catholics in England 153
Erasmus, Desiderius 72
Essex, Sheriff of 52
Eton College 170
Evans, Philip 143
Execution Dock, Wapping 124
Exeter College, Oxford 217

F

Farnese, Alessandro, Duke of Parma 222
Fawcett, Edward 210, 211
Felton, John 23
Fenn (Fen), James 62, 85, 189, 197
Fetters or Manacles 36, 55, 57, 77, 85, 129, 198, 203, 207
Fettiplace, Master 107
Filby or Filbie (Philbie), William 44, 48, 49, 53, 80, 81, 83, 92, 93, 109, 110, 185, 190, 213
Financial Year 87
Fitzgerald (FitzMaurice), James 28
Fitzgerald, Gerald, 11th Earl of Kildare (and Baron Offaly) 37, 77, 190
Fitzgerald, Gerald, Earl of Desmond 28
Fitzgerald, Henry, 12th Earl of Kildare (and Baron Offaly) 37, 77, 190, 191
Fleet Marriages 113
Fleet Prison 35, 76, 112, 113, 118, 150-152, 154, 157, 195, 209, 210, 212, 214, 215, 225
Fleet River 115
Fleet Street 112
Floggings at the Bridewell 116
Fogaza (Fogaca, Focatio or Fugatius), Anthony or Antonio 52, 82, 89-92, 191
Foot Irons 36, 77
Ford, Thomas, alias Satwell or Saltwell 44, 47, 48, 53, 80-82, 92, 93, 106, 110, 191, 194, 217
Forty Martyrs of 1970 141
Foster, Master 108
Foxe, John 26, 43
Framlingham Castle 212
France 139

François, Duke of Alençon and Anjou 27
Freeman, John (Yeoman Warder) 168
Fry, Elizabeth 117
Futterell, James (Yeoman Warder) 69

G

Garnet, Thomas 143
Gascoigne, Ralph (Yeoman Warder) 167
Gatehouse, Westminster 35, 51, 76, 111, 181, 182, 186, 195, 196, 200, 213, 227
Gauntlets or Manacles 128, 129
Gennings, Edmund 142
Gerard, John 63, 121, 128, 129, 172, 198
Germany 205
Getter, John. *see* Jetter
Giltspur Compter 117
Gittyns, Robert 117
Godmanstone, Dorset 174
Godsalf (Godshall, Godsafe or Goodsalf), George 44, 62, 80, 85, 92-96, 192
Goldwell, Thomas, former Bishop of St Asaph 29, 30
Goodsalf, George. *see* Godsalf, etc
Gordon 'No Popery' Riots 113, 115, 118, 120
Grand Storehouse Fire 1841 126
Gravesend 207
Great Crosby, Lancashire 212
Great Fire of London 112, 114-117
Greenwich 208
Gregory XIII, Pope 22, 23, 28, 176
Grenville, Sir Richard 72
Gresham Street 117
Guildhall 60, 171, 173, 219, 220, 223
Gwyn, Richard, alias White 142

H

Haddock, George. *see* Haydock
Hall, Anthony 131
Hall, Hugh 58-60, 84, 98, 99, 192, 219, 220
Hammon, William 202
Hammond, John 47
Hardinge, Thomas 88-91
Harpsfield, Nicholas 181
Harris or Harrys, John 45, 56, 80, 83, 193, 225
Hart Hall, Oxford 175
Hart, John 19, 30, 31, 37-40, 42, 43, 45, 47-51, 53, 55-61, 63, 64, 66, 68-73, 78, 81-83, 86, 90, 91, 92-98, 100, 118-120, 124, 128, 129, 132, 133, 147, 149, 152-155, 163-165, 171-175, 178, 182, 184, 189, 191-195, 198, 204, 208, 209, 213, 215, 219, 220, 224, 225
Hartley, Thomas 210
Hartley, William, alias Garton 45, 56, 66, 80, 83, 132, 133, 194, 195
Harvey, John 45, 56, 80, 83, 195, 225
Hatton, Sir Christopher 132-134
Hawkins, John 125
Haworth Castle 214
Haydock (Hadcock or Haddock), George 52, 62, 82, 85, 92-96, 195, 196, 211
Haywarde, John (Yeoman Warder) 168

Hemerford (Humerford or Humberford), Thomas 62, 85, 197
Henley on Thames 109, 177
Henry III 115
Henry VII 120
Henry VIII 13, 21, 24, 25, 112, 115, 127, 142
Heywood (Haywood), Jasper 66, 86, 98, 100, 132, 133, 138, 196
Higbye, Henry (Yeoman Warder) 167
Higgins, Mr 198
Hildesley (Ilsley), William 44, 53, 80, 82, 110, 197
Hille, Henry (Yeoman Warder) 167
History of Ireland 179
History of the World 67
Hodges, William (Yeoman Warder) 167
Holand or Holland, Henry, 4th Duke of Exeter 125
Holand or Holland, John, 3rd Duke of Exeter 125
Holinshed's Chronicles 179
Holloway Prison 116
Hopton, Cicely 120, 221
Hopton, Sir Owen 37, 40, 41, 47, 78, 79, 88-99, 109, 120, 121, 129, 149, 162, 163, 170, 172, 186-189, 191, 207, 208, 214, 217, 221, 224, 227
Houghton, John 142
Hounslow Heath 202
Howard, Lord Charles 132-134
Howard, Philip, 17th Earl of Arundel (and Surrey) 46, 131, 142, 216
Howard, Thomas, 17th Duke of Norfolk 23
Humerford, Thomas. *see* Hemerford
Hunsdon, Henry, Lord 132-134
Hyde, Mrs 91

I
Ilchester Gaol 189
Ilsley, William. *see* Hildesley, etc.
Infanta Henrietta Maria 183
Ingatestone Hall 208
Ireland 28, 179, 204
Iron gauntlets 36, 77

J
Jackson, Master 171
Jacob, John (or James) 44, 80, 83, 110, 197, 198
James VI of Scotland (I of England) 28, 143, 173, 222
Jaroslow, Poland 194
Jenkins, David 102-105, 107-109
Jesuits 22, 24, 29, 43, 173
Jetter or Getter, George 198, 199
Jetter or Getter, John 55, 56, 83, 94-96, 198, 199
John Harvard and Local Studies Library 119
Johnson, Robert 38, 48, 53, 78, 81, 82, 89, 91-93, 194, 199, 217
Johnson, William 90

Johnsone, William (Yeoman Warder) 167
Jones, John, alias Buckley 142

K
Kaines or Keynes, Edward and Humphrey 44, 80, 110, 199
Kalisz, Poland 175
Kemble, John 143
Kennet or Kent, Samuel (Yeoman Warder) 69
Kettleby, Lincolnshire 147, 224
Keynes, Edward and Humphrey. *see* Kaines or Keynes
Kildare Cathedral 190, 191
Kildare, Earl of. *see* Fitzgerald, Gerald, 11th Earl, and Fitzgerald, Henry (12th Earl)
King's Bench 35, 76, 117, 118, 188, 196, 197, 206, 213
King's Bench Prison 35, 76, 117, 118, 188, 213
Kirby, Luke 38, 48, 51, 53, 78, 81-83, 89-93, 142, 185, 190, 200, 213
Knight Marshal 118
Knollis, Sir Francis 132-134
Krems, Austria 174

L
Lady Day 88
Lancaster 64, 66, 85, 86, 100, 132, 133, 178, 182, 200, 207, 226
Lancaster, Mr 182
Lancaster, Thomas. *see* Worthington, etc.
Laon 206, 218
Launceston, Cornwall 26
Laurens, Henry 69
Lawrence, Robert 142
Layton or Leighton, Thomas 64, 85, 99, 200, 201
Leg Irons 62, 129
Leicester, Earl of. *see* Dudley, Robert, 14th Earl 131
Leslie, John, Bishop of Ross 169
Letherbor or Leatherborough, Ralph or Rudolph 56, 83, 201
Leveland Family 112
Lewis, David 14, 15, 18, 143
Lewis, Thomas 119
Liege 221
Lieutenant's Lodgings 121
Limbo Dungeon 198
Lincoln College, Oxford 182
Lincoln, Bishop of. *see* Cooper, Thomas
Lincoln, Dean of. *see* Wykeham or Wickham, William
Lincoln, Earl of. *see* Clinton (or Fiennes), Edward, 16th Earl
Line, Anne 142
Lingard, John 15
Lisbon 24
Lithuania 174
Little Dorrit 118
Little Ease 36, 55, 58, 77, 83, 84, 124, 125
Lloyd, John 143

INDEX

Loes or Lous, Joan 201
Loes or Lous, Philip 44, 80, 92-94, 201
London Bridge 60, 117, 119, 219
London, Chatham and Dover Railway 113
Lorraine 173, 213
Lott, Kapitanleutnant Werner 69
Louvain 182, 186, 222
Lovelace, Richard 111
Loyola, Ignatius de 22
Ludgate 35, 76, 112
Ludgate Prison 35, 76
Lydcot, Christopher 108, 109
Lyere, Catherine de 222
Lyford Grange 44, 105, 177, 180-182, 185, 190, 191, 197, 199, 201, 226, 227
Lyford, Berkshire 105
Lyons 30, 184, 187, 188

M

Macclesfield, Cheshire 217
Mackay, Robert 112
Malone, Simonde (Yeoman Warder) 167
Manacles 36, 48, 49, 55, 57, 77, 81, 85, 128, 129, 198, 203, 207
Manacles. *see* Gauntlets or Manacles
Manfield or Mansfield, John 44, 80, 108, 110, 202, 226
Marshalsea Prison 35, 38, 56, 61, 62, 76, 118-120, 137, 172-174, 182-184, 189, 192, 193, 195, 197, 198, 201, 205-207, 210, 211, 215-218, 221-223, 225, 226
Martin Tower 126, 127, 129, 152, 187, 214
Mary I 26, 28
Mary, Queen of Scots 18, 23, 28, 58, 84, 200, 222, 223
Mayne, Cuthbert 26, 142, 208
Meares, Thomas (Yeoman Warder) 167
Memoirs of Priests... that have Suffered in England 153
Mendoza, Bernardino de 223
Mercer, William (Yeoman Warder) 167
Mermaid Court 118
Miagh, Thomas. *see* Myagh or Miagh
Michaelmas Quarter 88
Midsummer Quarter 88
Mildmay, Sir Walter 132-134
Mile End Green, London 188
Mile End, Theatre at 195
Milverton, Somerset 182
Modest Answer to the English Persecutors 171
Monden, John. *see* Munden
Moravia 174
More, Edward 98, 99
More, Sir Thomas 13, 72, 196
Morell, Nan 181
Morris, Robert (Yeoman Warder) 167
Morse, Henry 143
Mountbatten, Lord Louis 69
Munday, Anthony 101-103, 110
Mundyn (Munden or Mundin), John, alias George Coryat 57, 62, 83, 85, 95-97, 202, 203

Myagh or Miagh, Thomas 37, 77, 91-95, 203, 204

N

Naas Gaol, Ireland 204
Naples 196
Nelson, John 27
New College, Oxford 202
New Fish Street, London 184
New King's Bench 118
New Marshalsea Prison 118, 119
New Prison 183
Newcomen Road 118
Newgate Prison 35, 56, 60, 76, 113-116, 170, 171, 178, 185, 195, 198, 199, 212, 213, 219, 220
Newgent, James. *see* Nugent
Newtown Compter 119
Nichols, John 40-42, 78, 79, 90, 200, 204, 205
Nonsuch 31, 193
Norfolk, Duke of. *see* Howard, Thomas, 17th Duke
Normandy 66, 86, 100, 131, 175, 183, 194, 196, 205, 207, 213, 215, 221-223, 226
Norris, Richard 66, 132, 133, 205, 210
Northumberland, Earl of. *see* Percy, Sir Henry, 8th Earl
Norton, Thomas 47, 125, 223
Notices and Remains of the Family of Tirwhit 150, 151
Nottingham, Earl of. *see* Blount, Henry, 9th Earl, etc.
Nowell, Nowel, or Noel, Alexander 158
Nugent (Newgent), James 37, 77, 92-95, 205, 206
Nugent, Sir Christopher, 14th Baron Delvin (Devlin) 37, 77, 205
Nutter, John 85, 183, 206, 207
Nutter, Robert, alias Askew or Rowley 61, 62, 65, 66, 85, 86, 98, 100, 132, 133, 206, 207

O

O'Neill, Hugh, 2nd Earl of Tyrone 205
O'Neill, Shane 205
Old Bailey 113
One Man Rack 125
Orford, Suffolk 174
Oriel College, Oxford 214
Orton, Henry 38, 39, 48, 66, 78, 81, 89-98, 100, 132, 133, 174, 199, 207
Osborne, Edward 152
Ostend 187
Oubliettes 124
Owen, Nicholas (Little John) 143
Oxford 24, 32, 51, 170, 175, 177, 179-182, 193, 197, 202, 214, 217

P

Page or Padge, William 88-91
Palmer, Andrew (Yeoman Warder) 168
Park Hall, Warwicks 171

Parma, Duke of. *see* Farnese, Alessandro
Parpoynt, Gervase. *see* Pierpoint
Parry, William 187
Parsons, Robert 18, 19, 31, 38, 41-43, 45, 47, 50, 53-55, 57, 60-62, 64-66, 68, 70, 71,79, 152-156, 172, 176, 177, 179, 180, 193, 196, 208, 211-213
Paschall, John 38-40, 78, 174, 193, 208
Paul VI, Pope 141, 176, 181
Payne (Paine), Jerome 208
Payne (Paine), John 44, 47, 52, 53, 80-82, 92, 93, 102, 142, 192, 208, 209
Peasants' Revolt 112, 118, 119
Peckham, Lady 209
Peckham, Sir George 38, 78, 209
Peine Forte et Dure 114
Pepys, Samuel 111
Percy, Sir Henry, 8th Earl of Northumberland 216
Perpoint, Gervase. *see* Pierpoint
Peterborough, Northants 208
Peters, John. *see* Colleton, etc.
Petre Family of Essex 208
Petts, Arthur. *see* Pitt or Pitts
Peverel, Thomas 124
Philbie, William. *see* Filby
Pickering, Maurice 111
Pickwick Papers 113
Pierpoint, Gervase 61, 65, 85, 86, 98, 99, 209-211, 216
Pit, The 36, 41, 42, 50-52, 55-58, 61, 62, 64-66, 77, 79, 82, 83, 85, 86, 124, 170, 171, 176, 180, 184, 198, 206
Pitt or Pitts, Arthur 52, 66, 82, 86, 92-97, 99, 132, 133
Pius V, Pope 23
Plasden, Polydore 142
Plessington, John 143
Poland 174, 194
Poland, King of 175
Poley or Pooley, Robert 186
Pollen, John Hungerford 19, 62, 87, 188
Pont-a-Mousson University, Lorraine 213
Popham, John 47
Pound or Pounds, Thomas 45, 80, 211, 212, 214
Powell, Richard (Yeoman Warder) 167
Prague 179
Prestall, John 88-93, 95-97, 99
Preston, Lancs 195
Privy Council 102, 104, 109, 131, 148-151, 156, 163, 174, 178, 221, 222, 224
Public Record Office 87
Punishment 123

Q
Queen's Bench 213
Queen's Bench Prison 118
Queen's Stairs 138

R
Rack, The 27, 36, 38-40, 42, 43, 45, 47, 52, 56, 58-60, 77-84, 125, 126, 128, 164, 170, 171, 176, 180, 191, 192, 194, 198, 199, 204, 208, 210, 214, 216,217, 223
Rainolds or Reynolds, John 32, 38, 50, 51, 57, 83, 193
Ralegh, Sir Walter 67, 111
Ransom, Stephen. *see* Rowsham, etc.
Rationes Decem 177, 180, 195, 221
Reade, Master 108
Red Rose (or Lion) Inn, Holborn 213
Reed, Isaac 126
Reynolds, John. *see* Rainolds or Reynolds
Reynolds, Richard 142
Rheims 24, 29, 30, 48, 50, 81, 139, 173, 176-178, 180, 182, 184, 185, 189, 193-196, 199, 200, 202, 206, 213-215, 217, 218, 220, 226
Richard II 119
Richardson, vere Johnson, Laurence 48, 53, 81, 83, 92, 93, 185, 190, 212, 213
Richmond, Duke of. *see* Blount, Henry, 1st Duke, etc.
Ridolfi Plot 216
Rigby, John 142
Rishton, Edward 13, 14, 17-19, 48, 66, 73, 81, 131-133, 194, 213, 214
Roberts, John 143
Rodesley, Derbyshire 217
Roe, Alban 143
Rome 24, 29, 30, 40, 41, 50, 57, 81, 154, 176-180, 182, 184, 185, 187, 194-196, 200, 204, 207, 211, 213, 217, 218, 226
Rookwood, Ambrose 152
Roper, Thomas 105
Roscarrock, Nicholas 38, 40, 78, 212, 214, 217
Rose Brothel, The 119
Rotherfield Peppard, Oxfordshire 211
Rouen 30, 56, 201, 217
Routhe, John 160
Rowley, Robert. *see* Nutter, Robert, etc.
Rowsham, Stephen 53, 55, 62, 82, 83, 85, 95, 96, 125, 173, 179, 192, 214, 215
Royal Armouries 126, 129
Rusham, Stephen. *see* Rowsham
Russell, Francis, 6th Earl of Bedford 131

S
Sacred Congregation for the Causes of Saints 141
Sadler, Sir Ralph 132-134
Saint Asaph, Bishop of. *see* Goldwell, Thomas, former Bishop
Saint John's College, Oxford 179
Saint Mary's University Church, Oxford 180, 214
Saint Omer 24
Saint Paul's Cathedral 115
Saint Peter ad Vincula, Chapel of 40, 187, 205
Saint Sepulchre's Church 113
Sainte-Menehould 214
Salt Tower 182
Saltwell, Thomas. *see* Ford, Thomas, etc.
Sander or Sanders, Nicholas 13, 18, 28, 202
Satwell, Thomas. *see* Ford, Thomas, etc.

INDEX

Savage, Robert (Yeoman Warder) 167
Scavenger's Daughter 36, 38, 43, 56, 61, 77, 78, 83, 85, 126, 127, 180, 184, 185,198, 200, 204, 207
Searle, Thomas (Yeoman Warder) 167
Second World War 141
Seville 24
Seymour, Thomas, Baron Seymour of Sudely 37
Shakespeare, William 126
Shawe, Robert (Yeoman Warder) 167
Sheffield, Edmund, 3rd Baron Sheffield 147-150, 156, 158-160, 224
Sheffield, John 160
Sheffield, Lady 148
Shelley, Richard 210, 215
Shelley, William 61, 85, 210, 215, 216
Sheppard, John 120
Shert (Shirt or Skert), John, alias Stalie 44, 48, 53, 81, 82, 92, 93, 194, 217
Sherwin, Ralph 15, 38, 43, 48, 50, 57, 78, 81, 89-91, 142, 163, 170, 176, 181, 193, 208, 217, 218
Sherwood, Thomas 27, 124
Shrewsbury, Earl of. *see* Talbot, George, 9th Earl
Sidney, Sir Henry 132-134
Simenes, William (Yeoman Warder) 167
Simpson, Cuthbert 43, 126
Singleton, Hugh 88
Skeffington, Leonard 127
Skeffington, Sir Leonard 126
Skeffington, Sir William 127
Skeffington's Yrons or Gyves. *see* Scavenger's Daughter
Slack or Slake, Richard 55, 66, 83, 86, 95, 96, 100, 131-133, 218
Sledd or Slade, Charles 30, 184, 199, 207
Smith, Richard 147, 148, 150, 155-161, 224
Smith, William 66, 132, 133, 218
Smithfield 60, 172
Society of Jesus 22, 24, 29, 38, 44, 50, 65, 66, 78, 86, 174, 176, 179, 184, 187, 194, 196, 211, 221
Soissons 184, 206, 214, 220
Somerset, Leonard. *see* Summesytte (Somerset), Leonard (Yeoman Warder)
Somerville or Somervyle, Elizabeth 58, 84, 98, 219
Somerville or Somervyle, John 58, 60, 84, 97, 171, 219, 220, 223
Somerville or Somervyle, Margaret (nee Arden) 98, 99, 219, 220
'Sophley', Leicestershire 218
South Maperton, Dorset 202
Southampton, Earl of. *see* Wriothesley, Thomas, 2nd Earl
Southwark 117, 118, 120
Southwell, Robert 142, 186
Southworth, John 143
Spain, Philip II of 23, 24
Spanish Armada 127, 216, 222, 226
Spanish Cravat, The 127

Staines 202
Stalie, John. *see* Shert, etc.
Standish, Lancashire 226
Star Chamber 112, 212
Stephenson, Thomas 62, 66, 85, 86, 98, 100, 132, 133, 220, 221
Stevens or Stephens, Jerome 38, 40, 78, 220
Stone, John 142
Stoney Street 120
Stonor Family 211
Stonor House 44, 45, 47, 56, 177, 180, 183, 193-195, 201, 221, 225
Stonor, (Sir) Francis 53, 221, 222
Stonor, John 45, 53, 80, 82, 221, 222
Stonor, Lady Cecilia 194, 221
Stonor, Richard 53
Stonor, Sir Francis 221
Stonyhurst College, Lancs 200
Story or Storey, John 50
Stow, John 119, 176, 218, 223
Stow's Annals 60
Strange, widow of Gloucestershire 215
Strappado 129
Suffolk Place 119
Summesytte (Somerset), Leonard (Yeoman Warder) 167, 168
Supplication to His Majesty for ... Defence of the Slandered Priests 183
Supremacy, Act of 21, 145
Supremacy, Oath of 21, 145
Sutton, Herefords 215

T

Talbot, George, 9th Earl of Shrewsbury 131
Tedder, William 66, 132, 133, 222
The Satisfaction of M. James Bosgrave...at his first coming into England 174
The Treatise of Schism 181
Thimbleby, Richard 210, 211
Thomson or Tomson, Christopher 40, 66, 78, 86, 90-93, 95, 96, 98, 100, 132, 133, 222, 223
Thornton (Thorneton) College 148, 150, 159
Throckmorton or Throgmorton Plot 223
Throckmorton or Throgmorton, Francis 58-60, 64, 84, 85, 125, 171, 200, 219, 223, 224
Throckmorton or Throgmorton, George or Thomas 58, 84, 224
Throckmorton or Throgmorton, Sir George 171
Throckmorton or Throgmorton, Sir John 58, 84, 223
Throckmorton or Throgmorton, Sir Nicholas 223
Thumbscrews 180
Tirwhit (Tiruit, Tirwight, Tirwright, Tyrrwhit), Elizabeth 152
Tirwhit (Tiruit, Tirwight, Tirwright, Tyrrwhit), Frances 160, 161
Tirwhit (Tiruit, Tirwight, Tirwright, Tyrrwhit), Goddard 155, 156, 158-161
Tirwhit (Tiruit, Tirwight, Tirwright, Tyrrwhit), John 149, 155, 156, 160

Tirwhit (Tiruit, Tirwight, Tirwright, Tyrrwhit), Marmaduke 149-151, 155-157, 160, 162
Tirwhit (Tiruit, Tirwight, Tirwright, Tyrrwhit), Nicholas 148
Tirwhit (Tiruit, Tirwight, Tirwright, Tyrrwhit), Robert 37, 77, 147-150, 152-157, 159-161, 224, 225
Tirwhit (Tiruit, Tirwight, Tirwright, Tyrrwhit), Sir Robert 37, 77, 147-156, 158-160, 224
Tirwhit (Tiruit, Tirwight, Tirwright, Tyrrwhit), Ursula 158-160, 224
Tirwhit (Tiruit, Tirwight, Tirwright, Tyrrwhit), William 37, 77,147-157, 161, 162, 224, 225
Tomson, Christopher. *see* Thomson or Tomson
Topcliffe, Sir Richard 129, 152, 226
Torture 123
Tothill Street 111
Tower Bills 87-100, 170-179, 181, 182, 184-192, 194, 196-201, 203, 204, 206, 207, 209, 212, 213, 215, 218-220, 223, 226
Tower Hill 37
Tower of London 31, 35, 76, 120
Tower Wharf 131, 173, 183, 188, 195, 205, 211, 213, 218, 221, 222, 226
Trinity College, Dublin 179
Tucker, John 45, 56, 80, 83, 225, 226
Tudor, Princess Elizabeth 37
Twigmore House. *see* Wigmore or 'Twigmore' House
Twyford, Matthew (Yeoman Warder) 168
Tyburn 27, 42, 50, 54, 60-62, 64, 113, 149, 163, 171, 172, 176, 181, 185, 189, 190,192, 194, 196, 197, 199, 200, 203, 206, 213, 217-219, 223
Tyler, Wat 112, 118, 119
Tyrone, Earl of. *see* O'Neill, Hugh, 2nd Earl

U

Uniformity, Act of 22
Unilever Building 116

V

Valladolid 24, 178
Verdun 206
Victoria and Albert Museum 181

W

Wall, John 143
Walpole, Henry 142
Walsingham, Sir Francis 18, 25, 30, 31, 38, 50, 51, 55, 70, 71, 102, 129, 132-134, 152, 156, 163, 171, 178, 179, 181, 184, 186, 187, 193, 194, 196, 199, 200, 202, 203, 207, 208, 211, 219, 223, 224
Walworth, William 119
Ward, Margaret 142
Warfield, Walter de 111
Warmington, William 66, 132, 133, 226

Warwick 60, 131, 133, 134
Warwick, Earl of. *see* Dudley, Ambrose, 21st Earl
Watten, 221
Waynewrighte, John (Yeoman Warder) 167
Webley, Thomas 170
Weblin or Webley, William 44, 80, 110, 226
Weblin, Thomas 108
Webster, Augustine 142
Well Tower 124, 174, 175, 190, 214
Wells, Peter (Yeoman Warder) 167
Wells, Swithun 142
Westminster 27, 35, 51, 62, 76, 111, 112, 135, 176, 181, 182, 185, 186, 189, 191, 193, 195, 196, 200, 213, 227
Westminster Abbey 112
Westminster School 112
Westmoreland, Thomas (Yeoman Warder) 167
White Lion Prison 35, 76, 119, 201, 212
White Tower 29, 121, 124-126, 128, 180
White, Eustace 142
White, Richard. *see* Gwyn, Richard
Whiting, Margaret 181
Whittington, Richard 114
Wickham, William. *see* Wykeham or Wickham
Wicklife, – 216
Wiggs, William 170
Wigmore or 'Twigmore' House 147-149, 155, 161
Wilkes, Thomas 223
William 'the Silent', Prince of Orange 187
Williamson, David 89
Williamson, Nicholas 186
Winchester College 202
Winchester House 120
Windleston, County Durham 220
Wisbech Castle 207, 210, 212
Wiseman, Master 108, 109
Wolsey, Thomas 14, 120
Wood Street Compter 42, 116, 117, 176, 210, 212
Worthington, Thomas, alias Lancaster 64, 66, 85, 86, 100, 132, 133, 226
Wray, Sir Christopher 132-134
Wriothesley, Thomas, 2nd Earl of Southampton 211
Wykeham or Wickham, William, Dean of Lincoln 149, 150, 157, 158, 224, 225

Y

Yate or Yates, Edward 44, 50, 51, 80, 82, 108, 110, 227
Yate, Master 105, 107, 109
Yate, Mrs 107
Yevele or Yeovil, Henry de 119
Young, Richard 125

Z

Zeeland, Admiral of 169